Palgrave Studies in Financial Instability and Banking Crisis Regulation

Editor-in-Chief
Riccardo De Lisa, University of Cagliari, Cagliari, Italy

Series Editor
Giuseppe Boccuzzi, University of Cagliari, Cagliari, Italy

This series aims to be a scientific hub and to act as a go-to resource for academia, policymakers, international supervisors, and financial institutions having an interest, from their respective viewpoints, in studies and research on financial stability, bank crisis, and deposit insurance issues. It will include theoretical, practical, and empirical studies on the economic, regulatory, legal, and technical aspects of financial stability and bank risks threats, banking crisis management and prevention, deposit insurance, and protection.

More information about this series at
https://link.springer.com/bookseries/16394

Giuseppe Boccuzzi

Banking Crises in Italy

An Application and Evaluation of the European Framework

palgrave
macmillan

Giuseppe Boccuzzi
University of Cagliari
Cagliari, Italy

ISSN 2662-3927 ISSN 2662-3935 (electronic)
Palgrave Studies in Financial Instability and Banking Crisis Regulation
ISBN 978-3-031-01343-0 ISBN 978-3-031-01344-7 (eBook)
https://doi.org/10.1007/978-3-031-01344-7

The English book is not a translation of the Italian version, but a new version of the Italian book: "*Le crisi bancarie in Italia (2014–2020). Insegnamenti e riflessioni per la regolamentazione*". Many parts of the Italian text have been restructured in the English version. Many topics have been updated according to the evolution of the events described in the Italian text.

This Palgrave Macmillan imprint is published by the registered company Springer Nature Switzerland AG
The registered company address is: Gewerbestrasse 11, 6330 Cham, Switzerland

When failures can turn into opportunities, if effectively analysed and managed

Preamble

Banking crises occur periodically, on a smaller scale locally and with a wider systemic reach, internationally. They all have much in common, but each has its own immediate causes and forms. The consequences are always grave and long-lasting for stakeholders, and for one group especially, the depositors. The headline concerns in every bank insolvency are: who loses and who pays? What private or public resources can be tapped into to restructure the single bank or the wider financial system and alleviate the costs for individuals and for society as a whole?

An immediate aftermath of a systemic banking crisis is often a rush to question why the existing legal framework was unable to foresee or counter the coming storm, increase national and international cooperation, curtail the harmful consequences and disruptive effects on the essential economic functions performed by banks and limit contagion from bank to bank, system to system and country to country.

The key concerns regarding banking crises are how to see them coming and what tools are available to offset and prevent them. After they happened, the questions are: what analysis should be done? How adequate were—and are—the rules? What mechanisms and procedures were—and can be—applied… In a word: where did it all go wrong and what can we do to stop it happening again? Our bookshelves are full and expanding as regulators, supervisors, central bankers, research departments and academics wade into the sea of speculation.

When banking crises occur, attention is focused on their causes, on how the events could have been foreseen and suppressed and how we can prevent their reoccurrence. What we learn today never fully prepares us for what may happen tomorrow. And while we do the autopsies on past dead banks or examine those that have been revived and those released from 'hospital' care back into normal business, we must be on the lookout for what new black swan may come swimming into view. The great question, both during and after a crisis, remains: how efficient were or are the operational and legal frameworks in achieving the ultimate objectives? What old and new lessons have to be learned and relearned?

The Italian crises have offered a critical testing ground for the effectiveness and consistency of the new European framework of bank resolution and deposit guarantee schemes. They have acted as the laboratory for a first examination of how well the new framework functions and stands up to the challenges. The laboratory specimens were sixteen small and medium-sized banks (with the exemption of MPS, which is a large bank) that went into crisis for a concatenation of contributing factors. Each in its way provides us with a broad range of legal and technical issues in the transactions carried out.

Among others, this study focuses on the work of the Italian Deposit Insurance System (FITD, Interbank Deposit Protection Fund) in confronting, successfully, those crises. The role of DGSs is expanding. Today, they are asked to be front-line doctors, to provide early intervention, diagnose, prescribe, perform life-saving surgery and not act just as family lawyers drawing up last wills and testaments. The DGSs must be creative and come up with alternative medicines. Traditional treatments, past remedies that served their purpose well and can still have their uses, may not be enough in a more complex world. Today, the DGSs have to walk a very fine line between innovation and established rules.

Events on the ground and as they unfold will demand flexible thinking. As this study is being written, for example, the Covid-19 pandemic has hit the world with an unprecedented economic shock. And it is not over yet. Economies, and consequently banks, will be dealing with the consequences of the pandemic for many years to come.

Our detailed study wishes to add the Italian experience to the debate on what measures to put in place to deal with future crises. What can we learn from this experience? Banking crises, when they occur, are disruptive. A crisis, big or small, must be a wake-up call. A frequently asked question is: 'Were the banks asleep at the wheel?'. The damage done to the real economy, to banks and to the broad social fabric must be blocked and limited as much as possible. To do that, we must have an appropriate box of tools, from heavy duty to precision instruments. And we have to be able to think and work 'outside the box'.

We point to the need for a clearer distribution of responsibilities between national and European authorities to ensure that all pursue the same target. Unity of purpose will ensure that action can be taken at the first signs of stress. In banking, as in all emergencies, early decisions and interventions are vital.

In Italy, like in all countries, public policy aims to preserve financial stability to the maximum extent possible. This is especially crucial in a less steady economy.

Italy successfully resolved sixteen banks in crisis over a period characterised by serious economic stress. It was involved in discussions with the Commission in the Tercas case, leading to the rethinking of State aid rules. Looking back, it may be quite legitimate to turn the usual question around and ask: what went right?

Contents

List of Figures

Chapter 2

Chapter 3

Chapter 4

Chapter 5

Chapter 6

Chapter 7

Chapter 8

Chapter 9

Chapter 11

CHAPTER 1

Introduction

1. Banking crises happen periodically, due to different causes and in different forms—a recurring story. They normally entail significant costs for the various stakeholders, primarily for depositors. A key issue is to determine who bears the costs (internally) of insolvent banks (shareholders and creditors) and what external financial support may be needed to resolve the institution.

The legal framework provides specific tools to reduce the disruptive effects of banking crises on the essential functions performed by banks and on the banking system as a whole. The mechanisms that generate these effects are complex and delicate given the all-encompassing nature of banking and the far-reaching implications of any disruptions and spillovers. The literature is vast and growing, from technical tomes for experts to 'Banking for Beginners' for the general public. We have come a very long way from a slim volume such as 'Lombard Street'.

In Italy, over the period 2014–2020, banking became almost a headline-grabbing hot topic, as banking crises followed one another, like aftershocks of the global financial meltdown, and the European authorities scrambled to produce effective banking reforms to contain the damage: in 2013, the State Aid Regulation; in 2014, the Bank Recovery and Resolution Directive (BRRD) and the Deposit Guarantee Schemes

G. Boccuzzi, *Banking Crises in Italy*, Palgrave Studies in Financial Instability and Banking Crisis Regulation,
https://doi.org/10.1007/978-3-031-01344-7_1

Directive (DGSD); in 2016, the Single Resolution Mechanism (SRM) and the Single Resolution Fund (SRF).

This new European regulatory framework was applied to the series of banking crises in Italy, which became the testing ground for the functioning, effectiveness and consistency of the new rules, and offered a unique opportunity to make a first critical assessment. This is the objective of this work.

2. This Book is Divided into Two Main Parts.

Part 1 is made up of six chapters and Part 2 of five chapters.

In Part 1, we give a brief overview of the banking crises in Italy over the years 2014–2020 and of the regulatory, institutional and market contexts in which they occurred. This section highlights the complexity of banking crises. It aims to provide a legal and technical framework for understanding individual crisis situations, the instruments applied, the objectives pursued and the cost implications for the stakeholders. We then proceed to an in-depth examination of the various crises: Banca Tercas (Chapter 2); the resolution of the 'four banks' (Chapter 3); orderly liquidation and precautionary recapitalisation (Chapter 4); the interventions of the Voluntary Scheme of the FITD (Chapter 5); and the preventive and alternative interventions of the FITD (Chapter 6).

We will examine 16 Italian banks in crisis, mainly small and medium-sized. Contributing factors range widely, from structural weaknesses that have characterised the Italian banking system since 2011–2012, a time of long economic crisis, low profitability, growth in impaired loans and fragile business models, to governance and management issues, particularly in more vulnerable banks.

Are we at the end of a cycle?

It is hard to say. Just as banks had begun to come to terms successfully with this cycle, Covid-19 came on the scene, giving an unprecedented shock to the national and global economy, and inevitably to banking, especially already fragile banks.

The novel situation has brought new concerns. Have we entered—and if so to what extent—a new tunnel of crises as shocks propagate from the real economy to banks, through an increase in non-performing loans and the worsening of profitability and efficiency indicators? What tools do we have to prevent and repair failures? Is the 'new' European framework up to the challenge? Is the recently tested resolution/liquidation process for insolvent banks enough? Or will we need once again to resort to extraordinary tools, preventive initiatives or even public intervention?

To answer these questions, analysing the Italian banking crises is particularly useful. Italian banking crises abound in legal and technical implications, which have paved the way for academics and policymakers to investigate the current operational framework. Banking crises always teach us lessons on how to perfect our objectives, instruments and procedures.

Our analysis shows that Italian supervisory and government authorities strove to reduce the disruptive impact of crises on banks of all sizes. Even in the case of very small banks, atomistic liquidation and reimbursement of depositors were replaced by transfers of assets and liabilities to other banks. This allowed the exit from the market of the insolvent bank while preserving the continuity of business functions.

In the weak macroeconomic context, the protection of savers was the primary objective. The banking sector, and especially the Interbank Deposit Protection Fund, acted to ensure stability and restore confidence in the financial system.

When banking crises occur, we usually ask 'What went wrong?'. We are quick to point the finger, and we often focus our analysis on the causes and the responsibilities. In this work, instead, we ask 'What went right'. We investigate those strategies that allowed us to successfully manage many complex crises and minimise their costs.

The measures adopted in Italy were many: (i) resolution pursuant to the BRRD; (ii) compulsory administrative liquidation, followed by the transfer of assets and liabilities to another bank with the support of the Interbank Deposit Protection Fund (Article 11.6 of the DGSD); (iii) compulsory administrative liquidation, followed by the transfer of assets and liabilities to another bank with government support through the use of public funds (*orderly liquidation*); (iv) precautionary recapitalisation by the government; (v) the intervention of the Voluntary Scheme of the Interbank Deposit Protection Fund; (vi) preventive interventions carried out by FITD pursuant to Article 11.3 of the DGSD. Alongside these measures, other public and private solutions were explored to facilitate the process (Atlante Fund, GACS, AMCO).

3. We begin with the Banca Tercas case in 2014. This was the first in the series of banking crises in Italy and became the watershed between the 'old' crisis management approach (aimed at broadly safeguarding the subjects involved[1]) and the 'new' approach (the reformed European Framework for banking crisis management, including State aid rules).

This case allows us to reflect on the European resolution framework, on the role of Deposit Guarantee Schemes and on the State aid provisions. The Tercas case has been definitively resolved by the ruling of the Court of Justice of the European Union of 2 March 2021, which dismissed the appeal brought by the EU Commission against the decision of the General Court of 19 March 2019 in favour of the Italian parties regarding the absence of State aid in the Banca Tercas case. In short, the General Court had found that the Commission had erred in law in taking the view that the Italian authorities had exercised substantial public control on the measures adopted by the FITD for the benefit of Tercas. As a result, the intervention of FITD could not be classified as State aid, since it was neither imputable to the Italian State nor financed through State resources.

This is a very important decision, but the position on State aid put forward here looks beyond the outcome of the legal proceedings in the Tercas case. Regardless of whether DGSs are considered to be public entities or rather, as upheld by the European Courts, private entities, we argue that the preventive and alternative interventions of DGSs should remain outside the scope of State aid rules, for several reasons.

First, because in the case of preventive or alternative interventions, the DGSs do not employ resources of the State but rather those of private banks. Second, those interventions are made on a voluntary basis when, in accordance with the least cost principle, they are less costly than the reimbursement of depositors. Consequently, they should be considered as DGSs' interventions and not as State interventions.

The Italian experience goes right to the heart of the debate on public and private intervention and suggests that the new direction taken by the European framework—moving from bail-out to bail-in—may be excessively simplistic and fail to fully consider the complexity of banking crises. Bail-in is too general a principle. Its application has to be carefully weighed against the overall financial and economic context in which the crisis occurs.

We argue that the objectives of crisis management in Europe are still unclear. The uncertainty about which tools to apply affects policymakers

[1] G. BOCCUZZI, *La crisi dell'impresa bancaria. Profili giuridici ed economici*, Giuffrè, 1998.

and hinders the crisis management process. In Italy, tensions between the objectives of financial stability and competition have emerged and have also affected public authorities. The banking system has often been called upon to bear the costs of the crisis to preserve confidence in the sector. Creative solutions—also referred to in this work—have been devised to overcome the rigidity of a framework unable to adapt to an increasingly complex macroeconomic and regulatory context. But these solutions have come at a high cost for the private sector.

The *Fondo Interbancario di Tutela dei Depositi* (Interbank Deposit Protection Fund) has been key in supporting interventions with such high costs for the banks. Costs were equally substantial when the Resolution Fund—managed by the Resolution Authority—was used. In some more serious cases, public intervention was also carried out. The use of private financing to cover the cost of crises raises important questions and reflections.

4. Part 2 evaluates these crisis events and focuses on the lessons learned and the open issues. We address the hot topics of improvement of the institutional structure and crisis management rules (Chapter 7), the harmonisation of insolvency rules in Europe (Chapter 8), the funding of resolution (Chapter 9), public intervention (Chapter 10) and, last but not least, the role of Deposit Guarantee Schemes in crisis management (Chapter 11).

In particular, we argue that the Banking Union framework should be revised to ensure a clearer distribution of responsibilities between national and European authorities, clarify any ambiguity in policy and achieve uniform application of rules and greater speed in decision-making. Time is of the essence in crisis management.

We also argue for a simpler and more flexible structure, more in line with an evolving and complex financial system, constantly changing markets and regulatory scenarios.

We take issue with the overly simplistic distinction in the current framework between resolution and liquidation (the first for systemic banks and the latter for small and medium-sized banks). In today's complex environment, liquidation may not always be the best solution for small and medium-sized banks because they too serve general interests that require an orderly exit from the market and continuity of essential functions.

Numerous policy suggestions are put forward.

The European crisis management framework cannot be a 'one size fits all' model given the complexities and peculiarities we have in Europe. We need original solutions that should draw on national best practices.

In the current European context, however, a supranational approach seems to prevail. This was the case with the BRRD, which followed a theoretical model without due consideration of national specifications. On the contrary, national experiences should play a greater role, because in crisis situations savings protection and trust in the banking systems are tied to national considerations, at least until a coherent and integrated European system is put in place.

The central theme of the book is the new bank resolution regime, applicable as an alternative to compulsory administrative liquidation. The essential element for the application of resolution is the existence of a 'public interest'. This notion, however, is not clearly defined in the legislation. This leads to uncertainty in its application, in particular as regards the choice between resolving and liquidating an insolvent bank. Indeed, for failing or likely-to-fail large banks, public interest is the precondition for triggering the resolution procedure. Small and medium-sized banks—the most numerous—can only undergo liquidation. This approach limits the concept of public interest to large banks and fails to acknowledge the need for the business continuity of smaller banks.

A closely related issue is bail-in. In the mind of legislators, bail-in was intended to be the key element of the reform. Yet, bail-in has never been applied due to its problematic nature, which caught off-guard the operators and, arguably, the authorities. The credibility and practicability of bail-in are under discussion. Although the participation of shareholders and creditors in covering insolvency losses is in principle justifiable, it cannot be unreserved, since it can also have destabilising effects.

With this in mind, this work delves into the ongoing debate on the harmonisation of national insolvency models and rules. The substantial differences between them may hinder the resolution—or liquidation—of cross-border groups.

We also analyse the resolution financing system, paying special attention to the principle of burden sharing between shareholders and creditors and to the role of resolution and deposit guarantee funds in ensuring solvency funding. Issues relating to liquidity funding, particularly relevant for the Italian experience, are also discussed. We highlight the lack of adequate tools to support liquidity in pre-resolution and post-resolution crisis management, including the preventive interventions implemented by the FITD. We argue that EU legislation aims mainly at providing solvency funding over liquidity funding.

This work focuses in particular on the role of the Interbank Deposit Protection Fund in crisis management. With over 30 years of activity, the Fund has been of fundamental importance in preserving financial stability and protecting depositors. However, it had to operate in a context of uncertainties in the European framework as regards the delicate functioning mechanisms of DGSs, their institutional mandate, the types of intervention that they can carry out and the conditions to which they are subject.

One controversial issue is the application of the least cost principle to preventive and alternative interventions with respect to depositor reimbursement. This rule is closely linked to another important principle: the *super-priority granted to DGSs* for participation in the liquidation estate following the reimbursement of insured depositors. Finally, we argue for the need to ensure funding for guarantee schemes, through public backstops or the single European deposit guarantee system.

The application of State aid rules is the main concern. The challenge is how and where to strike the right balance between financial stability and competition rules. In Europe, State aid rules put constraints on the freedom of DGSs to act quickly and successfully. This is not the case in other jurisdictions.

Lastly, we shall also look at the return to the market of those banks that had been nationalised, sold to a bridge bank in the context of resolution or acquired by the DGS in the context of preventive interventions. These external support operations focus on the restructuring and recapitalisation of banks in crisis and are temporary. 'Temporary' means that the acquisition lasts only for the time strictly necessary to restructure the bank and put it back on the market.

A brief distinction should be made between banks acquired by the State and banks acquired by DGSs or bridge banks. When nationalised banks are returned to the market, flexibility is necessary to have sufficient time for the bank's restructuring so as to recover as much of the investment as possible. The State must be able to behave like any private investor. There are many banking systems, including European ones, in which banks have been put permanently in public hands.

This is why public intervention is crucial as an instrument of last resort, as stated by the BRRD itself. The BRRD provides for the temporary acquisition by the State, the nationalisation of the insolvent bank and, in some cases, the precautionary recapitalisation of solvent banks. But the regulatory provisions often make it difficult to implement any of these.

The European debate also focuses on the incompleteness of the regulatory framework, particularly on the failure to implement the third pillar of the Banking Union, the European Deposit Insurance Scheme (EDIS). Together with the reform of the ESM, this issue is a priority on the political agenda.

The European banking system is fragmented. Risks are not equally distributed between countries.[2] A public backstop is missing and the market continues to rely on the State to ensure the capacity of DGSs to repay depositors up to the protected amount. We need to reflect on the role of public intervention in crisis management, considering that private resources are limited. Time is of the essence: public intervention requires time to be applied and to achieve political consensus. The timing of politics is not compatible with the urgency of a crisis. A pre-established toolkit and activation procedure should be agreed upon in order to avoid 'opportunistic' behaviour based on the search for the most practicable solution rather than the best solution.

Regulators, academics and practitioners should come together to learn from the best national experiences of banking regulation and resolution. The problems of bank insolvency must be addressed openly, without a priori nationalistic arguments, to expand the tools and range of solutions and, above all, to reduce unnecessary constraints. We must create a new and resilient regulatory framework, fit for the present and the future.

[2] See G. BOCCUZZI, R. DE LISA, The Changing Face of Deposit Insurance in Europe: From the DGSD to the EDIS Proposal, XXI Rapporto sul Sistema Finanziario, The Changing Face of Banking, Ass. Rosselli, 2016.

PART I

The Management of Banking Crises in Italy: Old and New Solutions in a Framework of Increasing Complexity

CHAPTER 2

The Overall Picture. System Weaknesses and Individual Problems

The Italian banking system emerged from the global financial crisis largely unscathed, since the Italian banks, which had a commercial banking business model, did not hold in their balance sheets the risky derivative products and other toxic assets which resulted in huge losses and the collapse of major banks in the United States and Europe. However, problems subsequently arose, in particular in the period 2014–2020, due to the interaction of a set of structural and contingent factors affecting the Italian economy and the banking sector.

This chapter covers the phenomenon of banking crises in Italy, explaining the regulatory and market environment in which they occurred, their scale and the solutions adopted, as well as the entities that paid the costs of the crises.

1 Background

The international financial system has experienced a period of severe turbulence since 2007, triggered by a succession of crises of financial institutions—some of systemic importance—which originated in the United States and rapidly spread globally. In the second half of 2008, the impact

G. Boccuzzi, *Banking Crises in Italy*, Palgrave Studies in Financial Instability and Banking Crisis Regulation,
https://doi.org/10.1007/978-3-031-01344-7_2

of the crises started to be felt by many European banks, although they were considered less vulnerable due to the stricter regulation of the financial sector than the United States.[1]

The global financial crisis soon transmitted its effects to the real economy. Italy was strongly affected: over the following years, the crisis had a heavy impact on the profitability of firms and banks, while the latter also experienced a growing deterioration in the quality of credit. The effects of the vicious circle between sovereign and banking risk were also heavy, affecting Italy and other European countries with structurally deficient public budgets.[2]

The many aspects of the global financial crisis were extensively investigated by economists.[3] Many studies were written to explain the phenomenon, and the resulting theoretical debate that emerged set in motion a process of reform that led to a global rethinking of the banking supervision and crisis management framework.[4] We will summarise briefly the main elements, to highlight the basic facts of that crisis that led to the Italian crisis events of recent years, together with other pathological phenomena that occurred over the same period.

[1] In the United States, the crisis followed a period of deregulation of the financial sector. Among the most important regulatory changes: (i) the Depository Institutions Deregulation and Monetary Control Act of 1980, which extensively modified the Glass-Steagall Act (1933) by removing constraints governing bank mergers and regulation of bank interest rates; (ii) the Gramm-Leach-Bliley Act 1999, which repealed the provisions of the Glass-Steagall Act that separated traditional banking from investment banking and reintroduced the universal banking model and removed barriers between financial institutions and insurance companies.

[2] ITALIAN MINISTRY OF THE ECONOMY AND FINANCE, *Relazione generale sulla situazione economica del Paese*, 2008.

[3] D. SMITH, *The age of instability. The Global Financial Crisis and What Comes Next*, Profile Books Ltd., 2010; A.R. SORKIN, *Too Big to Fail. The inside story of How Wall Street and Washington Fought to Save the Financial System—and Themselves*, Penguin Group, 2009; V. ACHARYA, M. RICHARDSON, *Causes of the Financial Crisis, Critical Review: A Journal of Politics and Society*, Vol. 21, Issue 2–3, 2009; T.F. GEITHNER, *Stress Test. Reflections on Financial Crises*, Crown Publishers, May 2015; J.F. BOVENZI, *Inside the FDIC. Trent'anni di fallimenti bancari, salvataggi e battaglie normative*, Wiley, 2015.

[4] G. BOCCUZZI, *Il regime speciale della risoluzione bancaria. Obiettivi e strumenti*, cit.

Thus, the Italian banking crises occurred at the end of a long process, which started with the global financial crisis, continued with the European crisis of 2011–2012 and resulted in the reforms that led to the new institutional, regulatory and market set-up in which these events occurred.

2 The Global Financial Crisis and the Crisis in Europe

During the turmoil of 2007/2009, banking crises occurred all over the world. The scale and size of the crises and their effects on the various categories of stakeholders (shareholders, creditors, other intermediaries, governments) were unprecedented.

The first signs of the financial crisis were felt in 2007, following the insolvencies of some banks and other financial institutions. The strongest shocks occurred in 2008, with a chain of insolvencies having their epicentre in the United States and culminating with the collapse of Lehman Brothers (September 2008), one of the largest financial institutions in the world. It was the first time that, inexplicably, a bank was allowed to fail.[5]

Other large banks operating in the major financial centres failed, causing a fall in confidence in the global financial system and the deepest recession since the Great Depression of the 1930s. Liquidity decreased

[5] L.G. MC DONALD, P. ROBINSON, *A Colossal Failure of Common Sense: The Inside Story of the Collapse of Lehman Brothers*, Crown Business, New York, 2010; A.R. SORKIN, *Too big to fail: the Battle to Save Wall Street*, Penguin, 2010; M. LEWIS, *The Big Short: Inside the Doomsday Machine*, Norton & Company, 2011; J.K. GALBRAITH, *The End of Normal. The Great Crisis and the Future of Growth*, Simon & Schuster, 2014; N. TALEB, *The Black Swan: The Impact of the Highly Improbable*, Random House, 2010; J. STIGLITZ, *Freefall: America, Free Markets, and the Sinking of the World Economy*, Penguin Books, 2010; P. KRUGMAN, *End this Depression Now!*, Norton & Company, 2012; B. Mc LEAN, J. NOCERA, *All the Devils are here: The Hidden History of the Financial Crisis*, Penguin Books, 2011; CONSOB, *La crisi finanziaria del 2007–2009*, http://www.consob.it/web/investor-education/crisi-finanziaria-del-2007-2009; F. TUCCARI, *La crisi economica mondiale 2007–2013*, Zanichelli, 2013; N. ROUBINI, S. MIHM, *La crisi non è finita*, Feltrinelli, Milano, September 2013; A. DELL'ATTI, F. MIGLIETTA, *Il sistema bancario e la crisi finanziaria*, Cacucci, 2014, F. CAPRIGLIONE, G. SEMERARO, *Crisi finanziaria e dei debiti sovrani: l'Unione Europea tra rischi ed opportunità*, Utet giuridica, 2012.

significantly, making it extremely difficult to finance banks and other market participants.

The crisis in the United States was triggered by the subprime mortgages bubble; these loans were packaged into risky and complex financial instruments, sold to financial institutions around the world. Those instruments no longer had a market in which they could be traded and became difficult to value, resulting in increasing balance sheet losses and insolvencies for large banks, even in Europe (Germany, United Kingdom, Belgium, Netherlands, Ireland, Spain and Greece).

The financial crisis put into sharp relief the crucial role of liquidity for banks and the negative effects that general illiquidity situations can have on systemic stability. In addition, it demonstrated the close link between banking and economic activities, as evidenced by the deep economic downturn in 2009 that followed bank failures.

Bank insolvencies were dealt with through massive recourse to State resources, at the expense of taxpayers, in amounts and with methods never experienced before.[6] The technical forms of intervention were also manifold (recapitalisations, guarantees, liquidity injections). Public money was mobilised in some countries through specific programmes: TARP in the United States; NAMA in Ireland; significant financial support to banks also occurred in Germany, Spain and Iceland. The impact on public finances was impressive.

As regards Europe, Fig. 1 shows the size of bank bail-outs with public funds in the period 2008–2013: the highest impact of government interventions as a percentage of GDP was observed in Ireland and Greece; in absolute terms, Germany and the United Kingdom were the European countries that used the largest amounts of State resources to support the banking sector.

In the UnitedStates, the total cost of TARP was about €444 billion[7]; from 2008 to 2013, FDIC intervened in support of about 500 banks,

[6] G. BOCCUZZI, *Towards a New Framework for Banking Crisis Management. The International Debate and the Italian Model*, Quaderni di ricerca giuridica della Consulenza Legale della Banca d'Italia, No. 71, 2011.

[7] CONGRESSIONAL BUDGET OFFICE, *Report on the Troubled Asset Relief Program*, March 2020. The amount of State aid granted to the banking sector, calculated as the amounts of recapitalisations and other measures to facilitate the disposal of non-performing loans (i.e. creation of bad banks), including guarantees and liquidity support measures, was around €5,029 billion.

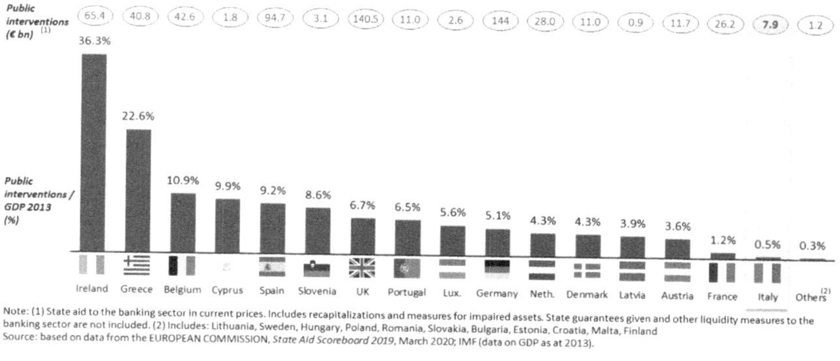

Fig. 1 Bank insolvencies in Europe: public intervention (2008–2013)

almost depleting the deposit insurance fund.[8] In Europe, based on data published by the European Commission, it is estimated that in the same period the total amount of public intervention in favour of the banking sector was approximately €633 billion.[9]

During the financial crisis, even the 'too big to fail' principle was betrayed; the crisis showed that even large banks could fail; moreover, some failing banks proved to be 'too big to be saved', since governments were unable to save banks whose balance sheets were larger than those of the State (Ireland, Greece, Iceland).

Despite the financial crisis and macroeconomic challenges, the Italian banking system came out of this phase unscathed, and public support for banks was negligible (in total €7.9 billion, equal to 0.5% of Italy's GDP).

A second wave of crises fuelled by the vicious circle between bank risk and sovereign risk affected Europe in 2010–2011 and especially those countries, including Italy, which were affected by a structural weakness of public finances. The spreads between the bonds issued by weaker

[8] Among the interventions carried out by the FDIC, only a small percentage of banks in crisis were put into liquidation with repayment of depositors, while 93% of banks were resolved through P&A operations with full transfer of deposits. G. MAJNONI D'INTIGNANO, A. DAL SANTO, M. MALTESE, *The FDIC Bank Crisis Management Experience: Lessons for the EU Banking Union*, Notes on financial stability and supervision, No 22, August 2020.

[9] EUROPEAN COMMISSION, *State aid Scoreboard 2019*, March 2020.

countries and those issued by stronger countries increased to unsustainable levels. In Italy, the spread with the German ten-year Bund peaked in November 2011, reaching 574 basis points. In the following years, also as a result of European monetary policies, the spread between the Italian BTP and the German Bund slowly decreased, but never returned to pre-crisis levels (from the early 2000s to September 2008 the spread had been below 80 bps) (Fig. 2).

Once the most acute phase of the crisis was over, the long economic recession that followed had a severe impact on weak economies, with negative effects on banks. These were affected by an exponential increase in non-performing exposures (NPEs), due to the typical business model of commercial banks, based essentially on the collection of deposits from retail clients and the granting of loans to the economy, enterprises and households.

These factors had a dual effect: on the one hand, public interventions in favour of failing banks entailed an abnormal cost for State finances; on the other hand, in countries with weaker public finances, the high sovereign risk affected the banks' balance sheets through the devaluation of the government securities in their portfolios. At the height of the crisis, the very survival of the euro was called into question (redenomination risk) (Fig. 3).

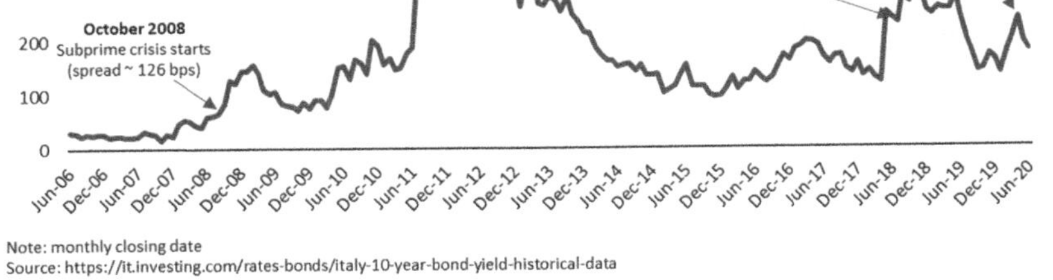

Note: monthly closing date
Source: https://it.investing.com/rates-bonds/italy-10-year-bond-yield-historical-data

Fig. 2 Spread between Italian and German ten-year bonds (2006–2020)

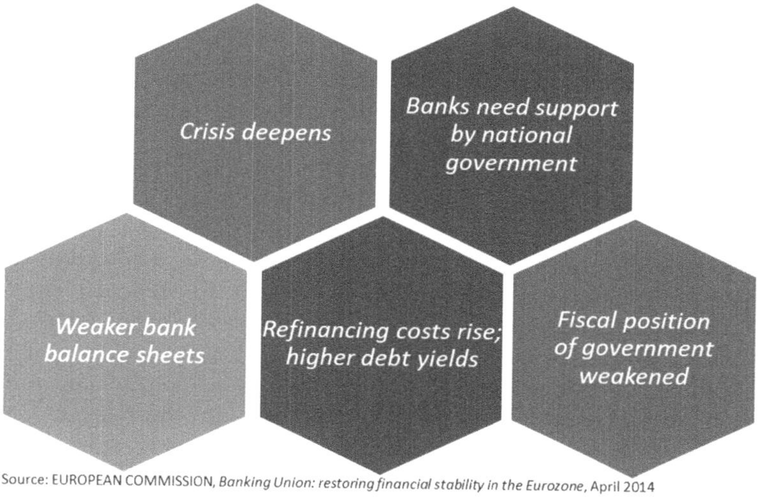

Fig. 3 Vicious circle between banking risk and sovereign risk

3 The Italian Banking Crises: Main Features

The overall phenomenon of banking crises in Italy, in terms of the number and size of banks involved, is in no way comparable with what happened in other countries during the global financial crisis. Italian crises were caused mainly by the long economic crisis and not by the excesses of speculative finance. However, the phenomenon was not negligible and required the use of a wide range of tools in favour of banks in crisis.

Describing the pathological events that affected the Italian banking industry is not an easy task, because of some distinctive features, not found in other countries, which can be summarised as follows:

i. The banking crises in Italy took place long after the global financial crisis, in the period beginning with the sovereign debt crisis (2011), which gave rise in Europe to the vicious circle between banking risk and sovereign risk. They were triggered by specific, interlinked structural factors that weakened the banking sector, including the serious deterioration in the macroeconomic environment and the resulting deterioration in the quality of credit to the economy, high operating costs and low profitability, and the low level of capitalisation;

ii. The crises occurred after the introduction of major changes in the regulatory and institutional framework in Europe, with significant changes—and more limitations and constraints—in the treatment of banking crises (BRRD, DGSD, SSM, SRM and State aid rules). The new regulatory environment is mainly based on the use of private resources, rather than on public support, as was the case during the global financial crisis; new institutional arrangements, principles, objectives and instruments were introduced. In particular, the new resolution procedure came into force and, within it, the bail-in tool and a stricter version, burden sharing;

iii. New complexities emerged: the previous crisis management toolkit could no longer be used, thereby limiting flexibility in crisis management. In the past, Italian authorities had a wide range of instruments, without significant limitations, because of the priority given to financial stability over other objectives of public regulation, including the pursuit of market competition. In addition, the decision-making process for crisis management became longer and more complex, given the multiplicity of authorities involved at both European and national level;

iv. There were strong reactions from different categories of stakeholders, especially those affected by burden-sharing measures, which led to the introduction—not without contradictions—of protective measures, to mitigate or eliminate the effects of insolvency on the subordinated bondholders affected by the write-off of their claims.

4 The Management of the Italian Banking Crises Before and After the European Reform

4.1 The Previous Regulatory and Operational Framework

The rules, strategies and practices of banking crisis management in Italy, as well as the market conditions in which they were applied, were very different in past decades from those in place when the crises of recent years occurred.

The Banking Law of 1936/38 introduced in Italy an administrative system of banking crisis management and resolution characterised by two main procedures: extraordinary administration and compulsory administrative liquidation, carried out under the direction and coordination of the Bank of Italy, in its capacity as regulator, supervisory and resolution authority for the banking sector. Therefore, the Special Resolution Regime has always been a distinctive feature of Italian banking law.

In this context, the crisis management and resolution function were not entrusted to an autonomous entity but was part of banking supervision.

For many decades, the banking market has been characterised as an 'administered market', where the supervisory authority played a key role in shaping the structure of the system and defining the exit arrangements for problematic banks. Instrumental to this institutional design was the exercise of some degree of moral suasion by the authorities. The doctrinal debate on the characteristics of banking supervision in those years was very intense.[10]

The 1993 banking reform, introduced by the Italian Banking Act (TUB - Consolidated Banking Act), confirmed and strengthened the special regime for bank insolvency as a regulatory and supervisory framework based on prudential rules (capital, liquidity and organisational requirements). The central role of the Bank of Italy in governing the insolvency and exit from the market of financial intermediaries remained unchanged.

In those years, the strategic choices of Italian banks were oriented to external growth, through mergers and acquisitions (M&A), even involving banks in difficulty. In this context, the solution of the crises was facilitated by the larger banks' high capacity to absorb struggling banks. The acquiring banks' interest in the acquisitions was also reflected in the recognition of goodwill (relating to branches, deposits, customer relationships, income potentials), which was intended to reduce the deficit of the insolvent banks.[11] Many banks that today are of medium-large size and national importance, at that time were small provincial and regional banks which over time also acquired banks in distress.

Even in cases where banks were subject to compulsory administrative liquidation, the transfer of assets and liabilities (P&A transaction) was an

[10] For an in depth analysis of the debate, G. BOCCUZZI, *La crisi dell'impresa bancaria. Profili economici e giuridici*, cit.

[11] G. BOCCUZZI, *La crisi dell'impresa bancaria. Profili economici e giuridici*, cit.

available tool to transfer the business or part of it to another bank, in order to reduce the disruptive effects of insolvency (Article 90 TUB).

The role of deposit guarantee schemes—the FITD and the scheme for cooperative banks (FGDBCC)—was crucial. Interventions of the guarantee schemes were designed to implement solutions other than the reimbursement of depositors, such as the bank's recovery or the transfer of its assets and liabilities in liquidation. There were very limited cases of payouts of depositors of banks in liquidation. This ensured broad deposit protection and continuity of the essential functions of the bank, without prejudice to the effects on shareholders (the first to suffer the consequences of the bank failure) and other parties at fault in a bank failure, through administrative sanctions, civil proceedings and criminal prosecution.

For the extraordinary crises involving large banks, a specific public intervention tool was introduced by Decree of the Treasury Ministry of 27/9/74 (DM 27/9/74), after the failure of Banca Privata Italiana. The decree provided that the Bank of Italy could grant special advances to those banks that stepped in to protect the depositors of other banks in liquidation. The instrument was used to solve major failures for over 20 years, including those of Banco Ambrosiano, Banco di Napoli and Sicilcassa. It has not been in operation since the early 2000s, when new rules regarding the recourse to central bank lending entered into force.

The broad protection afforded to the various stakeholders resulted in a low perception of crisis situations on the part of depositors and market operators; there was certainty that the authorities would in any event take appropriate measures to protect creditors from the consequences of the failure. This certainty also operated *ex-ante*, through the strong conviction that the crisis would be resolved without serious consequences for savers, except for the shareholders and managers responsible for the failure and for those categories affected by the restructuring measures. In this context, even the extraordinary administration procedure did not have undesirable effects on funding and liquidity, since it was perceived as an element of stabilisation and safety. The management of the bank under this procedure was entrusted to administrators appointed by the Bank of Italy, having the specific function of assessing the business situation, removing irregularities and promoting the solution of the crisis in the interest of depositors (Article 72 TUB).

4.2 *New Rules of the Game: The New European Regulatory Framework*

A key element in banking history is that when financial crises occur, reform processes follow. This also happened after the financial turmoil of 2007/2009, at a global level, which also involved the European Union. New prudential regulation (Basel 3), the bank recovery and resolution framework (BRRD) and deposit guarantee schemes (DGSD) entered into force. Together, the reforms created a new regulatory framework (the Single Rulebook), consisting of measures and mechanisms to strengthen the capacity of the banking system to cope with external shocks and maintain its stability.

In the Eurozone, the institutional architecture of banking supervision and crisis management was reshaped by major innovations, through a wide-ranging project: the European Banking Union, which marked the transition from coordination and exchange of information between national authorities to centralisation of decisions in the European supervisory and crisis management authorities, in coordination with the national authorities.

The Banking Union is composed of three pillars: the first two, the Single Supervisory Mechanism (SSM) and the Single Resolution Mechanism (SRM), have been implemented. The third pillar, represented by the Single European Deposit Guarantee Scheme (EDIS), is struggling to take shape due to the opposition of some countries.[12] Thus, we are dealing with an unfinished design.

Among the key innovative elements of the new regulatory framework for bank crisis management, the central principle is that the costs of bank failures should no longer be borne by taxpayers, but by the insolvent banks' shareholders and creditors. Where external support measures are needed to cover losses and restructuring costs, the resources must be provided by the banking sector as a whole. The intent, therefore, is to reduce the moral hazard, by dropping the principle that banks are private when they are alive (resulting in the privatisation of profits) but become public when they are insolvent, through the socialisation of losses.

The core of this new principle is the bail-in—a term that has now become common language—which means that when a bank is insolvent

[12] G. BOCCUZZI, *L'Unione Bancaria Europea, Bancaria Editrice*, 2015.

and needs to be restructured and recapitalised (as part of the resolution procedure) the coverage of losses and the increase in capital must be borne by the shareholders and other capital instrument holders; if these are not sufficient, other creditors of the bank, excluding depositors protected by deposit guarantee schemes, must contribute proportionally to the losses (Article 44(2)(a) of the BRRD).

The bail-in rules, while consistent in principle with the new crisis management guidelines, have nevertheless raised doubts and concerns relating to the effects on those bearing the losses and to the fact that the tool itself may cause instability.[13]

In addition to bail-in, resolution funds and deposit guarantee schemes are also involved in the financing of the resolution, with resources made available by the banks.

The Resolution Fund can intervene for the purposes and with the forms regulated by the BRRD (transposed by Article 79 of Decree No 180/2015). Where the bail-in tool is applied, if some liabilities are excluded from its scope (Article 44 BRRD), the Fund may intervene to cover losses and recapitalise the bank in resolution, provided that contributions by shareholders and creditors are at least 8% of total liabilities, including own funds; in any event, the contribution from the Fund may not exceed 5% of total liabilities, including own funds.

DGSs intervene to reimburse depositors in the event of liquidation or to contribute to the financing of resolution. They can also intervene—on a voluntary basis, if provided by their Statutes—with preventive and alternative measures. In practice, however, the role of DGSs in bank recovery

[13] F. PANETTA, *Finanza, rischi e crescita economica*, Equita SIM *Benchmarking the UK market: A way to create an efficient and effective capital market in Italy*, Milan, 27 January 2016; G. BOCCUZZI, *La risposta europea alla gestione delle crisi bancarie: alcune riflessioni critiche*, Bancaria, No 4, 2016; B. INZITARI, *BRRD, bail-in, risoluzione della banca in dissesto, condivisione concorsuale delle perdite (d.lgs. 180/2015)*, Ildirittodegliaffari.it, 13 May 2016; G. SANTONI, *La disciplina del bail-in, lo stato di dissesto e la dichiarazione dello stato di insolvenza*, in R. LENER, U. MORERA, F. VELLA, *Banche in crisi. Chi salverà i depositanti*, Analisi Giuridica dell'Economia, Il Mulino, February 2016; F. FIORDIPONTI, *Le aspettative restitutorie di azionisti e creditori ai tempi del bail-in*, in *Analisi Giuridica dell'Economia*, il Mulino, pages 527–550, 2016; I. DONATI, *La ricapitalizzazione interna delle banche mediante bail-in*, in R. LENER, U. MORERA, F. VELLA, *Banche in crisi. Chi salverà i depositanti*, cit.

and insolvency prevention measures has been reduced by the new State aid rules and their extensive interpretation and application.[14]

Indeed, the EU rules deeply changed the national framework. The new directives (transposed in Italy by Legislative Decrees No 180 and 181 of 16 November 2015 and No 30 of 8 March 2016) introduced new strategic guidelines, objectives and tools. Notably, the instruments previously applied in our system to avoid insolvency and limit its harmful consequences on savers and on the economy can no longer be used. And when there are profound changes, if not carefully introduced with calibrated and well-managed tools, they can give rise to unwanted effects. They may not be accepted and also spark negative reactions against the institutions that designed and implemented them.

4.3 Changes in the Banking Market and in Operators' Strategies

Another important element of the context of the Italian banking crises is the profound change in bank growth strategies. In the past, the strategies of Italian banks were oriented to external growth, through mergers and acquisitions (M&A), even of banks in difficulty. Over the last decade, as conditions in the banking market and in the consolidation of banks have changed, the banks' willingness to acquire banks in crisis has decreased significantly.

External growth is no longer considered an objective unless it creates value for shareholders and other key stakeholders. Banks are now looking more closely at the effects of potential consolidation on their economic, financial and equity situation, credit quality and prudential requirements, which are closely monitored by market participants and rating agencies. Market operators are increasingly focusing on these factors, as demonstrated by the low level of the banks' price/book value ratio (price quotations/net balance sheet equity), which is attributable to the banks' low profitability and high level of non-performing loans.

Today, in order to be willing to acquire a bank in crisis, banks demand far-reaching compensatory measures, not limited to covering the failing bank's losses, but including an adequate capital endowment to ensure the maintenance of the pre-existing capital ratios.[15] This is a major critical factor in crisis management.

[14] G. BOCCUZZI, *The European Banking Union: Supervision and Resolution*, Palgrave Macmillan, 2016.

[15] G. BOCCUZZI, *Quali regole nella gestione delle crisi bancarie: la complessità in una fase di transizione*, in Tempo Finanziario, No. 2, Year VI, April-June 2016.

5 Vulnerabilities of the Italian Banking System

As mentioned, the Italian banks came out of the first phase of the financial crisis largely unscathed, since they did not have high-risk derivatives in their balance sheets. At that time, banking crises were a very marginal phenomenon, in terms of both number and size.[16]

However, in the following years, the Italian banking sector was hit by a wave of crises, fuelled by structural factors and vulnerabilities which affected banks from 2011. Thus, it is important to analyse in greater depth this context of structural weakness, in order to better understand the real factors and the scale of the crises that have occurred. The analyses conducted have identified the following context factors:

i. **The significant accumulation of non-performing exposures (NPEs) in the banks' balance sheets**

The main cause of the considerable growth of NPEs is the long period of economic crisis: as shown by the evolution of GDP in the last two decades, in Italy the economic recession began in the early 2000s, well before the global financial crisis, with weak signs of recovery in the years 2005–2006. During the financial crisis, GDP plunged steeply (in the first quarter of 2009, −10% in Italy and −12% in the Eurozone compared to the previous year) and started to recover from the second half of 2009. However, it returned to negative in the years 2011–2013. Thereafter, Italian GDP recorded sluggish growth, below the Eurozone average.

Overall, compared with 2007, the last year before the start of the global crisis, in 2008 GDP was about three percentage points lower in the Centre–North Italy and ten percentage points in the South; at national level, the reduction in GDP was about 4 percentage points[17] (Fig. 4).

The Italian banks, which had a business model focused on traditional activities, were severely affected by the long economic recession, due to the deterioration of loans to businesses and households. From the beginning of the global financial crisis in 2008 to the end of 2015, the Italian banks' stock of NPEs has almost tripled: in terms of gross value, in 2008 total NPEs amounted to about €117 billion, equal to 5.7% of total gross

[16] In the period 2007–2009, nine small banks were subject to the extraordinary administration procedure. The FITD intervened in respect of only one of them, for an amount of approximately €5 million, to cover the capital deficit in the context of the transfer of the assets and liabilities of a bank under compulsory administrative liquidation.

[17] BANK OF ITALY, Annual Report, 2018.

Note: Annualized percentage change in GDP compared to the previous period, Source: Eurostat

Fig. 4 Evolution of GDP in Italy and the Eurozone

loans. In 2015, NPEs reached a peak of approximately €360 billion, equal to 18% of total gross exposures. In 2015, bad loans (exposures in default) were about €200 billion, 10.6% of total exposures (€83 billion in net value, 4.8% of total exposures). The increase in NPEs was due both to the worsening of default rates (more pronounced for businesses, which accounted for about 74% of total bad loans) and to difficulties in disposing of bad loans, resulting from the inefficiencies of recovery procedures and the lack of a market for non-performing exposures[18] (Fig. 5).

In Europe, the increase in NPEs was lower than in Italy, as shown in Fig. 6. Italy was the EU country where the phenomenon of non-performing exposures was most acute. Between the end of 2015 and the first half of 2016, the stock of Italian NPEs made up around 29% of total European exposures. In 2019, the percentage of Italian NPEs stock on aggregate European NPEs remained the highest among EU countries, at around 23%.

In this context, the action of the Italian banks was clear and decisive, through a de-risking process, also at the initiative of the supervisory authority. In particular, in March 2017, the European Central Bank

[18] According to a study by the Council of Europe of 2018 (on 2016 data), a civil case in Italy that goes through all three levels of judgement (Court of First Instance, Appeal and Cassation) lasts on average eight years, against an average of less than two years in the Council's member countries. EUROPEAN COUNCIL, *European Judicial Systems, Efficiency and Quality of Justice*, Cepej Studies No. 26, 2018.

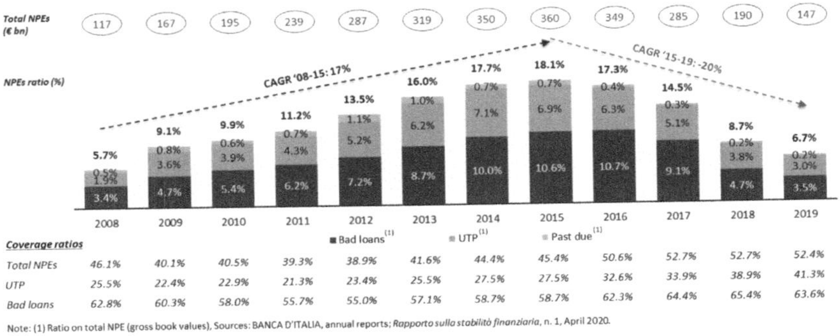

Fig. 5 Trend of non-performing exposures in Italy

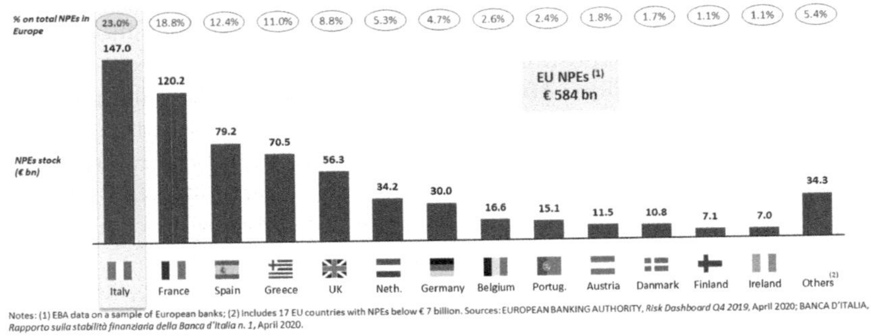

Fig. 6 Stock of non-performing exposures in Europe (2019)

published specific guidelines[19] asking banks to define and achieve targets for reducing their stock of NPEs. In addition, the capital market began to show the correlation between the value of banks and the quality of their credit portfolios: banks with high levels of NPEs (generally above 15–20%) started to pay a significant discount in terms of capitalisation compared to the book value of equity (price/book value).

The sale of NPEs on the market has been the main option for the management of banks. In recent years, the growth in NPE disposals has

[19] EUROPEAN CENTRAL BANK, *Guidance to Banks on Non-Performing Loans*, March 2017.

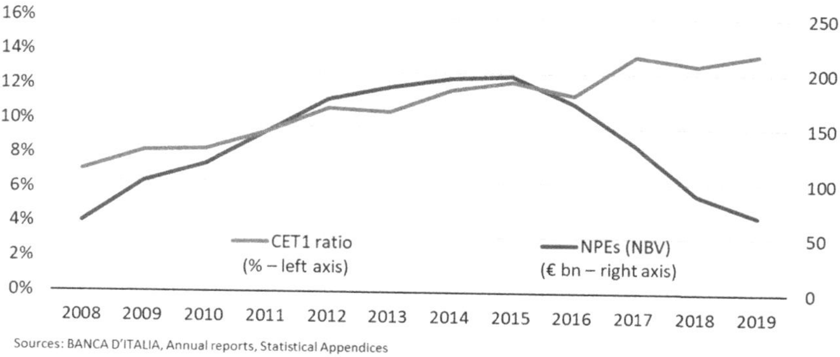

Fig. 7 Capital and NPEs of Italian banks

led to the progressive reduction of the NPE ratio in Europe and, to a greater extent, in Italy.

In particular, between 2015 and 2017, sales transactions for a gross value of over €130 billion were carried out in Italy, highlighting the primacy of the Italian market in the NPEs sector. In that period, the sale of NPEs in Italy rose steadily in both value and number of transactions, reaching a peak in 2017 with a gross value of about €80 billion, more than double compared to 2016 and four times higher than in 2015.[20]

As a result of the de-risking process, the NPE ratio decreased significantly. However, the impact of this process on the profit and loss account and capital levels of the banks was strongly negative.

In Europe, only Spain had to handle values close to the Italian ones, while the sales transactions recorded in the rest of the European countries were significantly lower. Despite the presence of an active market, the NPE ratio in Italy is still significantly higher than in other European countries: at the end of 2019, the European average was 2.7%, compared to 6.7% in Italy (Fig. 7).

ii. **The low profitability of the sector**

[20] KPMG, *I Non Performing Loan in Italy, Trend in Progress and Future Prospects*, 2018; PWC, *The Italian NPE Market, Ready to Face the Crisis*, June 2020.

Another critical issue for Italian banks was the prolonged period of low profitability, despite the improvements made since 2017. Cyclical and structural factors have negatively affected the profitability of the banking system.

In particular, the following should be considered:

- Reduction in total operating income, caused by decreasing revenues in the period 2013–2018, mainly attributable to low interest rates. These negatively affected net interest income, which makes up about 50% of total revenues. Revenues from commissions, mainly related to the provision of investment and asset management services, also decreased from 2013 to 2017. The operating income of the Italian banks, equal in aggregate to approximately €93 billion (3.12% of total assets), fell to approximately €80.5 billion in 2017 (2.7% of total assets of the system). Signals of improvement were recorded in the following years: in 2019, operating income stood at about €82.3 billion (2.74% of total assets);
- Increase in cost/income. Despite the cost reductions following the implementation of restructuring plans, achieved through the closure of branches (-23% in the last 7 years) and staff cuts (-12% in the last 7 years), the average cost/income ratio of Italian banks rose in the period 2013–2019 from 62% to 65.5%,[21] mainly due to the effect of extraordinary costs related to restructuring processes (costs of staff leaving incentives). The increase was especially marked for small banks (those with protected deposits of less than €5 billion), from 78.5% in 2013 to 86.74% in 2019, reaching a peak of 90.93% at the end of 2016[22];
- High cost of credit. The deterioration in credit quality led to a sharp rise in the cost of risk, in terms of adjustments and provisions. The cost of credit risk of Italian banks, calculated by comparing the net provisions on loans with the total amount of exposures to customers, stood at levels above 2% in 2013–2014 and above 1% in the following years.

[21] The average cost/income ratio in 2019 was 65.3% for banks and banking groups headed by joint-stock companies, 68.9% for cooperative banks and banking groups (*banche popolari*), and 71% for cooperative credit banks. The average ratio of significant banks is 65.6%. Source: BANK OF ITALY, *Appendice alla Relazione annuale sul 2019*, May 2020.

[22] FITD data.

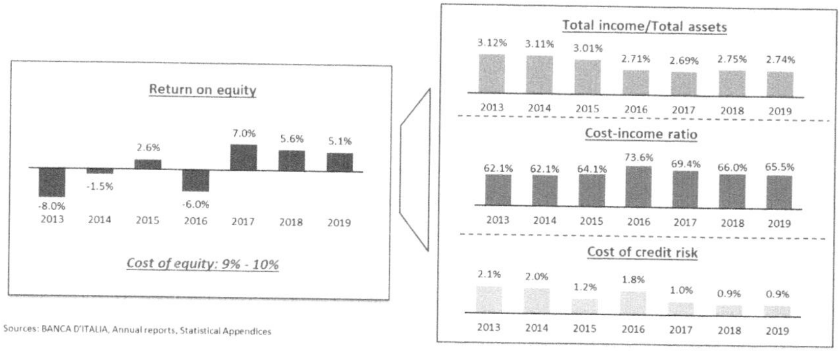

Fig. 8 Profitability of Italian banks (2013–2019)

Profitability, calculated in terms of return on equity (ROE), was significantly lower than the estimated cost of capital for most Italian banks (Fig. 8).

iii. **The business models**

In the new macroeconomic and financial environments, the low profitability of the banking sector is considered to be a consequence of an outdated business model that requires broad strategic review by banks. Supervisors have also focused their attention on this issue, including in the context of SREP.[23] This has also had serious consequences in terms of capitalisation and market values of the shares of listed banks. Figure 9

[23] M. BARAVELLI, *Dalla crisi al rilancio economico: evoluzione dei modelli di business delle banche italiane. Il ruolo del cambiamento organizzativo*, Banche e Banchieri, April 2015; G. FORESTIERI, *I modelli di business delle banche italiane. Alla ricerca della sostenibilità*, Banche e Banchieri, April 2015; M. COMANA, *SREP 2019: i business model delle banche al centro delle valutazioni della Vigilanza*, Diritto Bancario, February 2020, M. PIERIGE', *Banche, il business model che verrà*, Risk Management Magazine, Year 13, No 3, September-December 2018, A. OSTERWALDER, Y. PIGNEUR, *Creare modelli di business*, Milan, FAG, 2012, M. DI ANTONIO, *I modelli di business nel settore bancario: un'analisi da ripensare*, Bancaria, 2018, S. COSMA (et. al.), *I modelli di business delle banche: letteratura, nuove regole e implicazioni strategiche*, Bancaria, 2016, E. PELGANTA (et.al.), *Le variabili determinanti della redditività e i loro fattori di cambiamento: profilazione delle banche nel contesto (new normal) post crisi*; intervention at the AIFIRM conference in Rome, 8 August 2018.

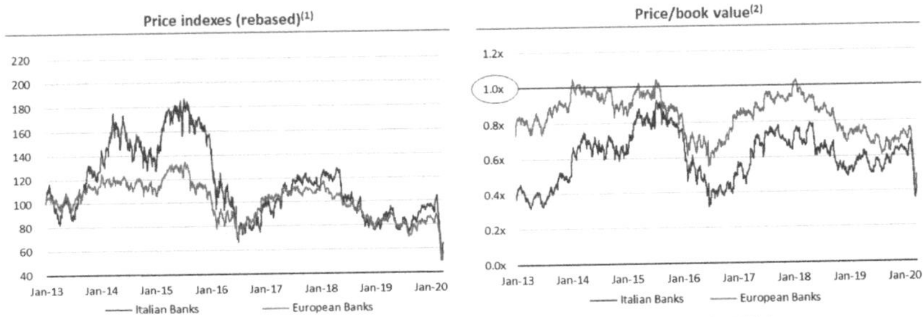

Notes: (1) Italian banks and European banks price indexes rebased at 100 starting from 2 January 2013; (2) Italian Bank Index: IT8300 Index; European Bank Index: SX7P Index.
Sources: BLOOMBERG, data as of 26 March 2020.

Fig. 9 Price indexes and relationship between price and book value of capital (comparison between Italian and European banks)

shows that the aggregate value of the price/book value of European banks has been stably below 1. The ratio has been especially low in Italy, where bank prices bottomed out in 2013 and 2016 and started to recover in 2017, driven by the reduction in non-performing exposures and personnel costs. However, the average market capitalisation of listed Italian banks is still well below their book value.

In the above negative context caused by a multiplicity of factors, the strategic objectives of policymakers and banks have been reoriented in two directions: first, to implement measures to address the structural problems of the banking sector as a whole; second, to provide an adequate toolkit and solutions for the crisis situations that inevitably ensued. The routes have been varied, complex and in some cases fraught with tensions, in a delicate phase characterised by the macroeconomic downturn and the transition to a new regulatory framework. All the ordinary instruments available were used, as well as extraordinary measures. In particular, preventive interventions have been carried out, mainly using financial resources from the banking system, to prevent weak situations from degenerating into insolvency. In the case of larger banks, public intervention was also activated combined synergistically with private sector involvement. In particular:

a. To manage non-performing exposures efficiently and remove them from the banks' balance sheets, measures have been taken to accelerate individual insolvency and enforcement procedures (Decree-Law No 59/2016, converted into Law No 119/2016);
b. Decree-Law No 18/2016 (converted into Law No 49/2016) introduced incentives for the securitisation of non-performing loans, through the use of public guarantees on senior bonds issued by the SPV (GACS)[24];
c. The financial sector created the Atlante Fund (Atlante I and Atlante II) to carry out investments in the banking sector, through the recapitalisation of banks and the participation to NPE securitisation transactions;
d. At the end of 2015, the banking system created a Voluntary Scheme within the FITD to carry out interventions in favour of banks in crisis, to overcome the constraints arising from the application of State aid rules. Subsequently, the statutory provisions and role of the scheme were strengthened. Its interventions were focused on prevention objectives. Priority was given to the recapitalisation of banks, provided that they showed concrete prospects for recovery, on the basis of effective and credible restructuring plans. The costs to the banking sector, however, were significant.

6 The Extent of the Crises

The extent of the crisis phenomenon can be measured by considering the total assets of the banks in crisis. Since 2014, Italy has seen 16 bank crises, 4 of which concerned significant banks (Veneto Banca, Banca Popolare di Vicenza, MPS and Carige) and 12 less significant banks (Fig. 10). Among the former, MPS qualifies as a systemically important bank, since

[24] The GACS (Guarantees on the Securitisation of Non-performing Loans) are guarantees granted by the State, in line with the guidelines of the European Commission, aimed at facilitating the disposal of non-performing loans. The guarantee is granted by the Ministry of Economy and Finance (MEF) on liabilities issued as part of securitisation transactions, against the transfer of the NPLs to a special purpose vehicle. The GACS are unconditional, irrevocable and on first demand and cover the holders of senior securities in the event of non-payment of the amounts due by the SPV for principal and interest.

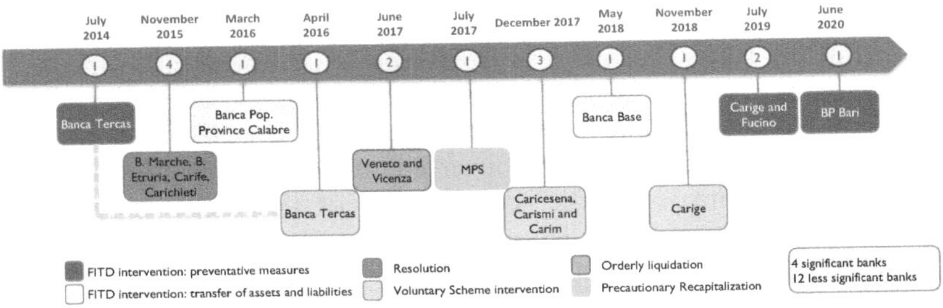

Fig. 10 Italian banking crisis 2014–2020

in December 2016 it had total assets of about €153 billion and protected deposits of about €34.5 billion.[25]

The total assets of the 16 banks amounted to approximately €294.8 billion, of which approximately €153 billion (52%) belonged to MPS. The total amount of the banks' protected deposits was around €82.2 billion. Excluding MPS (whose protected deposits in December 2016 were 42% of the total of the banks concerned), the remaining banks, all of small and medium size (protected deposits of less than €10 billion) had total protected deposits of approximately €47.7 billion. The impact of these banks on the Italian system was about 10% in terms of total assets (of which about 5% is attributable to MPS) and 15% in terms of protected deposits (Fig. 11).

7 Instruments

It is important to underline that all the instruments of the new European framework were applied to address the above banking crises (Fig. 12):

- Resolution according to the BRRD, with use of the Resolution Fund (Banca delle Marche, Banca Etruria e del Lazio, Cassa di Risparmio di Ferrara, Cassa di Risparmio di Chieti);
- Compulsory administrative liquidation, followed by the sale of assets and liabilities to another bank, with the FITD's intervention to cover

[25] MONTE DEI PASCHI DI SIENA, *Relazione finanziaria e Bilancio Consolidato 2016*.

	Total Assets (€ mln)	Covered Deposits (€ mln)	Tot. Assets of bank / Tot. Assets of italian banks (%)	Covered deposits of bank / Covered deposits of italian banks (%)
Tercas	4,466.7	1,857.6	0.2%	0.4%
Banca Marche, Etruria, Carichieti, Ferrara	26,315.4	13,236.2	1.1%	2.6%
Banca Pop. delle Province Calabre	15.3	7.8	0.0%	0.0%
Veneto Banca, Popolare di Vicenza	62,502.5	13,879.3	2.1%	2.4%
MPS	153,178.5	34,490.2	5.1%	6.0%
Carim, Caricesena, Carismi	11,353.0	4,149.7	0.3%	0.8%
Banca Base	47.8	26.8	0.0%	0.0%
Banca Carige	22,094.6	9,006.9	0.7%	1.5%
Banca del Fucino	1,224.1	491.8	0.0%	0.1%
Banca Pop. di Bari	13,636.4	5,065.0	0.5%	0.8%
Total	294,834	82,211	10%	15%

Fig. 11 Scale of the crisis: the size of the banks (*Source* Calculations based on FITD and other official data)

the sale imbalance, pursuant to Article 11.6 of the DGSD (Banca Popolare delle Province Calabre, Banca Base);

- Compulsory administrative liquidation, followed by the transfer of assets and liabilities to another bank, with the government's support through the use of public funds (orderly liquidation). This measure was made possible by the application of the State aid guidelines laid down in the Commission Communication of 1 August 2013 (Banca Popolare di Vicenza, Banca Popolare del Veneto);

	Measure implemented	Burden Sharing on subordinated bondholders	Supporting Authority/Entity	NPEs investor	Acquiror
Tercas	Preventative intervention	×	Voluntary Scheme of FITD	-	Banca Pop. di Bari
Banca Marche, Etruria, Carichieti, Ferrara	Resolution	✓	Resolution Authority	REV and Atlas Fund	UBI and BPER
Banca Pop. delle Province Calabre	Transfer of assets and liabilities	✓	FITD	-	Banca Pop. di Bari
Veneto Banca, Popolare di Vicenza	Orderly liquidation	✓	Ministry of Finance	AMCO	Intesa Sanpaolo
MPS	Precautionary recapitalization	✓	Ministry of Finance	Atlas Fund and AMCO	Ministry of Finance
Carim, Caricesena, Carismi	Preventative intervention	×	Voluntary Scheme of FITD	Atlas Fund and Voluntary Scheme of FITD	Crédit Agricole-Cariparma
Banca Base	Transfer of assets and liabilities	✓	FITD	-	Banca Pop. di Ragusa
Banca Carige	Preventative intervention	×	FITD and Voluntary Scheme of FITD	AMCO	BPER Banca
Banca del Fucino	Preventative intervention	×	FITD	AMCO	Igea Banca
Banca Pop. di Bari	Preventative intervention	×	FITD	AMCO	Mediocredito Centrale - MCC

Fig. 12 Variety of instruments applied

- Precautionary recapitalisation, provided for by the BRRD, applied to resolve the crisis of Monte dei Paschi di Siena;
- Intervention of the FITD's Voluntary Scheme for the recapitalisation of banks (Banca Tercas, Cassa di Risparmio di Cesena, Cassa di Risparmio di Rimini, Cassa di Risparmio di San Miniato, Banca Carige);
- The preventive measures carried out by the FITD pursuant to Article 11.3 of the DGSD, transposed into Italian law by Article 96a(1a) of the TUB and set out in Article 35 of the FITD Statute (Banca Carige, Banca del Fucino, Banca Popolare di Bari).

8 Who Paid?

When a crisis occurs, some fundamental questions arise: what was the cost of the crisis and who paid for it? What was the contribution of the public sector and what was that of the private sector?

The cost of banking crises in Italy in recent years has been significant. As shown in Fig. 13, the total amount of transactions carried out amounts to €43.6 billion, of which €22.5 billion was borne by the public sector and €21.1 billion by the private sector.

In particular, the distribution of the total cost was as follows:

i. Approximately €8.5 billion (19%) were borne by the shareholders and subordinated bondholders of the banks in crisis (burden sharing). Under the burden-sharing principle, shareholders are the first to pay the cost of the crisis, bearing all losses within the limit of the existing equity, while subordinated creditors contribute subsequently, under certain conditions. However, quantifying the amount of the losses borne by shareholders is not a simple exercise, since the effects on the bank's equity normally begin to occur well before the bank's entry into an overt crisis.[26] For the purposes of this exercise, we considered the equity of the banks at the time of the adoption of the crisis solution measure;

ii. **€12.6 billion (29%) by the Italian banking system and other private entities;**

iii. €22.5 billion (52%) by the Italian State.

Not counting the value of the guarantees—partially still not activated—issued by the public sector in connection with the rescue of the two Veneto banks, amounting to approximately €12.4 billion (29% of the total value of the interventions), the share of the private sector is higher than that of the public sector. **The total disbursement for the solution of the crisis of the 16 banks was €31.2 billion, of which approximately €12.6 billion (40%) was borne by the Italian banking system and other private parties, €8.5 billion (27%) by shareholders and subordinated bondholders and €10.1 billion (33%) by the State.**

[26] For example, the equity of Banca Marche at the end of 2012 amounted to approximately €936 million. At the end of the first half of 2015, i.e. a few months before the start of the resolution procedure, the bank's equity was practically zero.

€mln	Shares and bonds holders	Banks and other private investors						Italian State	Total
	Burden Sharing	Resolution Fund	FITD	Voluntary Scheme	Atlas Fund	Other Investors	Total	Public Intervention	
Cover of losses	8,463 *all Banks*	4,798 *4 Banks*	1,177 *Prov. Calabre, Base, Pop. Bari*	1,044 *Tercas, Carim, Carismi, Caricesena*	3,427 *Veneto Banks*	--	**10,446**	4,785 *Veneto Banks*	**23,694**
Equity instruments	--	--	831 *Carige*	318 *Carige*	--	1,028 *Tercas, Carige, Fucino, Pop. Bari*	**2,177**	5,400 *MPS*	**7,577**
Guarantee	--	--	30 *Fucino*	--	--	--	**30**	12,342 *Veneto Banks*	**12,372**
Total	**8,463**	**4,798**	**2,038**	**1,362**	**3,427**	**1,028**	**12,653**	**22,527**	**43,643**
								AMCO	**Totale**
NPEs investments	--	--	--	*12* *Carim, Carismi, Caricesena*	*2,425* *4 Banks, MPS, Carim, Carismi, Caricesena*	*335* *Carim, Carismi, Caricesena*	**2,437**	*7,003* *Carige, Fucino, Pop. Bari, Veneto Banks*	**9,440**

Fig. 13 Distribution of the costs of the bank crises in Italy (*Note* The cost of private interventions does not include the disbursement incurred by the Solidarity Fund, borne by the FITD as provided by the law, for the indemnities to subordinated bondholders of the four banks in resolution and the two Veneto banks in liquidation, for a total amount of approximately €280 million. This amount reduces the burden sharing, which is shown in column 1)

The largest interventions concerned the two Veneto banks and MPS: they added up to about €30 billion, or 76% of the total interventions carried out in Italy between 2014 and 2020 (65% net of guarantees).

Moreover, the main instrument that accompanied the restructuring of banks was the hive-off of a huge amount of NPEs. Figure 13 also shows the total of the interventions carried out for the hive-off of NPEs: disbursement by public (AMCO) and private entities (Atlante Fund and other institutional investors, including the FITD's Voluntary Scheme) was about €9.4 billion.

From SGA to AMCO: a successful story

Società per la Gestione di Attività—S.G.A. S.p.A. was established in 1989, operating according to Law No 588 of 19 November 1996 (Conversion into law of the Decree-Law No 497 of 24 September 1996, containing 'Urgent provisions for the reorganisation, restructuring and privatisation of Banco di Napoli').

In this context, on 31 December 1996, pursuant to Article 58 TUB, the SGA acquired the receivables and other deteriorated assets of Banco di Napoli (this transaction was followed by the purchases of NPEs from other entities of the Banco di Napoli banking group).

Over the years, the company has carried out its activities both directly and through a mandate given to the transferring company (Banco di Napoli, which has been succeeded by Intesa Sanpaolo and ISGS, also part of the Intesa Sanpaolo banking group).

In June 2016, pursuant to Article 7 of Decree-Law No 59/2016, converted by Law No 119/2016, SGA was placed under the control of the Ministry of Economy and Finance, and its corporate object was extended to include the purchase and/or management of receivables of other institutions.

Therefore, the mandate of SGA is now the purchase and the management, according to criteria of cost-effectiveness, of deteriorated assets originating from banks. The company may also acquire on the market equity and other financial instruments.

The SGA also pursues judicial and out-of-court recovery management activities on non-performing loans originating from banks.

On 19 july 2019, sga was renamed amco—asset management company s.p.a., to reflect its new mission and activity as a full-service credit management company.

The transactions carried out recently by AMCO have regarded almost all the major banking crises in Italy, through the acquisition of NPE portfolios: in 2018, Veneto Banca and Banca Popolare di Vicenza, amounting to approximately €18 billion; in 2019, Banca del Fucino (approximately €314 million, at a price of €101 million); Carige Bank (€2.8 billion, at a price of approximately €1 billion) and Banca Popolare di Bari (€2 billion, at a price of approximately €500 million).

In June 2020, amco managed approximately €33 billion of assets under management.

The evolution of AMCO is again under evaluation, in the context of the possible regulation and establishment of asset management companies, at national or European level, to hive off from banks' balance sheets the NPEs that could emerge as a consequence of the pandemic.

CHAPTER 3

The Tercas Case: A Watershed

The case of Banca Tercas concerns the crisis of a small provincial bank which has become prominent at European level following the European Commission's negative assessment of the preventive intervention carried out by the FITD, for alleged infringement of State aid rules. The issues raised by this case are still debated due to their many legal and institutional implications.

The issue has definitely been resolved in favour of the Italian parties by the European Court of Justice, in an appeal filed by the Commission against the judgement of the EU General Court which upheld the appeal brought by the Italian authorities, the FITD and Banca Popolare di Bari, which is the bank that acquired Tercas. The decision of the Court of Justice has an importance that goes beyond the Tercas case.

This case has generated a wide-ranging debate in europe about the operation of deposit guarantee schemes and the need to review the regulation governing them.

G. Boccuzzi, *Banking Crises in Italy*, Palgrave Studies in Financial Instability and Banking Crisis Regulation,
https://doi.org/10.1007/978-3-031-01344-7_3

Tools Applied

- Special administration of the Bank, pursuant to Article 70(1)(b) of the TUB.
- Acquisition by a private bank through a capital increase.
- Preventive intervention of the FITD, consisting in covering the losses and issuing guarantees on certain liabilities of Tercas.
- Approval of the transaction by the bank's shareholders' meeting.

The Main Steps

- **Apr. '12**: the bank is put under special administration.
- **Oct. '13**: the special administrators send to the FITD a formal request for intervention, pursuant to Article 29 of the Statute, accompanied by the offer of Banca Popolare di Bari (BPB) to acquire Banca Tercas.
- **Nov. '13–Mar. '14**: the FITD performs a due diligence on the economic, financial and equity situation of Banca Tercas to determine the capital needs of the bank.
- **May '14**: the FITD approves the support measure for Banca Tercas, after assessing, inter alia, the least cost condition.
- **Jul. '14**: the coverage of losses and the capital increase are approved by the shareholders' meeting of Banca Tercas, in the terms proposed by the special administrators.
- **Feb. '15**: the European Commission notifies Italy that it has opened an investigation under Article 108 TFEU, for alleged infringement of the State aid rules, in relation to the FITD's support for Banca Tercas.
- **Dec. '15**: the European Commission declares that the intervention of the FITD constitutes State aid incompatible with the rules of the internal market and orders the repayment of the amount provided by the FITD.
- **Apr. '16**: Banca Popolare di Bari returns the amounts received to the FITD. The Voluntary Scheme intervenes in favour of Banca Tercas for the same transaction and amount.

1 Banca Tercas: General Background Information

Banca Tercas was the parent company of the banking group of the same name, operating mainly in the Abruzzo region. It controlled another regional bank, Banca Caripe S.p.a., as well as a small insurance company.

The Tercas Group had a network of around 150 branches and 1,200 employees. On 31 December 2013, its total assets amounted to €4.5 billion and its covered deposits to approximately €1.8 billion (Fig. 1).

The crisis of Banca Tercas was started in 2012. The Bank was put under special administration by the Minister of Economy and Finance, by decree of 30 April 2012, on a proposal of the Bank of Italy, for serious administrative irregularities and regulatory violations, following the negative outcome of a supervisory inspection.

Consolidated data as of September 2013 (€ mln; %)	
Direct funding	
o/w: covered deposits	1,858
% FITD total covered deposits	*0.4%*
Total assets	4,467
NPEs ratio (GBV)	31.7%
Cost-Income ratio	90.3%
Net profit (loss)	(427)
ROE	(100.2%)
CET 1 ratio	negative
Total capital ratio	negative
Employees	~ 1,200
Branches	~ 150

Fig. 1 Banca Tercas: main data (*Source* Elaborations on FITD data)

The main factors of the Bank's crisis were the high deterioration of asset quality, negative profitability and capital shortfall, together with governance issues. On 31 September 2013, the Tercas Group had a NPEs ratio of 31.7% and a Cost/Income ratio of 90.3%.

The bank's difficulties were such that the provisions made on assets (loans, participations, etc.) by the special administrators, together with other provisions, led to a significant negative equity.

In October 2013, Banca Popolare di Bari (BPB) expressed an interest in the acquisition of Tercas, to be carried out through recapitalisation, provided that Tercas and its subsidiary Caripe underwent a due diligence enquiry and that the FITD covered Tercas' negative equity in full.

After positive assessment of the transaction from a strategic point of view, BPB decided to acquire the control of Tercas, under the conditions proposed, to be negotiated with the FITD.

Both BPB and the FITD carried out their own due diligence on Tercas and, at the end of this phase, an agreement was reached: the capital needs of Tercas were estimated at €495 million, of which €265 million to cover the shortfall and €230 million for the restoration of the minimum capital required by the supervisory authority (CET1 ratio at 8.5%).

On 30 May 2014, the FITD, after having ascertained, inter alia, that the preventive measure was less costly than the depositor pay-out in a compulsory administrative liquidation, decided to provide financial support to Banca Tercas in the following terms:

i. cash disbursement of €265 million to cover the bank's capital shortfall, as determined during the due diligence carried out by FITD and Banca Popolare di Bari;
ii. issue of guarantees up to a maximum amount of €30 million, to participate in the coverage of further losses resulting from the special administration procedure, due to the tax burden generated by the cash intervention of the FITD;
iii. additional guarantee to Banca Tercas of €35 million against certain high-risk credit exposures.

It was therefore an intervention by the FITD to cover losses and risks, with the aim of enabling Banca Tercas and its subsidiary Banca Caripe to be integrated with Banca Popolare di Bari; an operation with the objective

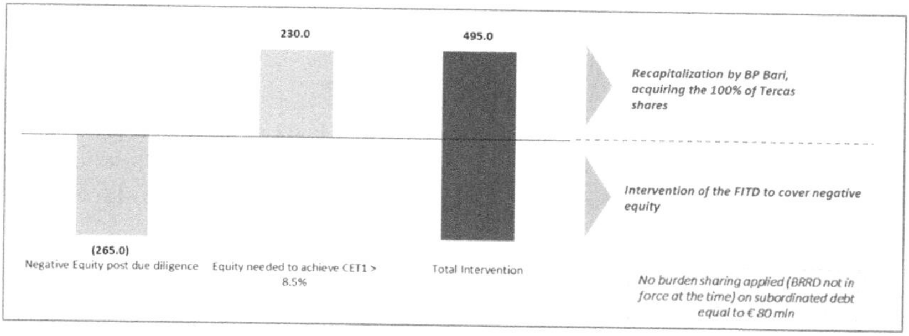

Fig. 2 Banca Tercas: the structure of the deal

of achieving a definitive solution to the crisis of Tercas, which would exit the market.

On 29 July 2014, the extraordinary shareholders' meeting of Tercas approved the capital increase and, on the same date, the Bank of Italy authorised the acquisition by Banca Popolare di Bari of the controlling stake in the capital of Tercas. On 31 July, the FITD implemented its capital injection and issued the required guarantees.

The bank's special administration ended on 30 September 2014, when the shareholders' meeting reappointed the ordinary governance bodies. At that point, Banca Popolare di Bari acquired the control of Tercas (Fig. 2).

2 The Regulatory Framework

The regulatory framework under which the measure was implemented was the one preceding the implementation of Directive 2014/49/EU on deposit guarantee schemes (DGSD), which entered into force on 2 July 2014. The directive was transposed in Italy by Legislative Decree No 30 of 15 February 2016. Therefore, when the directive entered into force, the Tercas case—with the intervention of the FITD (30 May 2014) and the approval of the Shareholders' Meeting (29 July 2014)—had been concluded.

Before the directive, Article 96a(1) of the Italian Banking Act (TUB) provided that deposit guarantee schemes: (i) were required to reimburse depositors in cases of compulsory administrative liquidation of a bank;

(ii) could apply other forms of intervention in the cases and under the conditions laid down in their statute.

Due to the broad mandate given them by the TUB, DGSs had discretion in the use of resources for interventions other than the reimbursement of depositors. In particular, the FITD's statute allowed it to implement preventive measures in favour of member banks under special administration.

The framework was significantly modified by the transposition of the DGSD, which however confirmed the approach of the previous legislative and statutory framework, as it provided for—and stressing its importance—the possibility of other interventions than the reimbursement of depositors, such as preventive interventions (Article 11.3) and alternative interventions (Article 11.6), provided that they were less costly than reimbursing depositors.

3 State Aid Rules: The EU Commission Decision

The Tercas case represented a watershed for the FITD's operations within the framework of banking crisis management.

On 27 February 2015, the European Commission opened an investigation against the Italian State, pursuant to Article 108 TFEU, for alleged infringement of State aid rules by the support measure carried out by the FITD in favour of Banca Tercas, not notified to the Commission.

At the end of a long procedure, on 23 December 2015,[1] the Commission adopted a decision that considered the FITD's support to be public and declared it incompatible with the internal market, pursuant to Article 108(3) TFEU.[2]

The Commission decision was based on a series of elements aimed at demonstrating the imputability to the State of the FITD's intervention and the use of State resources. In particular, the Commission emphasised the following main factors: (i) the existence of a public mandate to protect

[1] EUROPEAN COMMISSION, *Decision No C (2015) 9526 final of 23 December 2015 concerning a proceeding pursuant to Article 108(2)TFEU and Article 62(1)(a) of the EEA Agreement* (case SA.39451 (2015/C) (ex 2015/NN)—Banca Tercas).

[2] P. DE GIOIA CARABELLESE, *Crisi Bancarie e Aiuti di Stato. La Sentenza Tercas: Brussels versus Italy?*, Ordine Internazionale e Diritti Umani 686–718, 15 October 2019; I. MECATTI, *L'organizzazione dei sistemi di garanzia dei depositanti in funzione degli interventi alternativi per la prevenzione e la gestione della crisi delle banche*, Il Mulino—Rivisteweb, Banca Impresa Società, 2 August 2020.

depositors, even if implemented through other intervention methods; (ii) the possibility for public authorities to influence all stages of the support intervention and to control the use of the DGSs' resources; (iii) the compulsory nature of the contributions paid by member banks to the FITD.

In its decision, the Commission also ordered the recovery of the resources, with the obligation on the part of Tercas to return the entire amount of the measure to the FITD. This caused great dismay and concern in the public opinion, as well as regulators and market operators, with serious consequences on the stability of the integration between the two banks, implemented more than a year earlier.

4 The Creation of the Voluntary Scheme and the Intervention

The Commission's negative decision resulted in a situation of great uncertainty and precariousness, as it radically changed the framework in which BPB carried out its assessments on the convenience of the takeover operation. In this context, the first objective of the banking system was to secure Banca Tercas and the completion of the business combination with BPB.

Hence, the decision taken by the member banks of the FITD, in line with the guidelines expressed by the European Commission[3] itself, to set up the Voluntary Intervention Scheme (SVI) for banks in crisis, according to a model already tested in other European countries and by the FITD itself, before the entry into force of the 1994 Directive, which made compulsory the participation of banks in a DGS. The Voluntary Scheme was in fact in line with the philosophy that always inspired the management of banking crises in Italy, aimed at the reorganisation and restructuring of banks instead of liquidation solutions, in the presence of concrete prospects of recovery, based on effective and credible business plans.

[3] While the Commission took a negative position on the use of the banks' mandatory contributions to the FITD in support interventions, which culminated in the decision taken in the Tercas case, on the other hand, it also pointed out that, if operations were carried out by the FITD on a voluntary basis and with private funds, it would not raise any objections from the point of view of State aid against such scheme even if set up within the FITD.

This initiative, therefore, was designed to solve the Tercas case and to provide support for any other similar situations, under the terms of the then-current Statute, in favour of banks in special administration.

The new instrument was fully in line with the interests of the Italian banking sector, as it helped to strengthen the safeguards and the scope for action in crisis situations that could otherwise undermine the reputation and stability of the system.

The Voluntary Scheme was set up with the participation of almost all the FITD's member banks (92.1%), representing 99.6% of covered deposits.

Following the Commission Decision of 23 December 2015, Banca Popolare di Bari and Banca Tercas asked the Voluntary Scheme to take action to shield them from the consequences of that decision.

On 25 January 2016, the Voluntary Scheme decided to intervene in favour of Banca Tercas, essentially in the same terms previously decided by the FITD: (i) disbursement of €265 million, plus commissions and interest (approximately €6.9 million). The SVI's intervention was carried out simultaneously to the 'payback' by Banca Tercas; (ii) a guarantee of €30 million to the bank, limited to six months, against the risk that the tax neutrality of the intervention of the Voluntary Scheme would fail. This latter commitment was not applied since fiscal neutrality was confirmed. The €35 million guarantee on high-risk performing loans also lapsed because of agreements between BPB and the debtors of Tercas.

The total intervention of the SVI amounted to €271.9 million.

5 The Appeal Brought by Italy and the Ruling of the EU General Court

In 2016, the Italian State, Banca Popolare di Bari and the FITD, supported by the Bank of Italy, appealed to the EU General Court of Luxembourg, asking it to annul the Commission's decision.

By judgement of 19 March 2019, the EU General Court[4] annulled the Commission's decision, ruling that the Commission had erred in concluding that the measures granted to Tercas entailed the use of State resources and was imputable to the State.

[4] Judgement of the EU General Court (Third Chamber, Extended Composition) of 19 March 2019 in Joined Cases T-98/16, T-196/16 and T-198/16.

In this regard, for a measure to be classified as 'State aid' within the meaning of Article 107(1) TFEU four conditions are met: (i) State intervention or State resources are involved; (ii) the measure may affect trade between Member States; (iii) it grants a selective advantage to its beneficiary; (iv) it distorts or threatens to distort competition.

According to the EU General Court's ruling, the evidence submitted by the Commission failed to demonstrate both that the measures in support of Tercas were imputable to the State, and that they were based on the use of State resources. Having annulled the decision on that basis, the EU General Court did not analyse the additional grounds of appeal put forward by the applicants.[5]

With regard to the criterion of 'aid granted by the State or through State resources', to qualify the measure as 'aid' within the meaning of Article 107(1) TFEU, certain advantages must, on the one hand, be granted directly or indirectly through State resources and, on the other hand, be imputable to the State. In that regard, the EU General Court ruled that it is necessary to carefully assess the cases in which the aid is granted directly by the State and those in which it is granted through a public or private body designated or established by the State. This is done by examining the evidence resulting from the circumstances of the case and the context in which the measure was taken.

In that regard, the EU General Court concluded that, since the measure in favour of Tercas was provided by a private entity, the Commission did not have sufficient evidence to establish the imputability of that aid to the State, since, on the contrary, there were numerous indications that the FITD acted autonomously at the time of its intervention.

The EU General Court decided that the mandate given by law to the FITD, as a deposit guarantee scheme, consisted exclusively in reimbursing depositors in the event of compulsory administrative liquidation of a member bank. Outside this framework, for support interventions—if they are less expensive than the repayment of depositors and there are prospects of recovery of the bank in difficulty, as in the Tercas case—the FITD does not act in accordance with a public mandate. These interventions are implemented within the framework of the provisions of Article

[5] They concerned the non-implementation or misapplication of the private market economy operator principle, the errors made by the Commission in assessing the compatibility of the alleged aid, the incorrect classification of the tax guarantee and the recovery of the benefit granted.

96-bis, paragraph 1, of the Italian Banking Act, according to which DGSs may put in place further cases and forms of intervention.

The EU General Court also ruled that the Commission did not demonstrate the involvement of the public authorities in the decision on the measure.

The FITD, in fact, is a consortium governed by private law that acts, under its Statutes, on behalf and in the interest of its member banks. In addition, its management bodies are appointed by the general meeting of the FITD and are composed exclusively of representatives of its member banks. The Bank of Italy's authorisation of the intervention by the FITD for the benefit of Tercas must be understood as a verification of its compliance with the regulatory framework, carried out as part of the prudential activity of the Authority.

Regarding the source of funding, the Court concluded that the Commission did not demonstrate that the funds granted by the FITD in support of Tercas were controlled by the Italian public authorities. The intervention of the FITD originated from a proposal made initially by the Banca Popolare di Bari and subsequently adopted by Tercas—in accordance with the FITD's Statutes, using the resources provided by the member banks—in implementing the decision taken by the FITD Board.

Therefore, in the light of the factual and regulatory background analysed by the EU General Court in its ruling, the amendments made since the Commission decision make it even less likely that undue interference by public entities in the FITD's decisions on preventive interventions might occur.

In particular, regarding the imputability of the measure to the State:

i. The private nature of the FITD and its bodies is clear. The FITD—as already mentioned—is a consortium between banks governed by private law, which operates in the interests of the banks when dealing with preventive interventions, to pursue its statutory purposes. The members of the governing bodies of the FITD are appointed by the general meeting of the banks. Public authorities may not designate any member of the governing bodies of the FITD. In addition, in the new set-up, the FITD's Statute no longer provides for—as before—a delegate from the Bank of Italy to attend meetings of the governing bodies as an observer;
ii. preventive measures, as well as alternative measures through the transfer of assets and liabilities of banks in liquidation—which always

pursue the reduction of costs and risks for the Consortium—are optional and, today, they are no longer even subject to the authorisation of the Bank of Italy; the relevant rules are contained in the Statute and the decision is left to the guarantee scheme. Therefore, there is no public mandate to carry out such measures, which are instead attributable to a choice of the banks belonging to a private consortium, in the full exercise of their autonomy. The current legislation requires the DGS only to carry out the reimbursement of depositors and interventions in resolution, in the cases and with the arrangements provided by law;

iii. the least cost condition, provided for by the applicable legislation and the Statute, ensures that such interventions are carried out only if they are consistent with the interests of the member banks, considering the 'the cost that the Fund would have to bear in order to carry out other measures provided for by the Statute' and the 'effects that liquidation of the bank could determine on the other banks in crisis and the banking system in general';

iv. the FITD may decide to implement a preventive intervention on its own initiative or on the request of private entities, without any involvement of public authorities; the opening of a special administration procedure is no longer a requirement for implementing a preventive intervention. Under the new regulatory framework, special administration is an early intervention measure that can be used when other measures are not sufficient. During this procedure, the FITD may carry out a preventive intervention, on the request of the special administrators.

The same considerations apply to the resources used for the interventions, which exclude the presence of State resources.

Moreover, other changes made to the regulatory framework (the removal of the authorisation of the interventions by the Bank of Italy, of the participation of one of its delegates in the meetings of the bodies of the FITD and of the requirement to open the special administration procedure) strengthen the conclusion that the FITD's resources are not under the State's control.

Additional circumstances are relevant. In accordance with the DGSD, the resources of the FITD are no longer provided ad hoc by the banks for individual operations but are provided under an *ex-ante* contribution system. The rationale for the new funding mechanism is precisely to provide the guarantee schemes with a greater degree of flexibility in their intervention, through the prompt availability of resources. Moreover, differently from depositor reimbursement and resolution financing, preventive measures are not subject to a public mandate, since the decision to implement them—as stated above—is attributable to the choice of the banks forming part of a private consortium, acting with full autonomy.

All these circumstances must lead to the conclusion that, following the ruling of the EU General Court and the subsequent regulatory innovations, the FITD is fully entitled to implement preventive and alternative interventions in favour of member banks, without the constraints of State aid rules.

5.1 The Commission's Appeal

On 12 June 2019, the Commission appealed to the Court of Justice (Case C-425/19 P.) asking it to annul the judgement of the General Court.

In its appeal, the Commission argued further the use of State resources by the FITD, as well as the imputability of the measures to State authorities. Suspension of the judgement pending the appeal proceedings was not requested.

During the proceedings, on 29 October 2020, Advocate General (AG) Evgeni Tanchev gave his opinion to the Court. He recommended dismissing the appeal lodged by the Commission, highlighting that the General Court had correctly concluded that the measures adopted by the FITD did not constitute State aid.

The opinion of the AG also confirmed the view that the public mandate of the FITD only consists in reimbursing depositors, but not in adopting alternative and preventive interventions, which are decided by the DGSD on a voluntary basis and in compliance with the least cost criterion.

Moreover, regarding the Bank of Italy's role in the matter, the AG believed that its participation was purely for information purposes and to control the compliance of the intervention with the rules, in line with its prudential supervisory functions.

These conclusions were not binding since the role of the AG is to propose a legal solution to the case in full independence. In any case, this opinion is of great importance, as it confirms the compliance of the FITD's work with the applicable regulatory provisions at European and national level.

5.2 *The Court of Justice Decision*

By decision of 2 March 2021,[6] the Court of Justice has definitely resolved the Tercas case in favour of the Italian parties, by dismissing the appeal brought by the Commission against the ruling of the General Court of 19 March 2019. The Court of Justice has clarified that in the case-law there were no conditions to consider the measures granted by FITD in favour of Banca Tercas as imputable to the State, since FITD is an entity governed by private law and not an organisation of the State or a public undertaking.

In that regard, the Court of Justice took the view that the General Court correctly stated that it is for the Commission to demonstrate, on the basis of a set of indicators, that the measures at issue were imputable to the State. Furthermore, it affirmed that there is no link of a capital nature between the FITD and the State.

The decision of the Court of Justice is of crucial importance, since, beyond the Tercas affair, which is now closed, it could give rise to fundamental legislative provisions for the management of banking crises carried out with interventions by deposit guarantee schemes.

[6] Court of Justice of the European Union, Judgement in Case C-425/19 P, Commission v Italy, Fondo Interbancario di Tutela dei Depositi, Banca d'Italia et Banca Popolare di Bari ScpA.

CHAPTER 4

The first application of the BRRD: the case of the four banks in resolution

After Banca Tercas, in the same period a similar case occurred for four Italian banks, for which specific recapitalisation and restructuring initiatives by the FITD were at an advanced stage. However, the realisation of these initiatives was prevented by an intervention of the European Commission, based on State aid rules.

The Commission stated that the FITD's preventive intervention would not have been possible under the new European regulatory framework governed by BRRD, as such intervention constituted State aid. The assumption was that the measures constituted 'extraordinary financial public support' provided to maintain or restore the solvency of the bank in crisis.

As a consequence, when extraordinary public financial support is provided, the bank is considered to be 'failing or likely to fail' (Article 32(4) BRRD) and thus to require the opening of liquidation proceedings or—in the presence of a public interest—resolution.

Based on this assumption, the four banks were declared failing or likely to fail and put into resolution.

G. Boccuzzi, *Banking Crises in Italy*, Palgrave Studies in Financial Instability and Banking Crisis Regulation,
https://doi.org/10.1007/978-3-031-01344-7_4

Banks in resolution	*Banca delle Marche* *Cassa di Risparmio di Ferrara* *Cassa di Risparmio di Chieti* *Banca Popolare dell'Etruria e del Lazio*

The tools applied

- Banks placed under special administration
- Banks put in resolution, applying the good bank—bad bank separation tool and setting up bridge banks
- Application of burden sharing
- Intervention of the Resolution Fund to cover losses and recapitalise the banks
- Compulsory administrative liquidation of the four banks in resolution
- Sale of the bridge banks

The main steps

- **May '13–Feb. '15:** the four banks are put into special administration
- **Apr. '15–Oct. '15:** the special administrators of three of the banks (Banca Marche, Banca Etruria and Banca Carife) send to the FITD formal requests for intervention. FITD opens discussions with the special administrators of the banks and conducts an analysis to assess the conditions and forms of a possible intervention
- **May. '15–Nov. '15:** the FITD approves the intervention for the recapitalisation of Banca Marche, Banca Popolare dell'Etruria e del Lazio and Banca Carife
- **Nov. '15**: the special administrators of Carichieti submit a request for intervention to the FITD, which starts an analysis to plan a support intervention
- **Nov. '15**: the European Commission communicates that the FITD's interventions constitute State aid and, as such, the beneficiary banks are to be considered as failing or likely to fail, which constitutes the condition for resolution or liquidation
- **Nov. '15**: The four banks are put into resolution by decree of Ministry of the Economy and Finance, which approves the measures taken by the Bank of Italy. The temporary administrators of the resolution are appointed, and in December 2015, they are appointed

as liquidators of the banks. The ordinary bodies (Boards of directors and of statutory auditors) of the four bridge banks are also appointed. The NPLs of the four banks (around €8.5 billion in terms of GBV, €2.1 billion in terms of NBV) are transferred to REV, a special vehicle established for this purpose

- **Jan. '16**: the Bank of Italy, as national resolution authority, starts the competitive process for the sale of the four bridge banks
- **Jan. '17–Jun. '17:** agreements are signed for the transfer of the bridge banks to UBI (Banca Marche, Carichieti and Banca Popolare dell'Etruria e del Lazio) and BPER (Banca Carife)
- **May '17–Jun. '17:** Atlante Fund acquires a portfolio of NPEs of the four banks having a GBV of €2.5 billion

1 The First Project: The FITD's Intervention

In 2014, four banks, located in northern and central Italy (Banca Marche, Banca Popolare dell'Etruria e del Lazio, Cassa di Risparmio di Ferrara, Cassa di Risparmio di Chieti), were in serious difficulties and were put into special administration by decrees of Ministry of Economy and Finance, on the proposal of the Bank of Italy. Following these measures, the management of the banks was entrusted to special administrators appointed by the Bank of Italy.

While each bank was placed under special administration at different times, the solution of their crisis occurred jointly, within a single package of measures. For this reason, we will analyse their cases together.

The banks were of small-medium size, classified as 'less significant' and, as such, falling under the competence of the Italian supervisory authority, the Bank of Italy. Together, their share of the national market amounted to 1% in terms of total assets (the largest bank was Banca Marche, with total assets of about €13.7 billion as of December 2015) and 2.6% in terms of deposits covered by the FITD. The main similarities between the four banks were: a gross NPE ratio of 40% (for Banca Etruria and Carife even above 50%) and a Cost/Income ratio significantly higher than 100%.

Figure 1 shows the key economic, financial and capital figures of the four banks as of December 2015, after the adoption of the resolution measures.

During the special administration, many attempts were made by the special administrators and the Bank of Italy to find an M&A solution

Consolidated data as of December 2015 (€ mln; %)	**Nuova B. Marche**	**Nuova B. Etruria**	**Nuova B. Carichieti**	**Nuova B. Carife**
Direct funding	11,567.8	5,121.6	2,486.5	2,808.4
o/w: covered deposits	7,865	2,810	1,049	1,511
% FITD total covered deposits	*1.5%*	*0.5%*	*0.2%*	*0.3%*
Total assets	13,758.8	6,144.4	3,084.4	3,327.8
NPEs ratio (GBV) (1)	41.8%	51.3%	39.8%	61.1%
Cost-Income ratio (2)	144%	127%	149%	133%
Net profit (loss)	(62.1)	(34.3)	(21.1)	(30.3)
ROE	(6.0%)	(0.1%)	(15.3%)	(15.9%)
CET 1 ratio (3)	11.9%	10.3%	9.5%	9.4%
Total capital ratio (3)	11.9%	10.3%	9.5%	9.4%
Employees	2,449	1,607	584	849
Branches	304	172	65	105

Fig. 1 The 4 banks: main data (*Notes* (1) 'Pro-forma' credit quality of the New banks, which includes assets subsequently transferred to REV; (2) Values include payments made by the Resolution Fund on the basis of provisional assessments to cover losses and to restore regulatory requirements (approximately €2 billion for Banca Marche, €725 million for Banca Etruria, €167 million for Carichieti, €624 million for Banca Carife). *Sources* NUOVA BANCA DELLE MARCHE S.p.A. situazione al 31 dicembre 2015; NUOVA BANCA ETRURIA S.p.A., Relazione e Bilancio 2015; NUOVA CASSA DI RISPARMIO DI CHIETI S.p.A., Bilancio di esercizio al 31/12/2015; NUOVA CASSA DI RISPARMIO DI FERRARA S.p.A., Bilancio separato al 31 dicembre 2015)

within the Italian banking system. Such attempts, however, were not successful[1], because of the complexities of the banks, each having its own peculiarities.

[1] I. Visco, *Indagine conoscitiva sulle condizioni del sistema bancario e finanziario italiano e la tutela del risparmio, anche con riferimento alla vigilanza, la risoluzione delle crisi e la garanzia dei depositi europea*, Audizione dinanzi alla Commissione permanente (Finanze e tesoro) del Senato, 19 April 2016.

With reference to Banca Marche, at the end of a long process of analysis and constant dialogue with the special administrators and the Bank of Italy, a comprehensive restructuring operation was delineated: it provided for the securitisation of the banks' NPEs and the acquisition of a shareholding by the FITD, in the context of a wider recapitalisation of the bank, to be finalised by an Italian industrial partner together with foreign investors. The intervention was authorised by the Bank of Italy in December 2014.

However, negotiations with the potential buyer encountered difficulties, especially in the search for other investors willing to recapitalise Banca Marche and underwrite securitisation tranches. In the first half of 2015, in the light of the deterioration of the Bank's situation and the impossibility to raise the financial resources necessary for the capital increase, the special administrators highlighted the need for an intervention different from that initially proposed.

The same situations occurred for the other three banks (Banca Carife, Banca Etruria and Carichieti). Between April and October 2015, the respective special administrators, considering the deterioration of the banks' situation and the difficulty in finding solutions on the market, sent to the FITD formal requests for interventions aimed at the reorganisation and recapitalisation of the banks.

Based on those requests and following the due diligences carried out, the FITD, in conformity with its statutory provisions, decided to intervene for the banks' recapitalisation, envisaging the application of burden-sharing measures, based on the write-down and the conversion of capital instruments (Article 59, BRRD), which were implemented in the Italian framework just a few months later.[2]

The decisions taken by the FITD were based on the business plans agreed with the special administrators. In particular, the FITD:

- On 6 May 2015 approved a support measure for the benefit of Banca Carife in the amount of €300 million, for the recapitalisation of the

[2] The prospect of resorting to 'burden sharing'—realisable only after the implementation of the EU Directive 2014/59 (BRRD)—was already taken into consideration at the time of the FITD's intervention in favour of Banca Marche and Banca Etruria: the capital instruments (shares) issued by the banks would have been utilised to cover losses; the subordinated bond would have been used partially to cover losses and, for the remaining part, to recapitalise the banks.

bank. The Bank of Italy authorised the FITD to carry out the intervention, in accordance with Article 96b of The Italian Banking Act. On 30 July 2015, the bank's extraordinary shareholders' meeting approved the capital increase proposed by the special administrators. Next, the FITD started the authorisation procedure with the ECB, pursuant to Article 19 of the Italian Banking Act, for the acquisition of a controlling stake in the bank;

- On 8 October 2015, it decided an intervention in favour of Banca Marche, for a maximum amount of €1.2 billion;
- On 1 November 2015, it decided an intervention in favour of Banca Etruria, for an amount of €426 million; and
- On 11 November 2015, it took the decision to appoint an advisor to analyse the economic and financial situation of Carichieti, prepare a business plan and verify the 'least cost' condition for the intervention. The financial support in favour of the bank was estimated at about €180 million.

The FITD's overall intervention, for a total estimated amount of €2.1 billion, would have been carried out through the recapitalisation of the four banks, in order to cover their losses and restructuring costs, as well as to restore capital requirements. Such operations were intended to fall under a wider project for the aggregation of the four banks. To this end, FITD worked on developing a unitary restructuring and relaunch plan. One of the various options examined was to create a Newco (SPV); the vehicle would act as operating arm and investment tool of the FITD, which would manage—according to a unitary and coherent logic—the equity investments in the four banks and the SPV, the latter intended for the management of the NPEs.

The project was based on the business and financial integration of the four banks, to exploit the synergies and economies of scale deriving from their combination and allow the FITD to recover more value than through the separate management of each bank's assets.

In view of this potential operation, the main conditions of a complex financing transaction with a pool of banks had already been agreed, at market conditions. This was intended to provide the FITD with the financial resources necessary to fund the operation, in order to avoid the immediate recourse to the contributions of its member banks. In agreement with the arranger banks, the structure of the financing would make it possible to put in place separate financing contracts, to be concluded at the time of each intervention. The overall amount of financing was €1.8 billion, to be reimbursed with the future contributions of the FITD's member banks, in line with the consortium's predefined funding plan of FITD, or with the proceeds of the sale of the shares that would be held in the four banks.

The whole operation regarding the four banks reached an advanced stage of definition and implementation. However, the Commission decision prohibited implementation of the project, based on the assumption that the FITD's intervention would constitute State aid, leading to the resolution or liquidation of the banks.

2 The Commission's Decision

The position of the European Commission was communicated through a letter sent on 19 November 2015 by Commissioners Hill and Vestager to the Italian Ministry of the Economy and Finance.[3]

The position moved along the lines already expressed by the Commission with regard to the Tercas case: the classification of the FITD's intervention as extraordinary public financial support, which the BRRD (Article 2(1)(28)) considers as State aid pursuant to Article 107(1) TFEU; this is one of the situations in which the bank is considered as failing or likely to fail (Article 32(4) BRRD) and must therefore be placed under resolution or liquidation.

Thus, the Commission excluded the possibility that the FITD could carry out preventive interventions in favour of banks, because in such case the banks would be considered as failing or likely to fail.

However, equating the FITD's intervention to 'extraordinary public financial support', hence to State aid, is highly questionable at various levels, given that the FITD's interventions constitute a completely different case from State aid, because they are decided by private subjects and implemented with private resources. Moreover, the Commission's position clearly contradicted the DGSD; Article 11(3) thereof regulates the preventive interventions of deposit guarantee schemes precisely to avoid the resolution or the liquidation of a bank.

Some clarifying considerations might be useful.

[3] M. Vestager, J. Hill, *Letter of the Commissioners on the solution of the crisis of the 4 banks*, 2015.

First, it should be considered that pursuant to the BRRD (Article 32), public intervention, and the subsequent qualification of the bank as failing or likely to fail, constitutes only one of the conditions under which the bank can be submitted to resolution or liquidation. The same article provides for a second condition, namely the impossibility of an alternative measure in a reasonable timeframe, including an intervention of the private sector or an Institutional Protection Scheme (IPS) or an action of the competent authority—including early interventions measures—that would avoid the failure of the bank. Thus, fulfilment of the 'failing or likely to fail' condition does not necessarily trigger resolution or liquidation, since the write-down or conversion of capital instruments (burden sharing), possibly in combination with the intervention of a third party (including a deposit guarantee scheme), may make it possible to avoid both resolution and liquidation.

In this sense, Article 59 BRRD provides that the power to write down and convert capital instruments can be exercised by the Resolution Authority even independently of the start of the resolution or the liquidation. This provision has been implemented in the Italian framework by Legislative Decree No 180/2015, which provides that the Bank of Italy, after determining that a bank is failing or likely to fail, may apply the burden sharing, even together with the intervention of third parties, to prevent the bank's failure and the enforcement of one of the two insolvency procedures.

Moreover, the preventive interventions of DGSs cannot fall within the scope of Article 56 BRRD (Government financial stabilisation tools), which regards direct support by the State, with properly public resources, in the context of a resolution and as a last resort, arranged by the Government in cooperation with the Resolution Authority. Thus, the classification of the FITD's measure as State aid is highly questionable and raises the more general problem of how the Commission's position can modify a specific provision of a Directive.

The approach followed by the Commission caused dismay and serious uncertainties and concerns for the fate of the four banks, especially considering the time spent managing the crises and the advanced stage of the initiatives taken by FITD.

In the situation, only the intervention of the FITD's Voluntary Scheme could prevent the resolution or liquidation of the four banks, in line with the guidance of the Commission itself, according to which, outside insolvency procedures, supporting measures should come from private entities, identified in conformity with State aid rules.

To that end, the Voluntary Scheme—then in the process of being established—was working on a specific initiative in support of the four banks; a project was under way to carry out the same operations the FITD had been prohibited to perform.

But the evolution of the events did not allow the realisation of the initiative taken by the banking system. The situation of the four banks was very serious, liquidity was precarious and the solution identified and its timing were considered incompatible with the severity of the situation.[4] Furthermore, the urgency to find a solution to the crisis of the four banks was also due to the fact that on 1 January 2016 the bail-in tool would enter into force, making its application mandatory before the involvement of the Resolution Fund for the funding of the resolution. Such acceleration made it possible to avoid sacrificing many creditors, in particular senior bondholders and other unsecured creditors, as would have happened in the case of bail-in or liquidation of the banks.[5]

3 The Resolution of the Four Banks

On 16 November 2015, Legislative Decree No 180 entered into force, implementing the BRRD in Italy. The bail-in tool, as said, was instead introduced starting from 1 January 2016.

On 21 November 2015, a few days after the introduction of the new resolution regime, the Government and the Bank of Italy opened the resolution procedure for the four banks in special administration, after the Bank of Italy had declared them to be failing or likely to fail and determined the existence of the other conditions for resolution, including public interest.

[4] I. Visco, *Audizione dinanzi alla 6ª Commissione Permanente del Senato (Finanze e Tesoro), Indagine conoscitiva sulle condizioni del sistema bancario e finanziario italiano e la tutela del risparmio, anche con riferimento alla vigilanza, la risoluzione delle crisi e la garanzia dei depositi europee*, cit..

[5] Banca D'Italia, *Domande e risposte sulla soluzione delle crisi delle quattro banche poste in 'risoluzione'*, 30 January 2016, https://www.bancaditalia.it/media/approfondimenti/2016/d-e-r-quattro-banche/index.html.

The assets and liabilities of the banks in resolution were transferred to four bridge banks and the national Resolution Fund was activated for the coverage of losses and recapitalisation. Moreover, burden sharing by shareholders and subordinated bondholders, in most part represented by retail customers, was applied.

The enforcement of burden sharing had a huge negative impact on public trust, because it was the first time in Italy that the creditors of a bank, even though subordinated, were subject to a haircut due to insolvency.

In particular, the resolution of the four banks was applied in compliance with the Commission Communication on State aid and implemented according to the following procedural steps.

The resolution was adopted by decision of the Bank of Italy of 21 November 2015 and approved by the Ministry of Economy and Finance. The existence of the condition of failing or likely to fail was verified through a temporary evaluation, given the situation of extreme urgency, also to quantify the costs associated with the resolution measures.[6] The resolution programme, considering the results of the temporary evaluation, was structured as follows:[7]

i) the special administrations of the four banks were closed and the mandates of the special administrators and the Surveillance Committees were terminated. Therefore, newly Temporary Administrators and Surveillance Committees were appointed by the Bank of Italy for each bank under resolution;

[6] C. Barbagallo, *Cassa di Risparmio di Ferrara, Banca delle Marche, Cassa di Risparmio della Provincia di Chieti, Banca Popolare dell'Etruria e del Lazio*, Senato della Repubblica - Camera dei Deputati, Commissione Parlamentare di inchiesta sul sistema bancario e finanziario, Legge 12 luglio 2017, No 107, Roma, 12 December 2017; https://www.bancaditalia.it/pubblicazioni/interventi-vari/int-var-2017/Barbagallo-12122017.pdf

[7] For an analysis of the resolution procedures applied to the four banks, see P. LEONE, S. NATALE, R. NICASTRO, (a cura di), *Risoluzione di una crisi. Le Good banks tra regole, mercato, territori e risparmiatori*, Bancaria Editrice, 2019; P. DESURY, C. ROVERA, *The Italian bail-over*, banks and Bankers, No 3, 2016..

ii) *burden sharing* was applied, by reducing the value of shares and subordinated bonds, to cover part of the losses determined by the temporary evaluation[8];
iii) four *bridge banks* were established, in the legal form of joint-stock companies, respectively, named Nuova Cassa di Risparmio di Ferrara Spa, Nuova Banca delle Marche Spa, Nuova Banca dell'Etruria e Lazio Spa and Nuova Cassa di Risparmio di Chieti Spa, to which nearly all the assets and liabilities of the respective banks in resolution were transferred. The capital of the bridge banks was provided by the Resolution Fund, for an amount corresponding to about 9% of the total risk weighted assets;
iv) the bridge banks were temporarily managed by administrators designated by the Resolution Authority, to maintain the continuity of the essential functions previously performed by the four banks and to transfer them to third parties, at market conditions, in order to allocate to the Resolution Fund the proceeds of the sale;
v) subsequently, the old banks in resolution were placed under compulsory administrative liquidation; and
vi) a single vehicle, a *bad bank*, REV Credit Management S.p.A., without banking licence, was created, and the NPEs of the four banks were transferred to it; the Resolution Fund injected financial resources for the constitution of the capital of the bad bank (€136 million).

Based on the temporary valuation, the value adjustments of the NPEs amounted to 75% for the secured exposures and 91.6% for the unsecured exposures, with subsequent total adjustments of €2.1 billion. This, in addition to the other adjustments already made by the old banks, led to a net value of the NPEs transferred to REV from €8.5 billion to €1.5 billion. Following the final valuation carried out by the independent valuers, adjustments of 68.9% for the secured exposures and of 92.7% for the unsecured exposures were applied, with subsequent transfer to REV

[8] Some categories of investors in subordinated bonds, in compensating some of the losses suffered, received a reimbursement from the Solidarity Fund, borne by the FITD, for approximately 254 million euros (95%).

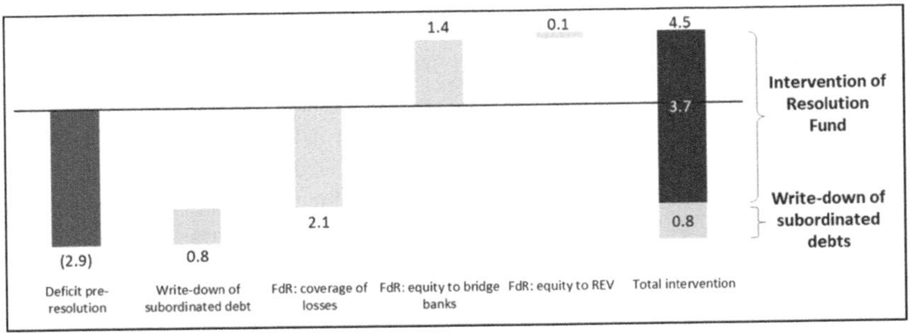

Fig. 2 The four banks: the key figures of the operation

of €2.1 billion of NPEs. REV's activity is still under way. It is managing those credits with the aim to maximise the recoveries or transfer NPEs to specialised companies.

The total disbursements of the Resolution Fund as of 22 November 2015, using financing provided by a pool of banks, amounted to about €3.7 billion, of which: €1.7 billion to cover losses of the old banks, €1.8 billion to recapitalise the bridge banks and 136 million to provide REV with the minimum capital necessary to operate. However, the final valuation carried out by the independent experts revealed further adjustments for €392 million, which increased the Resolution Fund's disbursement for the coverage of losses from €1.7 billion to about €2.1 billion and an adjustment of the value of shareholdings in the bridge banks from €1.8 billion to €1.4 billion (Fig. 2).

4 The Sale of the Bridge Banks

The second phase of the resolution procedure, concerning the sale of the four banks on the market, was also very complex. The European Commission established a too short deadline for the sale of the four banks, which was incompatible with market conditions.[9]

[9] The deadline for the sale of the bridge banks, initially established by the Commission at 30 April 2016, was postponed to 30 September, but was still too close for organising a new sale procedure with a call for tenders; the deadline was then postponed to December 2016, when the final phase of the negotiations with the potential investors had already started. Cfr. Banca D'Italia, *Rendiconto del Fondo Nazionale di Risoluzione*, Rome, 31 March 2017.

Negotiations with banks potentially interested in the acquisition ended in January 2017, through two distinct transfer operations: three bridge banks (Nuova Banca delle Marche, Nuova Banca dell'Etruria e Lazio e Nuova Cassa di Risparmio di Chieti) were acquired by UBI Banca; Nuova Cassa di Risparmio di Ferrara was acquired by Banca Popolare dell'Emilia-Romagna. To enable the transfer, the Resolution Fund intervened again to satisfy the additional capital need determined by the intervening banks after their due diligence. When factoring in the disbursement of about €1 billion for the second recapitalisation of the four banks, the total cost of the intervention for the Resolution Fund came to about €4.7 billion.

Between May and June 2017, the spin-off of the NPEs of the four bridge banks was realised, through the securitisation of a portfolio of €2.2 billion, at a price of €713 million (NPEs of Nuova Banca Marche, Nuova Banca Etruria and Nuova Carichieti) and the transfer of a NPE portfolio of Nuova Carife of €343 million at a price of €65 million. Said portfolios included both the 'unlikely to pay' positions of the four banks and the new bad loans that came to existence after the intervention of the Resolution Fund and the transfer of the old NPEs to REV. Quaestio Capital Management SGR joined both spin-off operations on behalf of the Atlante II Fund (Fig. 3).

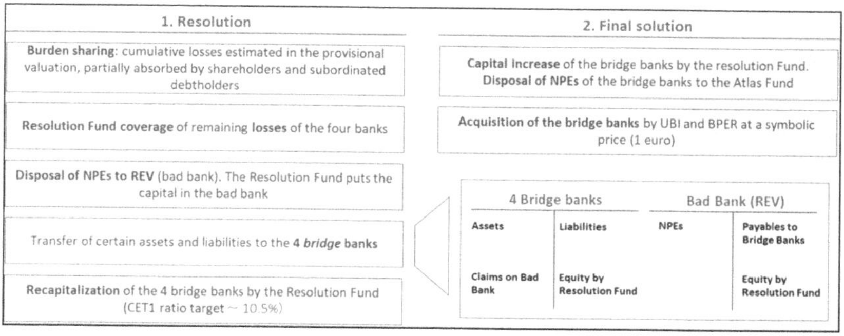

Fig. 3 The four banks: the structure of the deal

Atlante Fund and Atlante II Fund

Atlante Fund was an alternative investment 'closed' fund, regulated by Italian law and reserved to institutional investors. The Fund, established in 2016, was managed by Quaestio Capital SGR S.p.A. Atlante was established with a financial endowment of €4.25 billion, contributed by 67 Italian and foreign financial institutions, including banks, insurance companies, banking Foundations and Cassa Depositi e Prestiti.
The Fund could invest in banks with a capital ratio lower than minimum requirements established within the SREP; on request of the supervisory authority, it carried out initiatives to strengthen the capital of and/or buy non-performing exposures from Italian banks.
A fundamental principle of the Fund was independence from its shareholders and investors.
Atlante II Fund was founded between 2016 and 2017. Differently from Atlante Fund, it could invest only in non-performing exposures and in instruments linked to NPE operations, for example, warrants, for the purpose of reducing risk, in line with parameters used by other institutional investors. The Fund invested in junior and mezzanine tranches issued by SPVs created for the acquisition of NPEs portfolios from Italian banks.
Atlante II Fund was created with a capital endowment of about €2.5 billion, granted by various institutional investors and Italian financial intermediaries.

REV - Gestione crediti s.p.a.

REV is a Special Purpose Vehicle, regulated by Articles 45-47 of Legislative Decree No 180 of 2015, created for the management of assets and legal relationships, with the objective of maximising value through the sale or liquidation of the SPV itself.
Between 2016 and 2017, in execution of the resolution programme, REV acquired non-performing loans from the four bridge banks.
For the funding of the acquisition, REV subscribed a financing arrangement with the four bridge banks; a specific contract regulated the terms and conditions of the financing. The exposure of REV to the pool of lenders is backed by an autonomous first demand guarantee, granted by the Resolution Fund, which has been evaluated by the Commission to be compatible with State aid rules.
In 2017, as a consequence of the acquisition of NPEs, REV incurred a reduction of its capital ratios, which required the intervention of the Resolution Fund through a further capital increase for an amount of €85.3 million.[10]

[10] Cfr. Banca D'Italia, *Rendiconto del Fondo Nazionale di Risoluzione*, Roma, 29 March 2018.

CHAPTER 5

Two Types of Public Intervention: Orderly Liquidation and Precautionary Recapitalisation

In Italy, the government intervened in two particularly complex cases, where private solutions were either not available or insufficient to provide the required amount of solvency funding.

The first case concerned the two Veneto banks: Veneto Banca and Banca Popolare di Vicenza. Since these banks did not meet the public interest condition for recourse to the resolution procedure, they were placed under compulsory administrative liquidation, accompanied by public support measures to ensure their orderly liquidation through the sale of their assets and liabilities to another bank, in accordance with the Commission Communication on State aid.

The second was the case of Banca Monte dei Paschi di Siena, which was resolved through precautionary recapitalisation by the Italian State, under the BRRD rules for those banks that, although experiencing capital shortfalls, are solvent.

These cases have prompted extensive debate and deserve to be examined in depth as part of a review of the procedures and conditions for State intervention in banking crises.

G. Boccuzzi, *Banking Crises in Italy*, Palgrave Studies in Financial Instability and Banking Crisis Regulation,
https://doi.org/10.1007/978-3-031-01344-7_5

Orderly liquidation:	*Veneto Banca and Banca Popolare di Vicenza*
Precautionary recapitalisation:	*Monte dei Paschi di Siena*

1 The Two Veneto Banks: Orderly Liquidation

The tools used

- Compulsory administrative liquidation and appointment of three liquidators
- Reduction of capital instruments and subordinate debt (burden sharing)
- Transfer by liquidators of assets and liabilities to the acquiring bank
- State aid under the Communication from the Commission on the application, from 1 August 2013, of State aid rules to support measures in favour of banks in the context of the financial crisis, paragraphs 65–86 (Specific considerations in relation to liquidation aid)

The main steps

- **May '16–Jun. '16**: the Atlante Fund subscribes the capital increases resolved by the two banks in the total amount of about €2.5 billion, acquiring a controlling interest of about 98% of total capital
- **Dec. '16**: the Atlante Fund subscribes further capital increase in the total amount of about €900 million to cover the two banks' capital shortfall
- **Mar. '17**: the two banks apply to the Ministry of the Economy and Finance (MEF) for access to precautionary recapitalisation. The application is rejected by the EU Commission
- **Jun. '17:** the European Central Bank (ECB) declares the two banks 'failing or likely to fail'
- **Jun. '17**: the Single Resolution Board (SRB) concludes that adopting a resolution measure is not in the public interest
- **Jun. '17**: the EU Commission approves the State aid measures taken by Italy for the market exit of Banca Popolare di Vicenza and Veneto

Banca, under national insolvency proceedings, through orderly liquidation and the sale of the good banks (including assets and liabilities) to Intesa Sanpaolo

- **Jun. '17**: on the proposal of the Bank of Italy, the Ministry of the Economy and Finance orders the compulsory administrative liquidation of the two banks. The ministerial decrees provide for continuation of the two banks' activities for the time required to sell them to Banca Intesa Sanpaolo and introduces aid measures for the orderly management of the crisis

1.1 The Banks: Background and Key Figures

The Veneto Banca Group was a medium-sized group, operating through a traditional distribution network, mostly in northern and central Italy. Through its subsidiary BancApulia, the Group was also present in some regions of southern Italy. As of 31 December 2016, it had total assets of around €28 billion and direct deposits of around €20 billion, including €6.5 billion in covered deposits.

At that date, the Group showed significant anomalies: a gross NPE ratio of 39%, a cost-income ratio of 105% and a CET1 ratio of 6.4%, the latter already including the €1 billion capital increase subscribed in 2016 by the Atlante Fund. The Group had a network of 480 branches and a workforce of 6,089 employees.

Banca Popolare di Vicenza, the parent company of the banking group of the same name, was also a medium-sized bank, operating in northern Italy and, to a lesser extent, in central and southern Italy. As of 31 December 2016, the Group's total assets amounted to approximately €34.4 billion, while direct funding was about €18.8 billion, including €7.3 billion of covered deposits.

At that date, the Banca Popolare di Vicenza Group was facing largely the same distress as the Veneto Banca Group: a gross NPE ratio of 35.8% and a cost-income ratio of 95.5%. Following the capital increase of €1.5 billion subscribed in May 2016 by the Atlante Fund, the Group's CET1 ratio at the end of the year stood at 7.5%. The Group operated through a network of 502 branches and 5,147 employees (Fig. 1).

Consolidated data as of December 2016 (€ mln; %)	**Veneto**	**Vicenza**
Direct funding	20,031	18,794
o/w: covered deposits	6,579	7,300
% FITD total covered deposits	*1.14%*	*1.27%*
Total assets	28,078	34,424
NPEs ratio (GBV)	38.7%	35.8%
Cost-Income ratio	105.0%	95.5%
Net profit (loss)	(1,502)	(1,902)
ROE	(49.0%)	(88.5%)
CET 1 ratio	6.4%	7.5%
Total capital ratio	8.3%	8.9%
Employees	6,089	5,147.0
Branches	480	502

Fig. 1 The two Veneto banks: key figures (*Source* 2016 Financial Statements of Veneto Banca Spa; 2016 Consolidated Financial Statements of Banca Popolare di Vicenza Spa)

1.2 *The Causes of the Crisis and the Attempts to Resolve It*

The crisis of the two Veneto banks followed similar paths and their ultimate solution was also devised jointly. For both banks, the crisis had been caused by multiple factors, including serious internal governance and management shortcomings,[1] which led to anomalous lending practices and a high incidence of non-performing loans.

Problems in the management of the two banks had already been flagged by the Bank of Italy during two inspections carried out in 2013 and 2015, which highlighted, among other concerns, the practice of

[1] Banca D'Italia, *La crisi di Veneto Banca S.p.A. e Banca Popolare di Vicenza S.p.A.: Domande e risposte*. Among the causes of the crisis, the document refers to inappropriate behaviour of directors and managers, in particular unsound lending practices and an inadequate method of determining share prices.

loans-for-shares (*operazioni baciate*), i.e. lending money to clients so that they would purchase the bank's shares. For both banks—but to a greater extent for Popolare di Vicenza—the requirement to deduct from regulatory capital the component linked to loans to shareholders had a significant negative impact on their capital, as well as on their reputation.[2]

In the course of 2015, the two banks' cash flow position deteriorated significantly: in the last months of the year, the funding of Popolare di Vicenza decreased by about €2.5 billion and that of Veneto Banca by about €4 billion.[3] In response to their difficulties, the two banks attempted to strengthen their capital position by raising funds on the market. Accordingly, in the same year, they prepared a relaunch plan which included: changing their legal form into joint-stock company (Società per Azioni)—as they later did; carrying out a capital increase of €1 billion for Veneto Banca and €1.5 billion for Banca Popolare di Vicenza; getting listed on the stock exchange.

However, the offer of the shares on the market was unsuccessful for both banks and, in the spring of 2016, the Atlante Fund, which had been set up in April of the same year,[4] subscribed the two capital increases in the amounts mentioned above, becoming the two banks' main shareholder.[5] At the end of 2016, the Fund made further contributions for capital increases totalling €938 million.

The impossibility of raising private capital on the market was confirmed in 2017 by the failure of the attempt to merge the two banks under a business plan prepared jointly by their respective managements. Moreover, to meet growing liquidity needs, in the early months of 2017 the two banks

[2] The supervisory inspections carried out in the period 2013–2015 found loans-for-shares transactions not deducted from own funds of approximately €300 million at Veneto Banca and €500 million at Popolare di Vicenza. See C. BARBAGALLO, *Veneto Banca e Banca Popolare di Vicenza*, Senate of the Republic - Chamber of Deputies Parliamentary Committee of Enquiry into the Banking and Financial System, Law No 107 of 12 July 2017, 2 November 2017.

[3] C. Barbagallo, cit., 2 November 2017.

[4] The Atlante Fund is a closed-end investment fund under Italian law reserved for professional investors, managed by Quaestio Capital Sgr. The initial subscriptions to the Fund amounted to approximately €4.2 billion, invested by banks, banking foundations, insurance companies, social security institutions and the Cassa Depositi e Prestiti. For more details, see Chapter 3.

[5] The Atlante Fund acquired 99% of the capital of Popolare di Vicenza and 97.64% of the capital of Veneto Banca.

issued government-backed bonds in the amount of about €8.6 billion, in accordance with the provisions of Decree-Law No 237/2016.[6]

In the light of the difficulties encountered on the capital market, in March 2017, the two banks filed a request for precautionary recapitalisation with the Ministry of the Economy and Finance. After extensive discussions, the EU Commission, which is responsible for verifying the compatibility of the measures with the EU rules on State aid, considered that the conditions for authorising precautionary recapitalisation were not met, in the light of the negative assessment on the existence of sufficient private resources to cover 'losses likely to be incurred in the near future', which is an essential condition for public recapitalisation.[7]

[6] Decree-Law No 237/2016, concerning urgent measures for the protection of savings in the credit sector, introduced: i) the granting of a State guarantee on newly issued liabilities, until 30 June 2017, in compliance with the EU legislation on State aid; ii) State interventions in support of banks and banking groups, through the subscription of shares, in order to avert or remedy a serious disturbance in the economy and preserve financial stability, pursuant to Article 18 of Legislative Decree No 180 of 16 November 2015, (precautionary recapitalisation). To this end, a fund was set up with an allocation of €20 billion for the year 2017.

[7] The conditions for access to precautionary recapitalisation are set out in the BRRD, the Commission Communication of 2013 and the policy stance adopted by the ECB in February 2018 as the competent authority on significant banks. The basic idea is that precautionary recapitalisation can only be allowed if the bank is prospectively solvent and viable, hence able to cover hypothetical losses under stress conditions, i.e. losses other than already established or highly likely losses. In particular, the BRRD provides that public funds supplied under precautionary recapitalisation cannot be used to cover current losses or losses expected to occur in the near future, including those determined by a possible AQR. Current and expected losses must be covered by private means, which include: CET1 in excess of the minimum requirement (4.5%), new capital generated by burden-sharing measures or new issues of AT1 and T2 and cash from confirmed disposals of non-core assets. If the above-mentioned losses cannot be covered by private means, this means that the 'private means test' is not passed and precautionary recapitalisation cannot be granted. The maximum amount of precautionary recapitalisation must be determined on the basis of the bank's capital shortfall under the adverse scenario in the latest EBA stress test, also considering any shortfall in the baseline scenario, which must be covered by private means and must be deducted from the maximum amount of recapitalisation that can be granted by the State. See EUROPEAN PARLIAMENT, Directorate-General for Internal Policies, *Precautionary recapitalisations under the Bank Recovery and Resolution Directive: conditionality and case practice*, 5 July 2017; European Parliament, Directorate-General for Internal Policies, *Precautionary recapitalisations: time for a review? In-depth analysis*, 6 July 2017.

On 23 June 2017, the ECB announced that the two banks[8] were deemed likely to fail and the Single Resolution Board concluded there was no public interest justifying a resolution action under Article 32 of the BRRD[9]. Specifically, in determining the absence of public interest in resolving the banks, the SRB remarked that both banks operated in limited areas of national territory; therefore, their crisis should be managed at national level.

SRB's decision concerning Veneto Banca and Banca Popolare di Vicenza[10]

On 23 June 2017, the Single Resolution Board (the 'SRB') decides not to take resolution action in respect of Veneto Banca S.p.A and Banca Popolare di Vicenza S.p.A

The SRB concludes that, while the conditions for resolution action of Article 18(1)(a) and (b) of Regulation (EU) No 806/2014 (the 'SRMR') are met, the condition of Article 18(1)(c) is not satisfied

·***Article 18(1)(a) of the SRMR: Failing or likely to fail***. *On 23 June 2017, the European Central Bank concludes that the banks are failing or likely to fail on the basis of Article 18(1)(a) in conjunction with Article 18(4)(a) of the SRMR*

In particular, there is material evidence to conclude that the banks infringe the requirements for continuing authorisation, in particular with respect to capital adequacy, in a way that would justify the withdrawal of the authorisation by the competent authority

·***Article 18(1)(b) of the SRMR: Alternative private measures and supervisory actions.*** *The SRB concludes that no such measures or actions can prevent the failure of the banks within a reasonable timeframe. The SRB reaches this conclusion taking into account several elements, including the banks' inability to raise sufficient additional private capital, the weaknesses and lack of credibility of their business plans, and the ineffectiveness of the application of the power to write down or convert the banks' capital instruments to remedy the breach of the capital requirements by them*

(continued)

[8] European Central Bank, *ECB deemed Veneto Banca and Banca Popolare di Vicenza failing or likely to fail*, Press Release, 23 June 2017.

https://www.bankingsupervision.europa.eu/press/pr/date/2017/html/ssm.pr170623.en.html.

[9] Single Resolution Board, *The SRB will not take resolution action in relation to Banca Popolare di Vicenza and Veneto Banca*, Press Release, 23 June 2017, https://srb.europa.eu/en/node/341.

[10] Single Resolution Board, *Summary of the SRB's decision in relation to Banca Popolare di Vicenza*, 23 June 2017.

(continued)

·***Article 18(1)(c) of the SRMR: Public interest.*** *The SRB concludes that, given the particular characteristics of the banks and their specific financial and economic situations, resolution action with respect to the banks is not necessary in the public interest, in accordance with Article 18(1)(c) in conjunction with Article 18(5) of the SRMR. This conclusion is based on the following grounds:*
-The functions performed by the banks, e.g. deposit-taking, lending activities and payment services, are not critical since they are provided to a limited number of third parties and can be replaced in an acceptable manner and within a reasonable timeframe;
-The failure of the banks is not likely to result in significant adverse effects on financial stability taking into account, in particular, the low financial and operational interconnections with other financial institutions; and
-Normal Italian insolvency proceedings would achieve the resolution objectives to the same extent as resolution, since such proceedings would also ensure a comparable degree of protection for depositors, investors, other customers, clients' funds and assets. The decision in respect of the banks is addressed to and is to be implemented by the Bank of Italy, in its capacity as National Resolution Authority. The banks will be subject to winding up under Italian insolvency proceedings

In the light of the decisions of the EU authorities, the Italian government considered that two separate winding-up procedures would entail very high costs and would produce heavy impacts on the productive, social and occupational fabric, with significant adverse effects on the economy of the two banks' catchment area, and came to the conclusion that the appropriate solution was an orderly liquidation of the banks, suitable to ensure the continuity of critical functions and preserve the value of the two banks, through the transfer of their assets and liabilities to another bank.[11]

1.3 The Orderly Liquidation of the Two Banks

It should first be noted that neither the primary EU legislation (BRRD) nor national legislation provide a definition and a specific regulation for orderly liquidation. This is not a new bankruptcy proceedings, but may simply be qualified as a particular way of conducting the winding-up procedure, governed by national law.

In Italy, orderly liquidation can be equated to the transfer of assets and liabilities and legal relationships identifiable *en bloc* governed by Article 90 of the Italian Banking Act (TUB), in the framework of the national rules

[11] Banca D'Italia, *La crisi di Veneto Banca S.p.A. e Banca Popolare di Vicenza S.p.A.: Domande e risposte*, op. cit.

on compulsory administrative liquidation (Articles 80–95 TUB). A similar framework can be found in Article 11(6) of the Directive on deposit guarantee schemes (DGSD), concerning alternative measures that can be used by deposit guarantee schemes in a bank winding-up procedure.

Orderly liquidation is governed by the EU Commission guidelines on State aid. It follows that, in relation to possible interventions in insolvency situations, which produce significant legal effects on the rights of third parties, acts of soft law, dictated by competition requirements, are of crucial importance with respect to the rules and procedures aimed at preserving the stability of the financial institution. Therefore, a more appropriate and coherent treatment of these situations within the EU legal framework seems essential.

In the case of the two Veneto banks, at the end of the long process summarised above, the Ministry of Economy and Finance (MEF), acting on a proposal of the Bank of Italy, by Decrees Nos 185 and 186 of 25 June 2017 placed the two Veneto banks under compulsory administrative liquidation pursuant to Article 80 of the TUB and Article 2(1)(a) of Decree-Law No 99/2017,[12] containing 'Urgent measures for the compulsory administrative liquidation of Banca Popolare di Vicenza SpA and Veneto Banca SpA'.

Decree-Law No 99/2017 also provided that business operations would continue for the time necessary for their transfer to the purchaser Intesa Sanpaolo SpA, selected through a tender process, and that public support would be given to ensure orderly management of the crisis.[13]

[12] The Decree was converted with amendments into Law No 121 of 31 July 2017 (Official Gazette of the Italian Republic No 184 of 8 August 2017).

[13] On the liquidation of the two banks in Veneto, see M. Rispoli Farina, *La soluzione della crisi delle banche venete nell'ambito della procedura di risanamento e risoluzione delle banche italiane. Uno sguardo di insieme*, in *Innovazione & Diritto*, No 2, 2018; A. A. Dolmetta, U. Malvagna, *Debiti (non) ceduti e insinuazione al passivo. A proposito delle 'banche venete', Rivista di Diritto Bancario, No 3, 2018*; A. Brozzetti, *Il Decreto Legge No 99/2017: un'altra pietra miliare per la 'questione bancaria' italiana*, in *Rivista Trimestrale di Diritto dell'Economia*, No 1, 2018; S. Bonfatti, *Crisi Bancarie in Italia 2015–2017*, in *Rivista di Diritto Bancario*, No 4, 2018; E. Cacciatore, *Riflessioni sull'efficacia verso i terzi del contratto di cessione previsto dal decreto 'salva banche venete'*, in *Rivista di Diritto Bancario*, No 4, 2018; and P. BONETTI, *Brevi note sui profili costituzionali dell'interpretazione conforme del decreto-legge No 99/2017 sulla liquidazione coatta amministrativa di due banche venete*, in *Rivista di Diritto Bancario*, No 10, 2018.

The solution was the simultaneous transfer, assisted by State support, of the assets and liabilities of the two banks (with some exclusions[14]) to Banca Intesa Sanpaolo; therefore, the cost of the crisis would be primarily borne by the shareholders (in particular the Atlante Fund, the value of whose capital increases subscribed in the two banks in the previous months, totalling about €3.4 billion was entirely wiped out) and the holders of subordinated bonds of the two banks, through the application of the burden-sharing measures, in the total amount of about €1.27 billion.

The Italian government's intervention was possible in the form of support to orderly liquidation under the Commission Communication of 30 July 2013 on State aid, in particular, paragraphs 65–86 on liquidation aid.[15] The Communication states that Member States should always consider liquidation when the credit institution cannot credibly return to long-term viability and adds that, in order to preserve financial stability, State measures to support the orderly liquidation of banks may be considered as compatible aid.

Thus, the EU guidelines on State aid show that the EU authorities favour the market exit of non-viable banks, allowing—under certain circumstances—the exit process to take place in an orderly manner, in order to minimise the negative impact of ordinary insolvency proceedings. Moreover, the winding-up process should be limited to the period strictly necessary for the orderly liquidation. Liquidation must as much as

[14] The perimeter of the sale included the two banks' assets amounting to about €43.7 billion. The sale did not include: non-performing loans (bad loans, unlikely-to-pay exposures and past-due exposures), the liabilities referred to in Article 52(1)(a)(i), (ii), (iii) and (iv) of Legislative Decree No 180/2015 (Common Equity Tier 1 and Tier 2 instruments subject to burden sharing), claims of shareholders and subordinated debt holders of the former Veneto banks arising from the sale of those financial instruments, liability actions against the former corporate officers of the two Veneto banks, legal actions against the banks relating to actions or events that occurred before the transfer, as well as all equity investments (except for some specifically identified investments). The assets and liabilities not acquired by Intesa Sanpaolo remained in the two banks under liquidation. Some items, such as non-performing loans, were subsequently transferred to the Asset Management Company—SGA (now AMCO). In line with the provisions of the Consolidated Bankink Act (TUB), the liquidators were entrusted with liquidating the residual assets and satisfying the creditors' claims by distributing the proceeds of said liquidated assets in the order of priority established by law. See Intesa Sanpaolo, *2017 Financial Statements*.

[15] G. Boccuzzi, *Il valore di una disciplina ben ponderata*, in Sole24Ore, 23 June 2017.

possible aim at selling off parts of the business or assets by means of a competitive process.

The Commission's Communication also states that approval of the State aid measures is conditional on compliance with the provisions on burden sharing, the submission of an orderly liquidation plan for the bank and the Commission's compatibility assessment.

Within the liquidation procedure, any sale of the business or assets must be carried out by means of a competitive process. Therefore, to determine whether State aid is provided to the buyer, the Commission examines whether the sale process is open, unconditional and non-discriminatory, the sale takes place on market terms and the sale price is maximised. If the Commission finds that there is aid to the buyer, it will assess its compatibility and may require measures to limit distortions of competition.[16]

1.4 Liquidation Support Measures

The public support measures relating to the two Veneto banks consisted of a cash disbursement to cover the buyer's capital needs resulting from the acquisition and the implementation of the planned restructuring measures, as well as the granting of guarantees to the same buyer against various risks.

In particular, the Decree-Law and the implementing ministerial decrees guaranteed the total neutrality of the acquisition with respect to the CET1 ratio and the dividend policy of the Intesa Sanpaolo Group, by means of[17]:

- a public cash contribution of €3.5 billion to offset the negative impact of the acquisition on capital ratios, resulting in a CET1 phased-in ratio of 12.5%;
- a further public cash contribution of €1.3 billion to cover the integration and restructuring costs of the acquisition, including the measures required by DG Comp to limit distortions of competition,

[16] European Commission, *Communication from the Commission on the application, from 1 August 2013, of State aid rules to support measures in favour of banks in the context of the financial crisis*, paragraphs 79–82, 30 July 2013.

[17] Intesa Sanpaolo, *Financial Statements 2017*, Press Release, 26 June 2017.

which involved the closure of about 600 branches and the voluntary exit of about 3,900 employees;

- State guarantees totalling approximately €6 billion, including about €2 billion against the risks, obligations and commitments relating to events that occurred prior to the sale or to assets and relationships not included in the transferred assets and liabilities, and about €4 billion to cover the risks associated with a portfolio of performing loans considered to be high-risk, which Intesa Sanpaolo may return to the banks being wound up if the loans are reclassified as bad loans or unlikely-to-pay loans[18];
- the coverage of the capital deficit, guaranteed by the State up to a maximum of €6.351 billion.[19]

Therefore, the State's intervention took the form of a cash payment of €4.8 billion and the granting of guarantees of a maximum value of about €12.4 billion. Those guarantees mainly made up for a number of information gaps at the time of Banca Intesa's bid, due to the speed with which the tender procedure was carried out.[20]

Article 5 of Decree-Law No 99/2017 also provided that the two banks' non-performing loans (having a provisionally assessed gross value of approximately €17.8 billion and a net value of €9.9 billion) would

[18] The due diligence carried out by Intesa Sanpaolo calculated the total amount of high-risk loans to be €3,692 million. On 11 May 2019, a first tranche of high-risk loans totalling €456 million was given back to the banks in liquidation. On 12 October 2019, the second tranche of high-risk loans classified as bad loans or unlikely-to-pay loans was returned, on the basis of agreements with the banks under liquidation and SGA (now 'AMCO'), against a consideration of €218 million. See Intesa Sanpaolo, *2019 Financial Statements*.

[19] Since the sales perimeter only included part of the assets and liabilities of the two banks, the accounting balance of the transferred business was achieved by recognising in the financial statements of the buyer, Banca Intesa, a loan to the banks in liquidation. Against this credit, Banca Intesa granted a loan to the banks in liquidation of €6.4 billion, for a term of 5 years at an interest rate of 1%, guaranteed by the State up to a maximum amount of €6,351 billion. The loan is repaid through the recovery of the assets of the liquidation procedure, including the proceeds of the non-performing loans transferred to AMCO, as these proceeds are periodically paid to the banks under administrative compulsory liquidation. See Intesa Sanpaolo, *Annual Report 2017*.

[20] Bank of Italy, *Informazioni sulla soluzione della crisi di Veneto Banca S.p.A. e Banca Popolare di Vicenza S.p.A.*, Report for the VI Financial Committee of the Chamber of Deputies, July 2017.

be transferred by the liquidator to AMCO, which is now managing and collecting the loans, to maximise their medium-long term collection.[21] The proceeds, net of costs, are returned to the banks in liquidation and are used to satisfy the creditors' claims, including the State's, in the order of priority established by law.[22]

Therefore, the total cost of the support incurred by the State will depend on the outcome of the realisation of the assets of the banks in liquidation (Fig. 2).

The EU Commission considered these measures to be in line with the EU rules on State aid to banks set out in its 2013 Communication.[23] In this respect, the Commission, in line with the provisions of Sect. 6 (paragraphs 71–78) of the 2013 Communication, concerning the conditions for application of State aid to the orderly liquidation of banks under national insolvency proceedings, assessed that the following conditions were met[24]:

- Limitation of costs of winding down: the amount of aid granted for the sale of the assets and liabilities of the two banks had been determined by the outcome of a competitive sale process, with the aim of minimising the amount of support needed for the sale. The Commission also stated that it had no information on alternative scenarios, in

[21] The consideration for the sale of the non-performing loans is a claim of the banks in liquidation from AMCO, equal to the carrying value of the assets in AMCO's portfolios, periodically adjusted to its lower or higher realisable value. As at 31 December 2019, the NPEs of the Veneto banks were recognised in the respective portfolios of AMCO at a net present value of €5,385 million. See AMCO, *Consolidated Financial Statements 2019*.

[22] Article 4(3) of Decree Law No 99/2017 provides that repayment of the loan granted by Intesa has lower priority than preferential claims—but is ranked on a par with the State's claim deriving from the possible enforcement of the guarantee (the so-called recourse claim)—and ranks higher than the other claims. As to the other payments made by the State, the Ministry of the Economy and Finance has a claim against the banks in liquidation, which ranks higher than unsecured claims, but lower than the claims relating to the coverage of the funding gap.

[23] European Commission *State aid: Commission approves aid for market exit of Banca Popolare di Vicenza and Veneto Banca under Italian insolvency law, involving sale of some parts to Intesa Sanpaolo*, press release, 25 June 2017.

[24] European Commission, State Aid SA.45664(2017/N) – Italy – *Orderly liquidation of Banca Popolare di Vicenza and Veneto Banca - Liquidation aid*, C (2017) 4501 final, Brussels, 25 June 2017.

Assets and liabilities acquired by Intesa			
Loans to banks	3.8	Due to banks	10.4
Performing loans	28.6	Due to customers	24.3
Financial assets	7.8	Securities issued	11.8
Other assets	3.6	Other liabilities	3.7
Claims on banks in lca (guaranteed by State)	6.4		
Total assets	**50.2**	**Total liabilities**	**50.2**

Banks in liquidation			
NPE acquired by AMCO	11.4	Payables to Intesa (guaranteed by State)	6.4
Other assets	1.4	Other liabilities	1.2
		Subordinated liabilities	1.2
		Pre-existing equity	4.0
Total assets	**12.8**	**Total liabilities**	**12.8**

State contribution to Intesa Sanpaolo to recapitalize the good banks	€3.5 bn
State contribution to cover restructuring costs	€1.3 bn
State guarantee to cover risks and representations and warranties, linked to the previous management	€6.0 bn
State guarantee to cover the transfer capital deficit	€6.4 bn
Total State intervention	**€17.2 bn**

Fig. 2 The two Veneto banks: the structure of the intervention (*Source* estimates based on public data from Bank of Italy and Intesa Sanpaolo. BANCA D'ITALIA, Informazioni sulla soluzione della crisi di Veneto Banca S.p.A. e Banca Popolare di Vicenza S.p.A., Memoria per la VI Commissione Finanze della Camera dei Deputati, luglio 2017; INTESA SANPAOLO, Annual Report 2017)

national insolvency proceedings, which could have allowed achieving the same objectives at a lower cost for the Italian State;

- Limitation of distortions of competition: the aid would not cause distortions of competition since the assets and liabilities (considered to be of a limited amount) would be sold by means of a competitive procedure and the two banks would exit the market;
- Burden sharing: shareholders and subordinate debt holders had to contribute to a maximum to the cost of the intervention. For both banks, the shares and the subordinated bonds would remain in their respective banks in liquidation and would not be transferred to the buyer[25];
- Restoration of long-term viability: the Commission considered Intesa Sanpaolo capable of absorbing the assets and liabilities of

[25] Certain categories of subordinated bondholders received, for the losses suffered, compensation from the Solidarity Fund, paid by the FITD, for approximately €26 million (80%), in addition to a voluntary compensation paid by Intesa Sanpaolo for the remaining 20%.

the two banks, since it was more than 15 times larger than the transferred activities in terms of total assets.

1.5 Some Considerations on the Two Veneto Banks' Case

The case of the two Veneto banks warrants reflection on the value of certain legal and economic conceptual categories applied to special insolvency proceedings[26]. First, when applying this instrument, more clarity is needed on the boundaries between solvency and insolvency in order to limit the authorities' discretion. How can we assess the existence of public interest in practice, given that the reference to the aims of resolution laid down in the BRRD is not fully satisfactory?

It is also necessary to regulate more precisely the application of the 'special' insolvency procedure related to orderly liquidation and to understand, from a systematic viewpoint, the Commission's approach to general compulsory administrative liquidations with the *en bloc* sale of assets and liabilities, implemented with the support of deposit guarantee schemes, which is the traditional approach to bank insolvency in Italy.

We should also consider the feasibility of carrying out the sales in the liquidation, which, being alternatives to repaying depositors, are considered by the Commission as State aid, and therefore require complex and time-consuming procedures to obtain the Commission's authorisation.

Consequently, overall review of the framework on State aid is necessary, by means of a well-balanced primary legal act, in order to establish a more solid legal basis, in the light of the effects of this legislation on the crisis resolution methods, EU and national decision-making procedures and the various categories of banking stakeholders.

[26] See G. Boccuzzi, *Il valore di una disciplina ben ponderata*, cit.

2 Monte Dei Paschi Di Siena: Precautionary Recapitalisation. A Public Intervention Measure not Originating from Failing or Likely to Fail

2.1 The Rules on Precautionary Recapitalisation in the Bank Recovery and Resolution Directive (BRRD)

Precautionary recapitalisation is a special public measure for banks that have a capital shortfall but are still solvent. This measure is an exception to the general rule in Article 32 of the BRRD which provides that the existence of extraordinary public financial support suffices to qualify the bank as failing or likely to fail and results in its resolution or liquidation.

Therefore, the injection of public equity is a precautionary and temporary instrument designed to overcome specific situations in which a bank, even though it is considered solvent, has a capital shortfall that it cannot correct with ordinary market instruments. Thus, the bank can be recapitalised with public funds in order to prevent disruption of the economy and preserve financial stability.

The provision of public funds automatically triggers the application of the State aid rules and, consequently, of the burden-sharing rules set out in the Commission Communication on State aid of 30 July 2013.

Precautionary recapitalisation is governed by Article 32(4)(d) of the BRRD, which states that public financial support granted to avert or remedy a serious disturbance in the economy and preserve financial stability does not constitute extraordinary public financial support—and hence the bank shall not be considered to be failing or likely to fail—when such support is granted in one of the following forms:

i) a State guarantee to back liquidity facilities provided by the central bank in accordance with the central bank's conditions;
ii) a State guarantee of newly issued liabilities;
iii) precautionary recapitalisation. This is the injection of capital or purchase of capital instruments at prices and on terms that do not confer an advantage upon the bank, if at the time of the injection or purchase the bank does not meet any of the conditions for resolution, and none of the conditions for write-down or conversion of capital instruments are met.

Given the exceptional nature of the support measures listed above, the provision also introduces certain constraints and limitations in order to limit the use of this instrument. To this end, the BRRD states that the bank is not considered to be failing or likely to fail where the public financial support:

a) is given prior approval under the State aid rules and, where granted in the form of a State guarantee, is reserved for banks with positive net value;
b) is adopted on a precautionary and temporary basis, in proportion to the disturbance to the economy;
c) is not used to cover losses that the bank has incurred or is likely to incur in the near future.

A further condition is that the granting of public financial support in the form of injection of own funds or purchase of capital instruments must be limited to addressing capital shortfalls established by national, EU or SSM-wide stress tests, asset quality reviews or equivalent exercises conducted by the European Central Bank, EBA or national authorities.

Public precautionary recapitalisation is associated with the application of burden-sharing measures between shareholders and creditors, which in the present case can only be expressed as conversion[27] of eligible liabilities (hybrid additional tier 1, subordinated tier 2 and other subordinated instruments) into new shares, in accordance with the Commission Communication of 2013, since in this case the public capital support can only be provided if a stress test under an adverse scenario demonstrates the need for capital.

This type of public support measure is clearly exceptional in the new regulatory framework, in terms of both applicability conditions and implementation methods. Therefore, while this provision adds flexibility to the prohibition on State aid, it is subject to very stringent conditions and strict controls by the EU authorities.

In particular, paragraph 43 of the Communication, which refers to banks that have an identified capital shortfall but whose capital ratio remains above the regulatory minimum, provides that subordinated debt

[27] The reduction in the value of instruments that can be included in regulatory capital can only be applied if necessary to absorb losses that also impact the bank's financial statements and exceed the bank's net book value.

must be converted into equity before aid is granted only if the bank is unable to restore its capital position on its own. If, instead, the bank no longer meets the minimum regulatory capital requirements, equity, hybrid capital and subordinated debt must have fully contributed to offset any losses before State aid can be granted (paragraph 44 of the Communication).

However, an exception to paragraphs 43 and 44 may be made where implementing said measures would endanger financial stability or lead to disproportionate results (paragraph 45 of the Communication). One possible way of addressing these risks is to reconsider the sequencing of measures to address the capital shortfall.

EBA has issued guidelines on the implementation of this legal framework, which set out the types of tests, reviews or exercises that may lead to this form of precautionary public equity injection[28] (Fig. 3).

2.2 *The Recourse to Precautionary Recapitalisation for MPS*

The tools used

- Precautionary recapitalisation by the Ministry of Economy and Finance, pursuant to Article 18 of Legislative Decree No 180/2015 (implementing the BRRD)
- Burden sharing ordered by Decree of 28 July 2017, in the form of conversion of subordinated bonds into ordinary shares, as part of the

[28] On this point, see European Banking Authority, *Guidelines on the types of tests, reviews or exercises that may lead to support measures under Article 32(4)(d)(iii) of the Bank Recovery and Resolution Directive*, EBA/GL/2014/09, 22 September 2014. According to the EBA, extraordinary public financial support taking the form of additional capital to a solvent bank in order to address a capital shortfall resulting from stress tests or capital adequacy reviews may not be considered a trigger for resolution when it is provided to remedy a serious disturbance in the economy of a Member State and to preserve financial stability. The EBA guidelines specify the main features of the stress tests or capital adequacy review exercises that may lead to support measures, which include the time horizon, scope, reference date, quality review process, common methodology and, where relevant, a macroeconomic scenario and hurdle rates as well as a timeframe to correct the capital shortfall.

However, the EBA also specifies that the guidelines do not affect or prejudice in any way the competent authorities' obligation to verify continuously whether an institution is failing or likely to fail, on the basis of the other objective conditions.

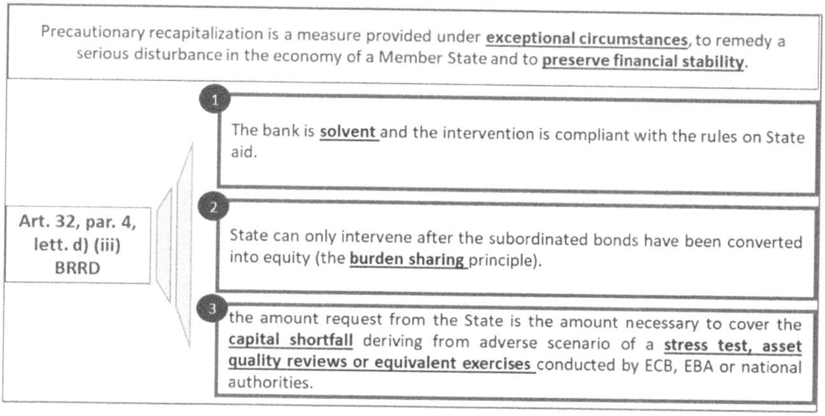

Fig. 3 Conditions for precautionary recapitalisation

procedure to strengthen the capital of MPS, pursuant to Decree-Law No 237/2016

- Disposal of non-performing loans through a securitisation transaction, in which the Atlante Fund took part
- Repurchase of the converted subordinated liabilities by the State against the granting of senior debt securities issued by the bank

The main steps

- **Jul. '16:** EBA's stress test shows a significant reduction in the Bank's CET1 ratio under the adverse scenario
- **Nov. '16:** the Bank's shareholders' meeting approves a €5 billion capital increase. However, the planned increase is soon abandoned, due to the difficulty in raising funds from the market
- **Dec. '16:** MPS applies to the ECB for access to precautionary recapitalisation
- **Jun. '17:** MPS and the Atlante Fund sign a binding contract for the securitisation of a portfolio of non-performing loans of approximately €24.5 billion
- **Jul. '17:** the Commission approves the restructuring plan associated with the precautionary recapitalisation

- **Jul. '17:** the Italian government publishes the Decree providing for the capital increase (precautionary recapitalisation) and the application of burden sharing
- **Nov. '17:** the Ministry of the Economy and Finance purchases the shares resulting from the conversion of the Bank retail investors' subordinated bonds, offering as consideration senior debt securities issued by MPS of a value of €1.5 billion

The framework on precautionary recapitalisation was applied in the case of Banca Monte dei Paschi di Siena,[29] following the negative result of the adverse-scenario stress test conducted by the EBA, whose results were published at the end of July 2016. This framework was introduced in Italy by Decree-Law No 237/2016 on urgent measures for the protection of savings in the credit sector.[30]

This measure has fully implemented the framework established by the BRRD as concerns the measures that can be carried out by the State (recapitalisation and issue of guarantees) and the conditions for their application. In particular, since the extraordinary public support measure was classified as precautionary recapitalisation pursuant to Article 18 of Legislative Decree No 180/2015, it did not trigger a resolution procedure for MPS.[31]

To implement the Commission's provisions, Decree-Law No 237/2016 requires the bank or parent company concerned to

[29] See Bank of Italy, *L'ammontare della 'ricapitalizzazione precauzionale' del Monte dei Paschi di Siena*, 29 December 2016; EUROPEAN COMMISSION, *Commission authorises precautionary recapitalisation of Italian bank Monte dei Paschi di Siena*, press release, 4 July 2017; L. Erzegovesi, *Il decreto 237/2016 e la ricapitalizzazione precauzionale di MPS del luglio 2017*, University of Trento, September 2017.

[30] See Decree-Law No 237 of 23 December 2016, published in the Official Gazette of 23 December 2016 and in force from the same day. The Decree was converted, with amendments, into Law No 15 of 17 February 2017. In particular, public capital-strengthening measures are regulated by Chapter II, Article 13 et seq. of the Decree. On this point, with regard to the measures adopted by the Decree-Law, see European Central Bank, *Opinion on the liquidity support measures, a precautionary recapitalisation and other urgent provisions for the banking sector*, 3 February 2017 (CON/2017/01).

[31] Among the common conditions required for both resolution and other crisis management procedures, Article 17(2)(f) of Legislative Decree No 180/2015 provides that a bank is considered to be failing or likely to fail if it receives public financial support, except for the cases set out in the subsequent Article 18.

submit to the supervisory authority a plan with an estimate of capital needs and the concrete measures to address them. To assess the appropriateness of the recovery plans, the supervisory authority can consider aspects such as the accuracy of the bank's estimate of its capital needs, the appropriateness of the planned measures to address those needs and the feasibility of the measures in the specific case.

Under the Decree-Law, the bank can access public support, by applying to the Ministry of the Economy and Finance,[32] if the measures set out in the plan to remedy the capital shortfall are not sufficient to meet its objective, or if the measures are assessed to be unsuitable either when the plan is submitted, or during its implementation.

In order to ensure compliance with State aid rules (paragraph 47 of the Commission's Communication), the Decree establishes a number of commitments and obligations of the bank, designed to prevent the outflow of funds, including a ban on paying dividends or coupons or repurchasing any of its own shares.

2.3 *The Case of MPS and the Technical Situation*

Monte dei Paschi di Siena is the world's oldest bank. It was established in 1472 as 'Monte di Pietà', 20 years before the discovery of America by Christopher Columbus. The long history of the bank as a State-owned bank is full of successful events, including internal and external growth.

In 1999, MPS was privatised and listed on the Milan stock exchange. Following a series of M&A operations, it became the fourth largest banking group in Italy. The Montepaschi Group operated mainly in Italy, focusing on traditional retail and commercial banking services. The Group was also active, through its own specialised companies, in business areas such as leasing, factoring, corporate finance and investment banking.

The bank had been showing signs of weakness for some time: someone attributes one of the main causes of the bank's problem to the acquisition of a medium-sized bank based in northern Italy, Banca Antonveneta, in 2007. In 2013 the Commission, for reasons of financial stability, approved, in line with State aid rules, a capital injection of €3.9 billion

[32] The Ministry of the Economy and Finance may make the capital injection conditional on the removal or replacement of board members or the chief executive officer of the bank requesting support, in line with paragraph 37 of the Commission Communication of 2013 on State aid.

in the form of hybrid capital instruments (the so-called Monti bonds), as well as a €13 billion guarantee granted by the Italian government on certain liabilities of the bank, on the basis of the restructuring plan presented by MPS, which the Commission considered to be capable of ensuring the bank's long-term viability.[33] By June 2015, the bank had repaid in full the State recapitalisation received in 2013.[34]

During 2016, the bank reported a reduction in the volume of business. In particular, total funding (direct and indirect) at the end of 2016 amounted to approximately €203 billion, down by approximately €23 billion from 31 December 2015.

The negative performance of direct deposits (about €104.5 billion, down by about €15 billion from the previous year) was influenced by the tensions linked to the negative results of the EBA's stress tests on the group and the recapitalisation planned by the bank's management. In December 2016, the MPS Group's covered deposits amounted to approximately €34.5 billion.

As of 31 December 2016, loans to customers amounted to about €107 billion, down by almost €5 billion from the end of 2015; non-performing exposures amounted to about €45.7 billion in gross terms (€20.3 billion in terms of net book value), corresponding to an NPE ratio of 34.5%.

The Group recorded a loss of about €3.2 billion in 2016—compared to a positive result of about €388 million in 2015—mainly due to write-downs in the non-performing loan portfolio.

The bank's capital situation deteriorated significantly. As of 31 December 2016, its Common Equity Tier 1 ratio was 8.2% (compared to 12.0% at the end of 2015), and its Total Capital ratio was 10.4%, down sharply compared to 16.0% at the end of December 2015[35] (Fig. 4).

[33] European Commission, *State aid: Commission authorises restructuring aid for Italian bank Monti dei Paschi di Siena*, press release Brussels, 27 November 2013.

[34] European Commission, State Aid SA.47677(2017/N) – Italy - *New aid and amended restructuring plan of Banca Monte dei Paschi di Siena*, Brussels, C (2017) 4690 final, 4 July 2017.

[35] Monte Dei Paschi di Siena, *Financial Statements 2016*.

Consolidated data (€ mln; %)	**2015**	**2016**
Direct funding	119,274	104,574
o/w: covered deposits	38,115	34,490
% FITD total covered deposits	*7.2%*	*6.0%*
Total assets	169,012	153,179
NPEs ratio (GBV)	34.8%	34.5%
Cost-Income ratio	50.4%	61.2%
Net profit (loss)	388	(3,241)
ROE	5.1%	(40.5%)
CET 1 ratio	12.0%	8.2%
Total capital ratio	16.0%	10.4%
Employees	25,731	25,566
Branches	2,133	2,032

Fig. 4 MPS: main data (*Source* MPS, Financial Report and Consolidated Financial Statements 2015 and 2016)

2.4 *The Results of the Stress Test and the Search for a Solution*

The MPS case began in July 2016 with the publication of the results of the EBA's EU-wide stress test, which showed a sharp contraction in the Group's CET1 ratio in the adverse scenario.[36]

In response, the Parent Company's Board of Directors approved the general terms of an operation to hive off the entire portfolio of non-performing loans (having a gross value of €27.7 billion) and recapitalise the Bank with a maximum estimated amount of €5 billion. In addition, the MPS Business Plan 2016–2019 set the following objectives: (i) relaunch the commercial business; (ii) boost operating efficiency by

[36] Monte Dei Paschi di Siena, *Financial Statements 2017*.

cutting approximately 2,600 jobs and closing about 500 branches; (iii) improve the management of credit risk.

However, in December 2016, the capital increase was not carried out, as the subscriptions received had fallen far short of the €5 billion necessary to achieve the objectives of the operation.

The failure to complete the capital increase also determined the failure of the securitisation of the non-performing loans and of the overall liability management project, which envisaged the voluntary conversion of subordinated bonds into shares for a total of €2.4 billion.

The application made by MPS for an extension of the deadline for completing the capital increase (to 20 January 2017) was rejected by the ECB due to fears of further deterioration of the Bank's capital position and, especially, its liquidity.[37]

Therefore, on 23 December 2016, the Bank applied to the ECB for access to the precautionary recapitalisation measure and to the Bank of Italy and the Ministry of the Economy and Finance for admission to the State guarantee, in order to issue new secured liabilities.

The ECB's assessment of MPS's application was positive. The ECB stated that the requirements for access to the precautionary recapitalisation measure were met, in accordance with current legislation, and highlighted that: (i) based on the consolidated situation at 30 September 2016, the parent company was solvent, as it complied with the minimum capital requirements established by the CRR, as well as with the Pillar 2 requirements; (ii) the results of the 2016 stress test had identified only under the adverse scenario a fully loaded CET1 shortfall at the end of 2018 of 2.44%, corresponding to a capital requirement of about €8.8 billion; (iii) the Parent's liquidity position had deteriorated rapidly between 30 November 2016 and 21 December 2016.

In the first half of 2017, after the granting of the State guarantee in support of liquidity pursuant to Decree-Law No 237/2016, the bank carried out two issues of bonds backed by the State guarantee, in the total amount of about €11 billion.

On 4 July 2017, the Commission announced the approval of the Group Restructuring Plan 2017–2021 to allow the Bank's precautionary recapitalisation, in line with EU legislation and with the SREP letter sent

[37] See C. Barbagallo, *Banca Monte dei Paschi di Siena*, Senate of the Republic – Chamber of Deputies. Parliamentary Committee of Enquiry into the Banking and Financial System, Law No 107 of 12 July 2017, 22 November 2017.

to the Bank by the ECB.[38] In greater detail, the restructuring plan set the following objectives to be achieved by 2021: (i) ROE exceeding 10%; (ii) cost/income ratio lower than 51%; (iii) cost of risk lower than 60 bps and gross NPE ratio lower than 13% in 2021; (iv) CET1 higher than 14%; (v) rationalisation of the Group's organisational structures, by cutting approximately 5,500 jobs.

On 28 July 2017, pursuant to Decree-Law No 237/2016, the MPS Group's capital was strengthened by €8.2 billion, through the following measures:

- Burden sharing, i.e. the forced conversion of all subordinated bonds issued by the bank, amounting to approximately €4.3 billion, through the issue of new shares;
- a capital increase of approximately €3.9 billion carried out by the Ministry of the Economy and Finance, completed on 11 August 2017.[39]

In addition, an exchange offer was planned, addressed only to subordinate retail bondholders affected by the burden-sharing measures and who met certain requirements. In this context, the Bank, in the name and on behalf of the Ministry of the Economy and Finance, purchased part of the ordinary shares resulting from the conversion of the subordinated bonds, for a value of approximately €1.5 billion. The recipients of the offer received in exchange senior debt instruments issued by MPS for the same amount.

After the completion of the precautionary recapitalisation and of the conversion of the subordinated bonds, the share of MPS capital held by the Ministry of the Economy and Finance increased from 4.024% in December 2016 to 68.247% in December 2017.

On 20 December 2017, the bank's bad loan portfolio, having a gross book value (GBV) of €24.5 billion, was sold through a securitisation

[38] EUROPEAN COMMISSION, State Aid SA.47677(2017/N).

[39] A special fund was set up in the State budget to cover the overall support measures for MPS. In particular, the Ministry of the Economy and Finance set up a fund with a budget of €20 billion for the year 2017 to cover the costs incurred for the subscription and purchase of shares to strengthen capital and the costs of the guarantees granted by the State on newly issued liabilities and on the provision of emergency liquidity to Italian banks and banking groups.

transaction at a price of approximately €5 billion, equal to 20.58% of GBV.[40] The transaction was carried out with the intervention of the Atlante Fund, which purchased 95% of the junior and mezzanine notes of the securitisation vehicle (about €1.3 billion) (Fig. 5).

2.5 The Sale of the Bank on the Market

As mentioned above, pursuant to Decree No 237/2016, in order to be able to request State support, MPS had previously submitted a capital-strengthening plan to the Bank of Italy and the ECB, which included the amount of capital needed, the planned measures to strengthen its capital position and the deadline for implementing the plan, which was the end of 2021.

Moreover, in line with Article 31 of Regulation (EU) No 575 of 26 June 2013, the Italian State had undertaken to exit the bank's capital. To this end, it was initially planned that the Ministry of the Economy and Finance would dispose of its shares by the end of the 2017–2021 restructuring plan, submitted at the time of approval of the precautionary recapitalisation measure.

In this regard, it was agreed with the ECB that a detailed plan for the Italian State's exit from MPS would be submitted by the end of 2019. In December 2019, the Commission and the Ministry of the Economy and Finance agreed to postpone submission of the plan to early 2020, also in view of the discussions with the ECB on the terms of the sale of a further portfolio of the Bank's non-performing loans.[41] To this end, on 29 June 2020, the Bank and AMCO approved a plan for the partial hive-off of a portfolio of bad loans (with a GBV of approximately €8.1 billion, including €4.8 billion of non-performing loans and approximately €3.3 billion of unlikely-to-pay exposures), deferred tax assets (DTA), other assets and certain liabilities of the bank.[42]

[40] Monte Dei Paschi di Siena, *Financial Statements 2017*.

[41] Ministry of the Economy and Finance, *A inizio 2020 presentazione piano dismissione partecipazione Mef in Mps*, Press Release No 234, 29 December 2019.

[42] Monte Dei Paschi di Siena, *Partial non-proportional demerger project with asymmetric option of a compendium of non-performing exposures from MPS in favor of AMCO*, Press release, 29 June 2020, https://gruppomps.it/en/media-and-news/press-releases/press-releasea-29-june-2020.html.

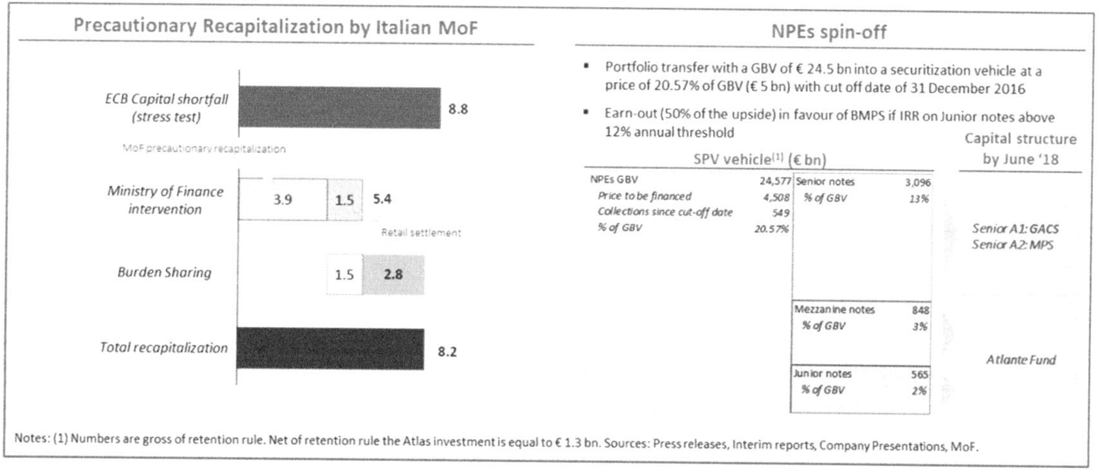

Fig. 5 MPS: the structure of the intervention

The political debate on the disposal of the State's controlling interest in MPS is still open; there is as yet no consensus about the future of MPS. The Government has started the disposal procedure as agreed with the Commission, but some argue that the State can still revise its position on the sale of the Bank, and has made alternative proposals, namely: postponing the sale; maintaining State control over the Bank; turning the Bank into a public instrument for the pursuit of economic policy objectives geared towards investment and growth (see Chapter 10); or including MPS in a merger between national banks.

CHAPTER 6

Establishment of the FITD's Voluntary Scheme and Interventions Carried Out

The Voluntary Scheme is an initiative taken by the Italian banking system to equip itself with an additional instrument against bank crises; this initiative is due to the negative decision taken by the European Commission on the FITD intervention in favour of Banca Tercas and to similar guidelines issued for other Italian banks in special administration, preventing early actions by the Deposit Guarantee Schemes, based on the State aid rules.

The Voluntary Scheme has carried out five interventions and is still operative, although its activities have been suspended following the resumption of FITD activity after the ruling of the EU General Court that annulled the Commission decision on Banca Tercas.

Voluntary Scheme Interventions	*Banca Tercas* *Cassa di Risparmio di Cesena* *Cassa di Risparmio di Rimini* *Cassa di Risparmio di San Miniato* *Banca Carige*

G. Boccuzzi, *Banking Crises in Italy*, Palgrave Studies in Financial Instability and Banking Crisis Regulation,
https://doi.org/10.1007/978-3-031-01344-7_6

1 Rationale, Structure and Functioning of the Voluntary Scheme

The Voluntary Scheme was an important initiative taken by the Italian banking system, within the framework of FITD structure and functioning, as a result of the Banca Tercas case. The initiative was also launched in the light of the suggestions made by the Commission in its decision on Tercas and the four banks in special administration, which asserted the public nature of the resources of the deposit guarantee schemes and provided operational guidance on how to remove obstacles to the intervention. In particular, the Commission stated that if private entities decide to support banks in difficulty according to their objectives and using their funds, without a State mandate, no State aid issues arise.

On the basis of this guidance, in 2015 the banking sector implemented an alternative, voluntary intervention scheme within the FITD, to overcome the problems raised by the State aid framework. The scheme also aimed to avoid the possible fallout on the banking system of traumatic solutions to bank crises, such as liquidation and its impacts on creditors and on the continuity of essential banking functions. In some circumstances, the liquidation of banks may result in negative externalities on the system, in addition to the direct costs of the procedure itself.

The possibility of setting up voluntary funds is also provided by Legislative Decree 30/2016, which transposed the DGSD, amending the Italian Banking Act. The Decree states that deposit guarantee schemes may, where provided for in their statutes and in accordance with arrangements between banks, carry out further interventions through resources paid on a voluntary basis by the participating banks and without recourse to the financial endowment accumulated on a compulsory basis. Further, it should be noted that voluntary schemes for resolving banking crises have also long been in place in other European countries—such as Germany and Austria—with large intervention capacities. These schemes have been operating for decades, with pre-established resources managed by the banks' associations.

The initial choice was to incorporate the rules of the Voluntary Scheme into the FITD Statute, also based on the guidance provided by the Commission. Over time, the structure and the functioning of the Scheme have been regulated more organically by Title II of the FITD Statute. This was done in response to developments in crisis-related needs and in order to reinforce the voluntary nature of the instrument within the framework of banking crises management.

The main characteristics of the scheme can be summarised as follows:

i) functional separation of financing mechanism and resources. The resources of the Scheme must be provided by the participating banks, independently and separately from those paid as compulsory contributions to the FITD for the setting up of the financial endowment, as required by law. Information about the separate management of said contributions can be found in a specific financial statement;
ii) absence of any control or authorisation by the State or other authority for the use of resources in support interventions;
iii) fully voluntary participation of banks in the scheme and its interventions;
iv) independent governance arrangements vis-à-vis the mandatory DGS. The Voluntary Scheme has its own governance and acts independently and separately from the FITD[1];
v) triggers for intervention. Support may be granted to participating banks in receipt of the Bank of Italy's early intervention measures or assessed to be 'failing or likely to fail'. Banks in compulsory administrative liquidation are not eligible for the scheme. Interventions can be made when the banks have reasonable prospects of recovery, based on adequate and credible restructuring plans. When a bank has been declared to be failing or likely to fail by the Bank of Italy, it can be supported by the scheme provided that, in accordance with the conditions laid down in the legislation, the Bank of Italy has taken prior measures to reduce/convert capital instruments onto CET1 capital;
vi) competence of the General Meeting of the participating banks for decisions on interventions in favour of banks in crisis, after a proposal of the Board of Management;

[1] The scheme has its own General Meeting of Participating banks and a Management Board, a volitive body consisting of 10 Representative Members and two Members by Law (FITD President and President of the ABI—Italian Banking Association). The Bodies of the scheme are completed by the FITD President, Director General and Board of Statutory Auditors.

vii) forms of interventions. The Scheme has a wide and diversified financial toolbox, including the issue of loans or guarantees, the acquisition of shareholdings and other technical forms; and

viii) resources for interventions. The financial resources are not collected in advance from the participating banks but are made available to the Scheme on call, in proportion to the banks' respective covered deposits. Furthermore, any recovery accruing from the interventions is allocated to the participating banks, in proportion to the amount paid in, deducting all charges and any loans—taken out at market conditions—extinguished.

2 Five Interventions in Case of Crisis

Since its establishment in November 2015, the Voluntary Scheme has carried out interventions in support of 5 participating banks, for an overall amount of approximately €1.4 billion (Fig. 1): Banca Tercas; Cassa di Risparmio di Cesena (Caricesena), Cassa di Risparmio di Rimini (Carim) and Cassa di Risparmio di San Miniato (Carismi); Banca Carige—Cassa di Risparmio di Genova e Imperia (Carige).

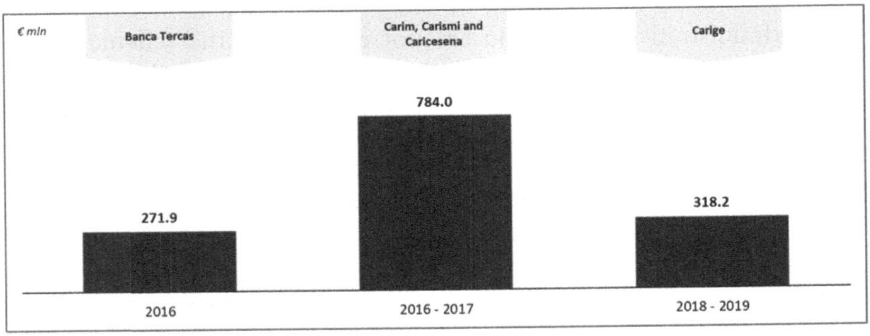

Fig. 1 Interventions of the Voluntary Scheme since 2016 (*Source* Annual Report and Financial Statement 2019 of the Voluntary Intervention Scheme)

2.1 *First Intervention in Favour of Banca Tercas Following the Commission Decision*

The Voluntary Scheme intervened to remedy the delicate situation that arose following the decision adopted on 23 December 2015 by the EU Commission against Banca Tercas. The decision ordered the recovery of the support granted by the FITD to Banca Tercas in 2014, on the grounds that it was incompatible with Article 108(3) of the Treaty on the Functioning of the European Union (TFEU). Following this decision, the Banca Popolare di Bari ('BPB') and Banca Tercas requested the support of the FITD's Voluntary Scheme, to protect them from the impact of the Commission decision, since implementation of the Tercas rescue operation had been based on the essential external support of the FITD.

After carefully analysing the application received, the Management Board of the Voluntary Scheme decided to intervene in the same terms as the original support measure approved by the FITD, structured as follows:

- disbursement of €265 million, in addition to a commission of €140,000 and the related interest (approximately €6.8 million), concurrently with the repayment of the alleged State aid by Banca Tercas;
- guarantee of €30 million with a limited duration of six months, against the risk of non-tax neutrality of the Voluntary Scheme's contribution; and
- guarantee of the Voluntary Scheme on a set of high-risk credit positions for an amount of €35 million.

Thus, the total cash support amounted to approximately 271.9 million. The two guarantees in favour of BPB were subsequently terminated, as the conditions for their activation did not occur.

2.2 *Second Intervention: Caricesena, Carim and Carismi*

Tools Applied

- Capital increase of the three banks by the Voluntary Scheme

- Spin-off of NPEs through a securitisation operation
- Acquisition by a third party of the capital subscribed by the Voluntary Scheme

Main Steps

- **May '16**: Caricesena sends to the Voluntary Scheme a request for support in the form of a capital increase necessary to provide an immediate solution to the bank's crisis situation
- **May '16**: the Voluntary Scheme expresses its willingness to support the bank, making any final decision subject to the results of a business due diligence and the approval of a rigorous and credible business plan
- **Sep. '16**: capital increase of €280 million by the Voluntary Scheme in favour of Caricesena
- **Oct. '16–Jan. '17**: Carim and Carismi request the support of the Voluntary Scheme
- **Sep. '17**: Crédit Agricole Cariparma, the Voluntary Scheme and the three banks sign a binding agreement governing the terms and conditions of the recapitalisation and simultaneous sale of the banks to Crédit Agricole Cariparma, together with the spin-off of non-performing exposures, to be finalised by the end of 2017
- **Dec. '17**: Spin-off of NPEs and setting up of an SPV (Berenice), recapitalisation of the three banks by the Voluntary Scheme and transfer of the banks to Crédit Agricole Cariparma

The second intervention of the Voluntary Scheme was carried out in support of the Cassa di Risparmio di Cesena, through the recapitalisation of the bank and, immediately after, in favour of the Cassa di Risparmio di Rimini and the Cassa di Risparmio di San Miniato. The Voluntary Scheme took control of the banks, subsequently selling them to Credìt Agricole Cariparma, at a price of €130 million.

The measures in favour of the three banks were completed in 2017, as part of an overall aggregation operation realised by Credit Agricole Cariparma (Fig. 2).

Consolidated data as of December 2015 (€ mln; %)	**Caricesena**	**Carim**	**Carismi**
Direct funding	3,603	2,804	2,432
o/w: covered deposits	1,692	1,448	1,010
% FITD total covered deposits	*0.32%*	*0.27%*	*0.19%*
Total assets	4,358	3,729	3,266
NPEs ratio (GBV)	35.8%	30.3%	26.8%
Cost-Income ratio	60.0%	73.4%	64.1%
Net profit (loss)	(252)	(38)	(68)
ROE	(70.0%)	(13.7%)	(27.2%)
CET 1 ratio	1.6%	8.5%	7.6%
Total capital ratio	3.8%	10.9%	11.7%
Employees	981	677	682
Branches	117	58	86

Fig. 2 Caricesena, Carim and Carismi: main data (*Source* Cassa di Risparmio di Cesena—Financial Statements at 31/12/2015; Carim, Financial Statement on 31 December 2015; Carismi, 2015 Financial Statements)

2.2.1 *The Case of Cassa di Risparmio di Cesena*

Cassa di Risparmio di Cesena S.p.A. (Caricesena) was a regional bank founded in 1841, which operated through a network of 117 branches located mainly in the Emilia-Romagna region and had 981 employees.

Between February and July 2015, the bank was subjected to supervisory inspections, as a result of which critical issues emerged, mainly attributable to deficiencies in the governance and control systems together with high credit risk; this significantly affected the bank's economic and equity situation.

The inspection revealed serious anomalies in the management of loans, in their classification and in the coverage of the associated risks. Shortcomings were also highlighted in different areas, such as strategic planning, risk management, compliance and internal auditing.

Following these negative results, the Bank of Italy, with two subsequent supervisory interventions, asked the bank to speed up the process of finding a banking partner or institutional investors interested in acquiring control. The implementation of a comprehensive intervention plan was also requested; this included the renewal of the governing bodies, the replacement of management, the full recognition of the credit losses that had emerged during the inspections, the implementation of an adequate capital increase, the revision of the organisational and control structure, the reduction of non-performing assets and the rationalisation of costs.

On 19 May 2016, Caricesena asked the FITD's Voluntary Scheme for a support intervention in the form of a capital increase, necessary to provide an immediate solution to the crisis situation and to ensure operational continuity in the interest of depositors.

In particular, the Bank reported severe difficulties in finding a banking partner, due to its issues and the capital shortfalls with respect to supervisory requirements.[2]

The Voluntary Scheme expressed its willingness to intervene, subject to a number of conditions, including, among others: the recognition in the 2015 financial statements of the results of the business due diligence conducted by the scheme; the approval of a rigorous and credible business plan; the proposal to the shareholders' meeting of an adequate capital increase, coupled with assumption of control over the bank by the Voluntary Scheme, through the acquisition of a control stake and the majority of voting rights. After an in-depth assessment of the bank's situation, the measure in favour of Caricesena was approved by the Voluntary Scheme's management board on 15 June 2016, and was structured as follows:

a. capital increase by the Voluntary Scheme of €280 million, aimed at ensuring compliance with the Bank's capital requirements, as part of the overall business plan for the restructuring and relaunch of Caricesena;

[2] The capital requirements imposed on the Bank at 31 December 2015 were as follows: CET1 ratio of 7.0%, Tier 1 ratio of 8.5%, Total Capital ratio of 10.5%. In this respect, on the same date, the bank had a CET1 ratio slightly higher than the requirement imposed by the supervisory authority. However, following the inclusion of the results of due diligence carried out by the Voluntary Scheme's advisor, the bank's CET1 ratio stood at 1.6%. *Source: Cassa di Risparmio di Cesena, Financial Statements at 31 December 2015.*

b. award to the former shareholders of Caricesena of free warrants, to be exercised in order to guarantee a future capital increase of the bank up to a maximum of €55 million.

On 23 September 2016, following the ECB's authorisation for the acquisition of the controlling stake in Caricesena, the capital increase was completed and the Voluntary Scheme became the majority shareholder of the bank with 95.3% of the share capital.

Subsequently, the Bank's Board of Directors was completely renewed by the Voluntary Scheme and the management was strengthened.

2.2.2 Carim and Carismi

The case of the two banks developed almost simultaneously with that of Caricesena.

Banca Carim was a regional bank founded in 1840, operating through a network of 58 branches located mainly in Emilia-Romagna, with strong roots in the province of Rimini.

The bank was placed under special administration on 29 September 2010; on 30 September 2012, it was returned to ordinary operations, following the restructuring action taken by the special administrators.

The bank's new management continued its reorganisation and relaunch. However, despite the actions taken to recover efficiencies, the bank continued to present structural capital shortfalls. On 9 June 2016, the bank approved a capital increase of €40 million, which was postponed following the start of a new supervisory inspection.

The inspection findings, which were recognised by the bank in its half year accounts at 30 June 2016, gave rise to significant impairments on loans, of approximately €90 million and a significant impact on the CET1 ratio, which stood at 6.4% compared to 8.5% in the previous half year)[3]; an aggregative solution was therefore necessary to strengthen its capital.

Carismi was a regional banking group operating mainly in Tuscany, with a network of 86 branches.

In the period October 2015–January 2016, Carismi was subject to supervisory inspections, which found significant capital shortcomings.

[3] Cassa di Risparmio di Rimini, *Financial Statement at 31 December 2016.*

Therefore, the Bank of Italy asked Carismi to make a capital increase; it also highlighted the need to revise the 2016–2020 strategic plan, by including a possible combination with potential investors.

In 2016, since the situation of both banks had worsened and the authority demanded an immediate solution to their crisis, Carim and Carismi applied for support to the FITD's Voluntary Scheme, respectively, on 4 October 2016 and 4 January 2017, given the impossibility of carrying out market solutions.

A search was launched for third parties willing to take part in the restructuring and relaunching of the two banks, with the support of the Voluntary Scheme, in order to avoid liquidation measures.

The Integration Operation with Credit Agricole Cariparma. The search for a solution to the crises of the two banks proved to be technically complex; various hypotheses were considered, proposed by non-banking entities and by international banking group Crédit Agricole Cariparma.

At the end of the evaluation process, Crédit Agricole Cariparma's proposal was accepted. The supervisory authority approved this decision, considering the Cariparma offer to be the safest and most effective solution to the Carim and Carismi crises. The proposal also expedited the sale of the Voluntary Scheme's stake in Caricesena, since Cariparma had also made its intervention for the two banks subject to the acquisition of Caricesena, which was at that time controlled by the Scheme. In addition, the sale of the scheme's stake in Caricesena was requested by the ECB when authorising the measure and was in any case provided for in Caricesena's Business Plan.

At the end of the due diligence carried out by Cariparma, the latter made a binding offer for the acquisition of control over the three banks.

On 28 July 2017, the Voluntary Scheme's management board approved the operation proposed by Cariparma and on 29 September 2017, a framework agreement was signed between Crédit Agricole Cariparma, the Voluntary Scheme, Caricesena, Carim and Carismi. The operation was structured as follows:

1. **Spin-off of NPEs**, through a securitisation transaction of a portfolio of approximately €2.8 billion, composed of unlikely-to-pay and non-performing loans, to bring the three banks' aggregate gross NPE ratio to no more than 9% on the transaction completion date. An additional portfolio of approximately €286 million was sold to a foreign fund.

The securitisation was carried out issuing approximately €335 million of senior notes, subscribed by national and international financial institutions, and through the issue of mezzanine notes for €505 million, subscribed by Quaestio Capital SGR, on behalf of the Italian Recovery Fund (formerly Atlante Fund). The Voluntary Scheme subscribed €12 million of mezzanine notes and €158 million of junior notes.

2. **Recapitalisation** of the three banks by the Voluntary Scheme. Based on the assessments carried out at the closing date, an overall capital increase for the three banks of €464 million was considered necessary to cover the extraordinary costs uncovered by the due diligence, align the value of the spun-off NPEs with their sale prices and reach an overall CET1 ratio for the three banks of 10.7%. This amount was in addition to the capital increase of €280 million in favour of Caricesena carried out the previous year.
3. **The sale of the three banks to Crédit Agricole Cariparma** for €130 million, carried out at the same time as the recapitalisations.

   Thus, the overall support provided by the Voluntary Scheme amounted to €784 million, of which:

- €170 million for the subscription of the tranches of the securitisation of the NPEs (€12 million of mezzanine securities and €158 million of junior securities);
- €614 million for the recapitalisation of the three banks.

The overall transaction was finalised on 21 December 2019, after the signing of the securitisation contracts and the verification of the conditions established in the framework agreement (Fig. 3).

2.3 *Banca Carige. Phase 1*

Tools applied

- Subscription of subordinated bonds by the Voluntary Scheme, as part of a subsequent operation to increase the Bank's capital

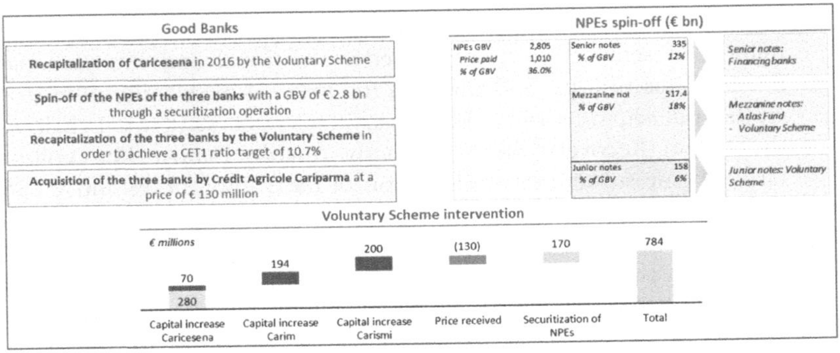

Fig. 3 Caricesena, Carim and Carismi: the structure of the deal

Main steps

- **Nov. '18**: Banca Carige applies for the Voluntary Scheme's support to comply with capital requirements
- **Nov. '18**: the general meeting of the banks participating in the Voluntary Scheme approves the support measure in favour of Banca Carige in the form of underwriting Tier 2 subordinated bonds
- **Dec. '18**: the bank calls an extraordinary shareholders' meeting to approve its capital increase. The operation is not approved because the meeting quorum is not reached
- **Jan. '19**: the Bank is placed under temporary administration
- **Jan. '19**: Legislative Decree No 1/2019 is published; it introduces urgent measures in support of Banca Carige, including extraordinary public financial support through a State guarantee on newly issued liabilities of the bank

The Bank: General Information and Main Data. Banca Carige was established in 1483, just a few years after MPS. It was a *significant* bank and the parent company of the Banca Carige Group, which also included Banca del Monte di Lucca, Banca Cesare Ponti and the companies Centro Fiduciario, Creditis Servizi Finanziari and Carige Reoco.

With its registered office in Genoa, as of 31 December 2018, it had a commercial network composed of 489 branches, with a strong presence in the Liguria region (market share of 25.8%) and northern Italy (market share of 4.3%). Banca Carige's difficulties started in 2014, due to economic and capital factors and governance issues.

As to economic factors, in the period 2014–2018 the bank's stock price tumbled to almost nil (dropping to €0.0015 per share at the end of 2018, compared to €0.5 at the start of 2014), mainly due to the low quality of its loan portfolio, which required significant and repeated write-downs. During this period, the Carige Group recorded total losses of approximately €1.6 billion. To achieve compliance with capital requirements, the bank resorted to three capital increases, for an overall amount of approximately €2.2 billion. With regard to governance, during the same period the bank underwent repeated changes of management and governing bodies, also due to diverging views regarding business management and governance (Fig. 4).

In early 2018, the bank underwent ECB inspections, which were followed by supervisory interventions on credit quality, profitability and governance.

On 11 November 2018, Banca Carige requested the intervention of the FITD's Voluntary Scheme in support of an overall recapitalisation aimed at ensuring compliance with prudential requirements and contributing to the group's consolidation process. The transaction involved the subscription of subordinated bonds amounting to €320 million, convertible into shares upon the occurrence of certain conditions.

The proposed capital operation was intended in response to the ECB's Decision of 14 September 2018 which, in view of the bank's many technical, organisational and management weaknesses, had requested the bank to submit a Capital Conservation Plan to restore and ensure sustainable compliance with capital requirements, by 31 December 2018. The plan had to evaluate all options, including a business combination.[4]

In the first part of 2018, the bank had made three unsuccessful attempts to find investors in Tier 2 bonds to be issued. Therefore, the capital operation proposed to the Voluntary Scheme was a necessary measure for implementing the Capital Conservation Plan requested by the ECB. This was also commensurate with the need to address further value adjustments and other negative elements existing on 30 September 2018.

[4] Banca Carige, *Report of the Board of Directors in item 3 of the Agenda of the Extraordinary General Meeting of Shareholders convened for 22 December 2018*, 30 November 2018.

Consolidated data as of December 2018; (€ mln; %)	
Direct funding	14,495
o/w: covered deposits	9,007
% FITD total covered deposits	*1.5%*
Total assets	22,095
NPEs ratio (GBV)	22.0%
Cost-Income ratio	93.7%
Net profit (loss)	(273)
ROE	(13.5%)
CET 1 ratio	10.7%
Total capital ratio	12.9%
Employees	4,282
Branches	489

Fig. 4 Banca Carige: main data (*Source* Banca Carige, Report on the consolidated financial and economic situation pursuant to Article 73, paragraph 4 T.U.B., 2018)

On 30 November 2018, the general meeting of the banks participating in the Voluntary Scheme approved the support to Banca Carige, in the form of underwriting Tier 2 subordinated bonds, for up to €320 million, to be converted into share capital in the amount necessary to enable a capital increase of €400 million. On the same date, the Voluntary Scheme underwrote €318.2 million; the remaining €1.8 million was subscribed by another Italian bank, Banco di Desio e della Brianza.

On 22 December 2018, the bank called an extraordinary general meeting of shareholders to approve its capital increase, to be carried out at the beginning of 2019. However, the operation was not approved because the meeting quorum was not reached.

To stabilise governance and pursue effective solutions ensuring the bank's long-term stability, on 2 January 2019, the ECB placed the bank under temporary administration and appointed temporary administrators to manage it.

On 8 January 2019, Legislative Decree No 1/2019 was published, introducing various measures in support of the bank, including the possibility for the Ministry of Economy and Finance (MEF) to grant public financial support through a State guarantee on newly issued liabilities of Banca Carige up to a nominal value of €3 billion.

On 18 January, the bank requested the MEF to grant a public guarantee on two bonds of €1 billion each, with a duration of 12 and 18 months respectively and interest rates of 0.5% and 0.75%, reserving the right to request the activation of an additional guarantee of €1 billion in the future. The bonds were issued on 25 January 2019, helping to secure the bank's liquidity position.

In the meantime, the temporary administrators, the Voluntary Scheme and FITD continued to talk to define the bank's capital increase and overall recovery and relaunch plan, with the involvement of an industrial partner.

Banca Carige also received subsequent support from the FITD. Details of this operation are given in Chapter 7.

CHAPTER 7

The FITD's Preventive and Alternative Measures

The FITD's preventive and alternative measures fall under the scope of Directive 2014/49/EU on deposit guarantee schemes (Articles 11.3 and 11.6). They are alternative to the reimbursement of depositors (payout) and the financing of resolution. The directive leaves to Member States the choice of whether to introduce these measures in their legislations. The national law transposing the directive allows implementation of these two types of measures, giving to Italian DGSs the option to introduce them in their Statutes and establish their rules.

The FITD's statutes provide for preventive and alternative measures, which are designed in line with the Directive. Consequently, the FITD has full discretion in this area to decide when and how to intervene. The decision is subject to the least cost test compared to depositor payout. Following the European General Court ruling of March 2019, which overruled the Commission decision on the Tercas case, the FITD decided to resume preventive and alternative measures, because it considered that State aid rules no longer apply to these two types of measures, as they are optional forms of support, carried out through private resources of FITD member banks and not attributable to a State decision.

G. Boccuzzi, *Banking Crises in Italy*, Palgrave Studies in Financial Instability and Banking Crisis Regulation,
https://doi.org/10.1007/978-3-031-01344-7_7

In the reporting period, FITD carried out 5 measures: 2 alternative and 3 preventive.

Alternative measures (Article 11(6) DGSD)	*Banca Popolare delle Province Calabre (BPPC)* *Banca Sviluppo Economico (Banca Base)*
Preventive measures (Article 11(3) DGSD)	*Banca Carige—Cassa di Risparmio di Genova e Imperia (Carige)* *Banca del Fucino (Fucino)* *Banca Popolare di Bari (BPB)*

1 The FITD's Mandate and Interventions

Since its establishment on a voluntary basis in 1987,[1] the FITD has carried out 15 measures to support banks in crisis, thanks to the broad mandate governed by its statutes. This has enabled the FITD to manage various kinds of measures, taking into account the specific features of each case. Even after the implementation of Directive 94/19/EC, which made the banks' participation in a deposit guarantee scheme mandatory and regulated its functioning, FITD maintained its legal status as a private law consortium and its broad intervention capacity in banking crises through various and flexible operating methods subject to the 'least cost' criterion compared to depositor payout.

Thus, the FITD's institutional objective of depositor protection was largely pursued indirectly through interventions other than the reimbursement of depositors of banks in liquidation, which was carried out only in two cases concerning very small banks. In the other cases, FITD intervened through alternative and less expensive measures: the sale of assets and liabilities of banks in liquidation (eight cases); or preventive measures, for the reorganisation of the bank, in order to avoid its liquidation, in the presence of concrete recovery prospects based on effective and credible restructuring plans (five cases).

In terms of time, the FITD's measures of these types can be divided into two periods: those carried out prior to Directive 2014/49/EU

[1] The FITD was established in 1987 with the voluntary participation of all Italian banks, with the exception of cooperative credit banks, which had their own guarantee fund, to protect themselves against the insolvency of their members, according to the stability of the banking system.

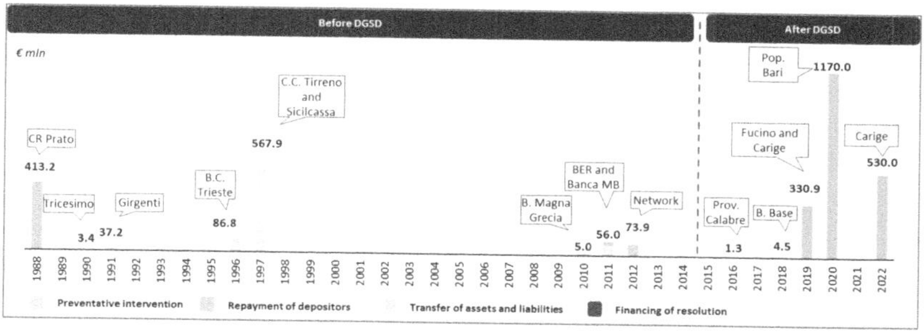

Fig. 1 FITD interventions from 1987 (*Source* FITD, Annual Reports)

(DGSD), which was adopted to strengthen the regulatory framework of deposit guarantees after the global financial crisis, and those carried out after its implementation[2] (Fig. 1).

For the purposes of our analysis, we will examine the FITD interventions carried out after the implementation of the DGSD.[3]

Since 2014, the FITD has carried out five measures, specifically two alternative measures, for banks under compulsory administrative liquidation (Banca Popolare delle Province Calabre and Banca Base), supporting the transfer of their assets and liabilities to other banks, and three preventive measures (Banca del Fucino, Banca Carige and Banca Popolare di Bari). The banks that received support for the sale of assets and liabilities in the context of liquidation were very small: the measures involved an outlay of €5.8 million, less than 1% of the FITD's total measures. The preventive measures concerned small and medium-sized banks and amounted to approximately €2,030.9 million (99% of the

[2] Following the severe bank failures that occurred during the financial crisis, a broad debate began at European level on the need to strengthen deposit guarantee systems, so as to improve their capacity to deal with large-scale bank insolvencies. The first initiative in this direction was the adoption of Directive 2009/14/EC of 11 March 2009, which remedied some weaknesses of the previous Directive 94/19/EC and achieved greater convergence of deposit guarantee schemes; in particular, the level of protection for each depositor was gradually increased to €100,000 and the term for depositor reimbursement reduced to 20 days. G. BOCCUZZI, *The Special Regime of Bank Resolution. Objectives and Tools*, op. cit.

[3] In 2021 FITD took the decision to provide 48.8 million euro for Aigis Banca in compulsory administrative liquidation, to make possible the transfer of assets and liabilities to Banca Ifis. For the purposes of our analysis, this recent case is not examined.

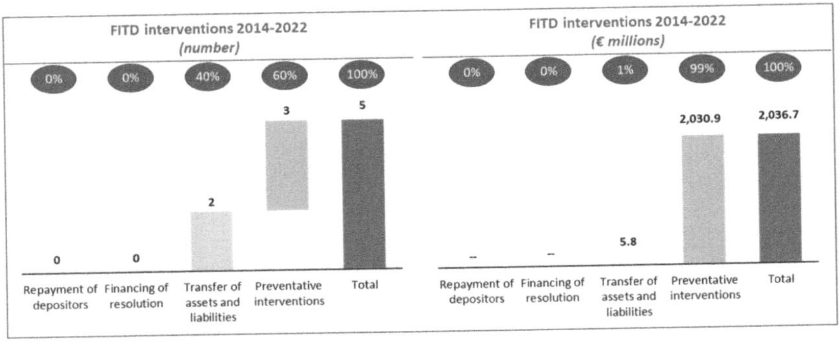

Fig. 2 FITD interventions in 2014–2022 (*Source* FITD, Annual Reports)

total disbursement supported by the FITD in the 2014–2022 period). See Fig. 2.

Directive 49/2014 (DGSD) gives a broad mandate to deposit guarantee schemes. Recitals 3 and 16 explicitly state that DGSs should go beyond the function of mere repayment of depositors, by carrying out measures to prevent bank failure and the related costs of reimbursing depositors, as well as other adverse impacts on financial stability and depositor confidence.

In line with this objective, Article 11 of the DGSD provides for a wide range of measures, to be activated in different phases of the crisis and in various forms. These methods of intervention can be divided into two categories: mandatory measures and discretionary measures.

The first category—mandatory measures—includes the repayment of depositors and the contribution to the financing of resolution (Articles 11.1 and 11.2 respectively).

The second category—discretionary measures—comprises:

i. measures to avoid the failure of a bank, under the conditions set out in Article 11(3), one of which is that the cost of the measure must not exceed the costs necessary to fulfil the statutory or contractual mandate of the DGS, (*preventive measures*);
ii. measures to preserve the depositors' access to covered deposits, through the transfer of assets and liabilities of banks in liquidation, as an alternative to the reimbursement of depositors (Article 11.6), provided that the cost associated with the intervention does

not exceed the cost that the DGS would bear for the payout of depositors (*alternative measures*).

It follows that in addition to the reimbursement of depositors in the event of liquidation and the financing of resolution, which are mandatory interventions, the DGSD also contemplates two other types of interventions, which allow the DGS to resolve the crisis of a bank by facilitating its sale or restructuring.

Following the transposition of the DGSD, the Italian legislation on deposit guarantee schemes has undergone a major reform. The new rules were introduced through amendments and additions to the Italian Banking Act (TUB) concerning the rules on deposit guarantee systems. The Italian legislation and the Statutes of the FITD and the Guarantee Fund of the Cooperative Credit banks (FGDBCC) have confirmed the wide range of measures that can be carried out, both mandatory and discretionary (Fig. 3).

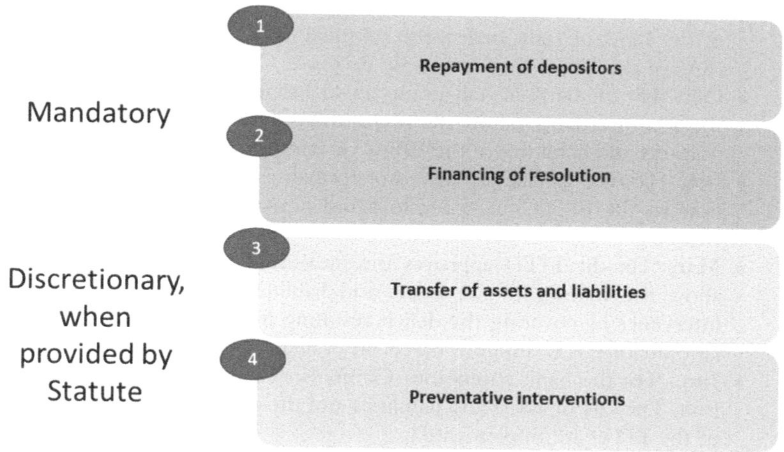

Fig. 3 Types of intervention of Italian DGSs

2 The FITD's Alternative Interventions

2.1 *The Case of the Banca Popolare Delle Province Calabre: Compulsory Administrative Liquidation with the Support of the FITD*

Tools Applied

- Special administration of the bank.
- Subsequent placing of the bank under compulsory administrative liquidation.
- Transfer of assets and liabilities of the bank in liquidation to another bank.
- Coverage by the FITD of the capital deficit, pursuant to Article 34 of the Statute.

Main Steps

- **Aug. '14:** the Ministry of Economy and Finance, on the proposal of the Bank of Italy, orders the submission to special administration (SA) of the Banca Popolare delle Province Calabre (BPPC).
- **Oct. '15:** the Bank of Italy grants a two-month technical extension of the SA, in order to allow the preparatory activity for the acquisition of assets and liabilities of the BPPC by Banca Popolare di Bari (BPB).
- **Feb. '16**: the special administrator formalises a request for intervention to the FITD, 'in order to avoid liquidation scenarios' of the BPPC.
- **Mar. '16**: the FITD approves the measure in favour of BPPC, to allow the transfer of the assets and liabilities to BPB. The FITD intervenes by covering the deficit resulting from the transfer with an amount of €1.37 million, based on evaluation of the *least cost*.
- **Jun. '16**: the bank enters into Compulsory Administrative Liquidation. The sale of assets and liabilities and the consequent intervention of the FITD are implemented.

The bank: general information and main data. Banca Popolare delle Province Calabre (BPPC) was a very small bank operating in the province of Catanzaro. It had the legal form of a joint-stock cooperative and had its registered office in the Reggio Calabria municipality. Its share capital on 30 September 2015 was approximately €8.9 million. The bank had 5 employees.

On 8 August 2014, a decree of the Minister of Economy and Finance, on the proposal of the Bank of Italy, dissolved the BPPC's governing bodies and placed the bank under special administration for serious capital losses, pursuant to Article 70(1)(b) of the TUB.

From 31 December 2013 (closing date of the last financial statements before the special administration) to 31 January 2016, the Bank had accumulated losses of €4.5 million, mainly due to provisions for NPLs made during the special administration procedure (approximately €7.4 million) and to the negative income trend, also connected to the bank's high operating costs.[4]

As a result of these losses, the bank's shareholders' equity contracted sharply, settling, on 31 January 2016, at €1.6 million, well below the minimum legal requirement for the constitution of a bank (€10 million).

In addition, the bank suffered a significant reduction in funding, which resulted in liquidity shortage. At the end of January 2016, total direct deposits amounted to €12.6 million. Covered deposits were €7.7 million; non-protected deposits were €3.9 million; the remaining part was mainly made up of deposits acquired as pledges by the bank for loans.

During the special administration, the bank carried out a gradual *run-off* of the loan portfolio and increased the levels of coverage.

The *NPE ratio* stood at around 87.3% and the coverage levels of the entire loan portfolio went from 22.8% at 31 December 2013 to 59.0% at 31 January 2016. The coverage ratio of non-performing exposures was 68.8% (Fig. 4).

The request for the FITD's support. After about a year of special administration, on 5 October 2015, the special administrators formalised a request for intervention to the FITD, 'in order to avoid any liquidation scenarios'. In the request, the administrator described the seriousness of the bank's situation in terms of capital shortfall, resulting from the write-downs of the loan portfolio made during the procedure, as well as the unwillingness of other parties to evaluate the possibility of intervention.

The FITD examined the situation of the bank and concluded that liquidation with reimbursement of depositors was the only feasible solution, unless alternative interventions subsequently materialised.

[4] Banca Popolare delle Province Calabre, *2013 Financial Statement*.

Data as of January 2016; (€ mln; %)	
Direct funding	12.7
o/w: covered deposits	7.8
% FITD total covered deposits	*0.0%*
Total assets	15.3
NPEs ratio (GBV)	87.3%
Cost-Income ratio	71.8%
Net profit (loss)	(4.5)
ROE	(73.3%)
CET 1 ratio	0.1%
Total capital ratio	0.1%
Employees	5
Branches	1

Fig. 4 BPPC: main data (*Source* Data provided by the BPPC)

On 26 February, the special administrator sent FITD a new request for intervention, pursuant to Article 31 of the FITD Statutes, in favour of BPPC, pointing out that the crisis was irreversible and the bank could not continue its activity autonomously. The administrator also reported that following talks with many banks, only Banca Popolare di Bari had offered to intervene by acquiring the BPPC's assets and liabilities, subject to its compulsory administrative liquidation and with the FITD support. The BPB made the operation conditional on the recognition of greater provisions on loans and staff reduction with respect to the special administration's assessments.

The special administrator, considering BPB's offer suitable to resolve the BPPC's crisis, in the interest of depositors, customers and creditors in general, requested an intervention of the FITD to cover the deficit resulting from the transfer for €1.37 million.

On 2 March 2016, the FITD approved an intervention in favour of BPPC supporting the sale of the bank's assets and liabilities. On 1 June 2016, the bank was placed under Compulsory Administrative Liquidation and on the same date its assets and liabilities were transferred to Banca Popolare di Bari. Applying the least cost criterion, FITD covered the transfer deficit for an amount of €1.37 million.

2.2 *The Case of Banca Base: The Compulsory Administrative Liquidation with the Support of FITD*

Tools Applied

- Special administration of the bank.
- Subsequent placing of the bank under compulsory administrative liquidation.
- Transfer of assets and liabilities of the bank in liquidation to another bank.
- Coverage by the FITD of the transfer deficit, pursuant to Article 34 of the Statute.

Main Steps

- **Feb. '18:** the bank is placed under special administration.
- **Mar. '18**: the special administrator begins to have contacts with FITD to verify the possibility of an intervention, as an alternative to the liquidation of the Bank.
- **Mar. '18:** Banca Agricola Popolare di Ragusa (BAPR) formalises a proposal for the acquisition of the assets and liabilities of Banca Base, on condition that FITD covers the transfer deficit and the costs of the compulsory administrative liquidation procedure.
- **Apr. '18:** the special administrator sends to FITD a request for a support measure, to cover the transfer deficit.
- **Apr. '18:** FITD approves a support measure of €4.5 million in favour of Banca Base.
- **Apr. '18:** the European Commission approves a general scheme of orderly liquidation, valid for 12 months, aimed at overcoming the crisis of small banks.

- **Apr. '18:** the bank is placed under compulsory administrative liquidation. The Bank of Italy appoints the liquidator, who transfers, with effect from 27 April 2018, the assets and liabilities to the BAPR.

The bank: general information and main data. Banca Sviluppo Economico S.p.A. (Banca Base) was a very small bank, established in 2007, with registered office in Catania and two branches.

The bank mainly offered credit products to customers operating in the healthcare sector and to micro-enterprises in the Catania area. It had a staff of 17 employees. In order to cover losses and comply with capital requirements, between 2012 and 2016 Banca Base carried out five capital increases, for a total amount of approximately €13.4 million.

In the period 2015–2017 Banca Base underwent several supervisory inspections, as a result of which, on 13 February 2018, it was placed under special administration.

As of 28 February 2018, Banca Base had the following balance sheet figures:

- shareholders' equity of €7.6 million, corresponding to a *CET1 ratio* of 18.0%; however, its capital level had fallen below the legal minimums for carrying out banking activities (€10 million);
- net loans to customers of €31.6 million, of which approximately €11.5 million of non-performing loans, corresponding to a gross NPE ratio of 50.9% (36.2% in net terms);
- direct funding of €37.1 million, of which €26.8 million of covered deposits.

The bank was characterised, in particular, by a serious shortage of liquidity, which in the first two months of 2018 had dropped by 55%, from €16.2 million to 7.4 €million. To contain the liquidity outflow, on 13 February 2018 the administrator suspended payments, pursuant to Article 74 of the Consolidated Banking Act (TUB).

On the basis of the assessments made by the special administrator and by the subjects potentially interested in the acquisition of Banca Base, the present value of the Bank's assets was considerably lower than the accounting value, such as to determine a capital deficit. Based on this evidence, the special administrator assessed the irreversibility of the crisis and the impossibility for the banks of continuing its activity autonomously (Fig. 5).

The solution to the crisis. During the special administration, the administrator had begun talks both with some of the bank's shareholders and with other parties potentially interested in intervening to resolve the crisis. At the end of this process, Banca Agricola Popolare di Ragusa (BAPR) declared its willingness to acquire the assets and liabilities of Banca Base, within the context of the bank's Compulsory Administrative Liquidation.

On 27 March 2018, the BAPR sent to Banca Base, the Bank of Italy and the FITD a proposal for the acquisition of the assets and liabilities of the distressed bank, conditional on the coverage, by the FITD, of the transfer deficit for an amount of €4.5 million. In this regard, the special administrator stated that, in consideration of the serious liquidity situation

Data as of February 2018; (€ mln; %)	
Direct funding	37.1
o/w: covered deposits	26.8
% FITD total covered deposits	*0.0%*
Total assets	47.8
NPEs ratio (GBV)	50.9%
Cost-Income ratio	125.2%
Net profit (loss)	(0.9)
ROE	(12.0%)
CET 1 ratio	18.0%
Total capital ratio	18.0%
Employees	17
Branches	2

Fig. 5 Banca Base: main data (*Source* Data provided by Banca Base)

and the high risk profile of the loan portfolio, this proposal appeared to be the only viable solution to the crisis of Banca Base.

The intervention in favour of Banca Base was approved by the FITD on 18 April 2018, pursuant to Article 34 of its Statutes, for an amount of €4.5 million. The FITD had applied the 'least cost' criterion by comparing the cost of BAPR's proposal with the cost of repaying depositors.

On 26 April 2018, the bank was put into Compulsory Administrative Liquidation and the liquidator transferred the assets and liabilities of Banca Base to BAP.

The Orderly Liquidation Scheme. The FITD's intervention in favour of Banca Base was part of a 'general orderly liquidation scheme', approved by the European Commission on 13 April 2018[5], valid for 12 months and aimed at overcoming the crisis of small banks with assets below €3 billion.

This scheme was deemed compatible with the State aid rules pursuant to Article 107(3)(b)of the TFEU, which allows the granting of aid to remedy a serious disturbance in the economy of a Member State, and to Section 6.4 of the 2013 Communication, which allows the granting of aid to ensure the orderly liquidation of distressed credit institutions, while limiting the negative spillover effects on the sector and on the economy as a whole. The granting of this support measure was subject to certain conditions (see Fig. 6).

In accordance with point 3.1.2 of the 2013 Communication, transactions falling under such a framework are subject to 'burden sharing', so that the shares and subordinated bonds are not transferred to the buyer, but remain in the bank in compulsory administrative liquidation.

To cover the transfer deficit, DGSs can decide independently on the basis of their statutes and, in any case, after successfully performing the least cost test, using the methodologies developed by the schemes themselves or with the support of an advisor.

Some considerations on the orderly liquidation scheme. The liquidation scheme approved by the Commission in 2013 concerned a type of solution to banking crises that had already been applied for decades in Italy, under Italian banking law. This tool is essentially based on the sale

[5] EUROPEAN COMMISSION, *State Aid SA.50640 (2018/N) - Italy*, published in the Official Journal on 23 November 2018.

- *In accordance with State aid rules, in April 2018, the European Commission decided not to raise objection to an Italian liquidation scheme for small banks with assets below €3 billion, which allows deposit insurers to contribute by providing compensation in the form of cash to the purchaser of the assets and liabilities of the failed bank.*
- *The objective of the liquidation scheme is to grant support in the orderly liquidation of non-viable small banks under national insolvency proceedings.*
- *Italy will ensure that costs borne by the deposit insurer do not exceed the net amount of compensating covered depositors of the failing institution.*
- *For the purpose of interventions under this scheme, the deposit insurer will ensure that there is a detailed calculation report with respect to the least cost assessment and will appoint an external advisor to support that assessment.*
- *The liquidation scheme is valid for 12 months.*

Fig. 6 A new intervention framework: the ex-ante authorisation of the Commission for a liquidation plan

of the assets and liabilities of the bank in liquidation to another bank, as allowed by Article 90 of the Consolidated Banking Act (TUB).

The case envisaged by the Commission is that Member States put in place support measures for the orderly liquidation of banks to protect financial stability; this option, according to the Commission, must always be taken into consideration when the bank is unable to credibly restore long-term profitability.

Thus, European authorities favour the exit from the market of inefficient banks, provided that the exit takes place in an orderly manner, i.e. by applying particular operations and procedures in the liquidation process to reduce the negative consequences of the application of the bankruptcy rules. This approach provides that, under certain conditions, the resources of the deposit guarantee schemes can also be used to ensure the orderly liquidation of the insolvent bank.

Orderly liquidation implies the cessation of the bank's activity and the impossibility of conducting new business with third parties; only the continuation or completion of activities with existing clients are permitted. Furthermore, the liquidation process must take place for the time strictly necessary to guarantee the orderly implementation of the operation. Moreover, as far as possible the sale of the business or assets should take place through a competitive process.

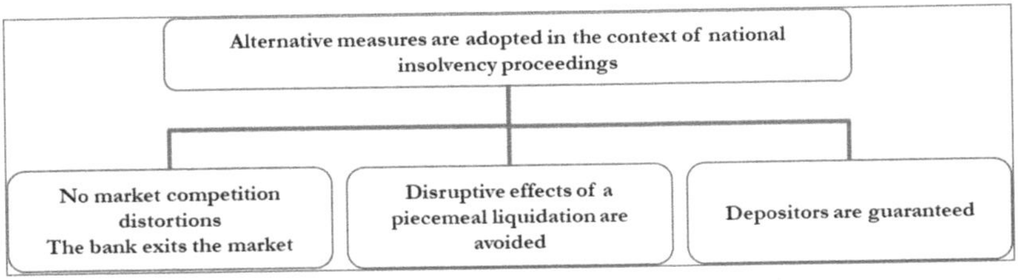

Fig. 7 The effects of alternative measures of deposit guarantee schemes

This includes the option, expressly provided for, that the scheme may be accompanied by State measures aimed at supporting liquidation, provided that the provisions on burden sharing by shareholders and holders of equity instruments are respected. According to the Commission, it is up to the Member States to decide whether a bank's exit from the market could have a serious impact on the regional economy, for example on the financing of small and medium-sized enterprises in the regional economy, and whether it is appropriate to use a DGS to mitigate these effects.

The activation of these measures is subject to the presentation of an orderly liquidation plan of the bank; furthermore, 'moral hazard' must be reduced to a minimum, avoiding the granting of additional aid that could benefit shareholders and subordinated creditors (Fig. 7).

3 The FITD's Preventive Measures

Following the European General Court ruling of March 2019, which upheld the appeal of the Italian State and the other parties involved in the matter (Bank of Italy, FITD, BPB), annulling the Commission Decision in the State aid case concerning Banca Tercas (see Chapter 3), the FITD resumed the application of preventive measures pursuant to Article 11(3) of the Directive and the Italian Banking Act. Thus, a support measure that has been part of the Fund's toolkit since its establishment was reactivated.

The Directive and the national transposition acts establish a comprehensive framework for preventive measures (Article 11.3 DGSD and

Article 96a(1b) of the Italian Banking Act), providing that the methods and conditions for the measures are to be governed by the DGSs' statutes.

The first condition for carrying out a preventive measure is the 'least cost' test. According to this principle, the cost of the preventive measures must not exceed, as reasonably foreseeable, the cost that the DGS would incur to carry out other measures provided for by its statutes. Another important condition is the verification, by the resolution and supervisory authorities, that: (i) no resolution action has been taken in respect of the bank receiving the preventive measure and the conditions for such an action are not met; (ii) the bank benefiting from the measure is able to pay the extraordinary contributions referred to in Article 96.2(3) of the Banking Act.

The use of preventive measures is also subject to the following additional conditions:

i. commitments must be established for the bank receiving the support, including at least stricter risk supervision and extensive monitoring powers by the DGS; the DGS establishes the methods and conditions of the intervention, in particular the beneficiary bank's commitment to strengthen its risk controls in order not to jeopardise the depositors' access to deposits;
ii. the DGS has appropriate procedures and systems to select the type of measure, execute it and monitor risks. The DGS must consult with the supervisory authority and the Resolution Authority on the measures and conditions imposed on the bank receiving the intervention and monitor the bank's compliance with its commitments;
iii. if the preventive intervention takes the form of equity participation, the shareholding by the deposit guarantee scheme must be limited to the time necessary to divest it in a cost-effective manner.

In terms of procedure, preventive measures must be activated by a specific request from the troubled bank, which must demonstrate its ability to overcome the risk of failure by submitting a clear and credible business plan covering at least three years. The business plan must be certified by a leading financial advisor. The overall project presented by the bank must also include the participation of an industrial partner (Fig. 8).

1. <u>*Preliminary assessment by the resolution and supervisory authorities*</u> *that*

- *no resolution action has been initiated and the conditions for it are not met (TUB, Article 96a(1c)(a); Statutes, Article 35(1)(a); DGSD, Article 11(3)(a) and forth subparagraph.*
- *the bank benefiting from the support is able to pay extraordinary contributions (TUB, Article 96a(1c)(b); Statutes, Article 35(1)(b); DGSD, Article 11(3)(f)*

2. <u>*Verification of the FITD's procedures and systems by the Bank of Italy*</u>

Verification by the Bank of Italy that the FITD has the appropriate procedures and systems to select the type of intervention, execute it and monitor the risks (TUB, Article 96b(1)(a); Statutes Article 35(3); DGSD, Article 11(3)(b)).

3. <u>*Least cost test*</u>

The burden of intervention through preventive measures must not exceed, as reasonably foreseeable, the cost that the Fund would incur to carry out other interventions envisaged by the Statute. To this end, the FITD also considers the effects that the compulsory liquidation of the bank could have on the other banks in crisis and on the system in general (indirect costs) (TUB, Article 96a(1b)(c); Statutes, Article 35(4); DGSD, Article 11(3)(c)).

4. <u>*Shareholdings.*</u>

If the intervention takes the form of equity participation, the holding of the investment by the Fund must be limited to the time necessary to divest it in accordance with an economy criterion.

5. <u>*Bank commitments*</u>

The FITD establishes the methods and conditions of the intervention (TUB, Article 96a(1b); By-laws, Article 35(5)), with particular reference to:

- *the commitments that the beneficiary bank must make to strengthen its risk management in order not to jeopardise the depositors' access to deposits (DGSD, Article 11(3)(e));*
- *verification by the FITD of compliance with the commitments made by the beneficiary bank.*

6. <u>*Obligations and commitments of the bank*</u>

The use of preventive measures is subject to obligations for the beneficiary bank, which include at least more rigorous risk supervision and extensive control rights by the FITD (DGSD, Article 11(3)(d)).

7. <u>*Consultation with authorities.*</u>

The FITD consults the supervisory authority and the resolution authority on the measures and conditions imposed on the beneficiary bank (DGSD, Article 11(3)).

8. <u>*Request for intervention and business plan*</u>

A prerequisite for the evaluation of the intervention by the FITD is that the bank concerned submits a specific request for support on the basis of a Board of Directors resolution, concerning the overall support project and the business plan underlying it – lasting at least three years – which demonstrates the bank's resilience and long-term viability. Intervention may be conducted provided that there exist real prospects for recovering the bank, on the basis of credible and feasible restructuring plans, capable of returning the bank to normal operating conditions within a reasonable time horizon.

The overall project prepared by the bank, of which the Fund's support forms part, must also include the participation of an industrial partner.

For the purposes of its decisions, the FITD carries out the necessary analysis to assess the credibility and sustainability of the business plan – possibly through its own advisors – and to assess the least cost (see point 4).

Fig. 8 The conditions for the preventive interventions of the FITD

9. Restoration mechanism for the financial endowment

Where the financial endowment is used for the alternative interventions referred to Article 35, the FITD members shall pay the Fund without delay. To this end, if necessary, the FITD shall recall the extraordinary contributions pursuant to Article 26, resources equal to those used for such measures, if:

a) the financial endowment of the Fund has been reduced to less than 25% of the target level;

or,

b) the financial endowment of the Fund has been reduced to less than two thirds of the target level and there is a need to repay the protected deposits.

Until the target level is reached for the first time, these thresholds refer to the effective financial endowment available for the year in which the intervention takes place (FITD Statutes, Article 25(6).

If the reduction in the Fund's financial endowment due to alternative measures does not bring it below the above-mentioned thresholds the resources are restored by 3 July 2024, through the additional contributions of the member banks at the date of each annual contribution (FITD Statutes, Article 25(7)).

10. Limits to interventions until 2024

Until reaching the target level of the financial endowment (0.8% of covered deposits by July 2024), the preventative interventions shall not in total exceed, in each year, 50% of the contributions paid in the year before. In exceptional cases, where the need exists to protect depositors and to ensure the continuity of essential functions, taking into account the role played by the bank in its context and possible impact on other member banks, FITD may decide to increase this limit in up to 20% of contributions paid in the year before. In any case, as a result of the intervention, the financial endowment of the Fund shall not reduce below the limit set in point 9.

Fig. 8 (continued)

3.1 *Phase 2 Intervention in Favour of Banca Carige*

Tools Applied

- Approval by the shareholders' meeting of Banca Carige of the capital increase and the issue of new subordinated bonds.
- Conversion of the subordinated bonds subscribed by the Voluntary Scheme into ordinary shares.
- Intervention by the FITD, pursuant to Article 35 of the Statutes, through the subscription of part of the capital increase.
- Participation by a third bank in the recapitalisation operation, with a minority stake and with a view to acquiring control.

Main Steps

- **Jan. '19**: the ECB appoints temporary administrators for Banca Carige.

- **Jan. '19/May. '19**: the special administrators start negotiations with potential investors interested in acquiring the bank. However, no binding offers are received.
- **Jul. '19**: the special administrators send a formal request for intervention to the FITD, pursuant to Article 35 of its Statutes, as part of a capital strengthening operation, with the participation of a banking partner.
- **Jul. '19**: the FITD's Board approves the intervention in favour of Banca Carige, on the basis of the business plan presented by the special administrators.
- **Dec. '19**: the capital increase of Banca Carige for €700 million and the issue of subordinated bonds for €200 million is completed.

  At the same time, the bank sells a portfolio of non-performing loans of approximately €2.3 billion to AMCO.
- **Jan. '20:** the special administration ends on 31 January 2020. The bank's ordinary shareholders' meeting appoints the new governing bodies.

After the intervention of the Voluntary Scheme through the subscription of a subordinated loan of €318.2 million, in support of the planned recapitalisation aimed at complying with the prudential requirements (see Chapter 6), the FITD intervened for the completion of the bank reorganisation project, in collaboration with a banking partner.

As mentioned, the transaction in the terms originally envisaged by the bank's *management* had not been approved by the shareholders' meeting of 20 December 2018 and the bank had subsequently been submitted to the temporary administration procedure by the ECB.

Immediately after taking office, the temporary administrators of Banca Carige started the search on the market for private partners willing to carry out a business combination; however, the attempts were unsuccessful. Consequently, on 24 June 2019, the FITD expressed its intention to intervene, even in a short timeframe, in the solution of the bank's crisis, after examining the technical and organisational structures of the Bank with the support of an independent advisor.

In July 2019, the temporary administrators sent a formal request for intervention to the Voluntary Scheme and, at the same time, to the FITD, for an operation that provided for the participation as an industrial partner of Cassa Centrale Banca (CCB),[6] which had the necessary economic, financial and capital solidity, and the underwriting of subordinated bonds by other institutional investors.

In particular, an overall capital requirement of approximately €900 million was identified, of which €700 million of CET1 capital and €200 million of subordinated *Tier 2* bonds, in order to guarantee capital ratios in line with the prudential requirements throughout the time horizon of the strategic plan.

The capital increase was divided into four tranches: the first tranche, of €313.2 million, was reserved for the SVI, through the conversion at par of the subordinated bonds subscribed in 2018; the second tranche, of €63 million, was reserved for Cassa Centrale Banca; the third tranche, of €85 million, was reserved for the bank's previous shareholders, with a guarantee on the subscription by the FITD; the fourth tranche, of €238.8 million, was reserved for the FITD.

In the meantime, with regard to the subscription of the third tranche, the administrators held discussions with the bank's shareholders to verify their willingness to participate in the capital increase. To this end, on the recommendation of the administrators, FITD signed confidentiality agreements with potential investors for the exchange of information on the assumptions and projections of the business plan and on the overall capital strengthening operation. However, the acceptances received were not sufficient to cover the entire capital increase reserved for Carige shareholders; therefore it became necessary to activate the commitment undertaken by the FITD to subscribe this tranche (Fig. 9).

The terms and conditions of the transaction, as well as the commitments undertaken by the bank and the other parties, were governed by a framework agreement signed on 9 August 2019.

[6] Cassa Centrale Banca—Credito Cooperativo Italiano S.p.A. (CCB) is the parent company of the cooperative banking group of the same name, established on 1 January 2019 following the reform of cooperative credit introduced by Decree-Law No 18 of 14 February 2016, converted with amendments into Law No 49 of 8 April 2016. The decree amended the TUB, introducing Articles 37-bis and 37-ter on Cooperative Banking Groups, which individual cooperative banks are required to join as an essential condition for the exercise of banking activity as cooperative credit banks, pursuant to Article 33 of the TUB. As of 31 December 2019, the Group was made up of 80 member banks, with approximately 1,500 branches in Italy and 10 local offices of the parent company. On the same date, the Group's fundamental financial indicators were solid: CET1 ratio of 19.72%, Total Capital ratio of 19.8%, Cost/Income ratio of 68.6% and NPE ratio of 9.3%.

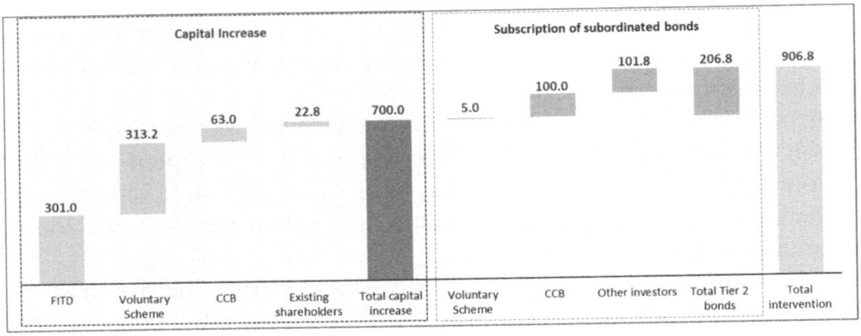

Fig. 9 Banca Carige: structure of the transaction

The option contract in favour of CCB. Simultaneously with the signing of the framework agreement, the FITD and the SVI signed an option contract with CCB for the purchase of all the Carige shares held by the FITD and the SVI, at a pre-established price, which can be exercised every six months starting from July 2020 and until December 2021.

Furthermore, as part of the transaction, SVI assigned to the bank's *retail* shareholders free shares—acquired as a result of the conversion of the bonds—for a total value of €10 million; the granting of warrants to the bank's pre-existing shareholders was also envisaged.

The transaction was approved by the extraordinary shareholders' meeting of Banca Carige on 20 September 2019.

In the following months, all the conditions envisaged by the framework agreement for the FITD's intervention were met: (i) the authorisations from the competent authorities; (ii) the transfer to AMCO of a significant portfolio of non-performing exposures of the bank; (iii) the signing by the bank of settlement agreements regarding distribution and outsourcing contracts; (iv) the signing of an agreement with the trade unions for the staff downsizing, under the terms set out in the business plan prepared by the administrators.

On 20 December 2019, the capital increase of €700 million and the issue of subordinated bonds for €200 million were carried out. The bonds were fully subscribed by public and private investors, including CCB. Taking into account the subscriptions made by the bank's shareholders—approximately €22.8 million, out of a total of €85 million in the tranche dedicated to them—the FITD's total support amounted to €301 million.

The agreement between FITD and the Voluntary Scheme. In order to ensure a uniform approach in the management of the bank, on 16 December 2019 the FITD and the Voluntary Scheme signed a securities lending agreement, which provided for the transfer to FITD of the ownership of the shares held by SVI following the capital increase.

In this way, the FITD acquired control over Banca Carige and, with it, the control of the companies belonging to the Banca Carige Group and the right to appoint the bank's board and statutory auditors. The ordinary shareholders' meeting held on 31 January 2020 appointed the new bodies and, as a result of these appointments, the bank's temporary administration came to an end.

3.2 *Phase 3 Intervention in Favour of Banca Carige*

The business combination of Banca Carige with Cassa Centrale Banca was unsuccessful. In March 2021, before the expiry of the option period (end-2021), CCB decided not to exercise the option call and, consequently, to withdraw from the transaction with Banca Carige.

A new phase was opening. The FITD, while continuing to monitor the bank's management, in particular the implementation of its business plan and its compliance with the commitments made under the framework agreement, initiated the procedures for the sale of the controlling stake in Banca Carige to another potential investor.

In parallel, during this delicate phase of searching for a new investor, the FITD and Banca Carige maintained close coordination. The management of the Bank was conducted according to criteria of prudence and improvement of operational and allocative efficiency. Despite the negative effects of the pandemic on the economy and banks, the Bank's performance was significantly improved, with the effect of creating the conditions for a business combination.

In fact, several expressions of interest in the Bank were received during 2021 and, at the end of a selection process, at the beginning of February 2022, the FITD accepted the proposal of intervention submitted by Banca Popolare dell'Emilia Romagna (BPER), one of the largest Italian Banks.

The operation envisages a further support intervention by the FITD of 530 million euros in the form of a capital contribution in Carige before the sale of the entire shareholdings of FITD and Voluntary Scheme (approximately 80% of Carige's capital) to BPER. Authorisation from Authorities is required for its completion, foreseen by mid-2022.

3.3 Banca del Fucino

Tools Applied

- Business combination of Banca del Fucino with Igea Banca.
- FITD's preventive intervention in support of the recapitalisation of the new banking group.
- Approval of the operation by the shareholders' meeting of the two banks.

Main Steps

- **Mar. '18:** the situation of Banca del Fucino is brought to the attention of FITD's Board.
- **Mar. '18–Sep. '18:** the possibility of intervention by other operators is examined by the bank, with negative results.
- **Sep. '18:** Banca del Fucino starts discussions with Banca Igea to evaluate possible industrial synergies between the two banks.
- **Dec. '18:** the two banks and their majority shareholders sign a framework agreement, which regulates the terms and the conditions of the merger.
- **Jul. '19:** Banca del Fucino, in agreement with Banca Igea, sends a formal request for intervention to the FITD, pursuant to Article 35 of the FITD's Statutes, together with the business plan.
- **Jul. '19:** FITD approves the support measure in favour of Banca del Fucino, through a guarantee of €30 million for the subscription of the capital increases planned for 2020–2022.

The bank: general information and main data. Banca del Fucino was the oldest private bank in Rome, founded in 1923. The bank mainly operated in the field of financial services, savings management and lending to small businesses and families.

In recent years, Banca del Fucino, to relaunch its business, had progressively shifted its focus to private banking; at the end of 2018, it had a commercial network of 32 branches located in 4 regions, of which 22 were in the province of Rome, and employed 309 resources.[7]

During 2018, Banca del Fucino suffered a significant reduction in assets and liabilities, in particular in the amount of direct funding. A severe liquidity crisis ensued: in April 2018, its liquidity coverage ratio bottomed at 35%; the minimum regulatory requirement of 100% was only restored in July 2018.

The reduction in direct funding by €295.8 million (-24.4% compared to 2017) concerned both covered deposits and uncovered deposits, albeit to different degrees. On 31 December 2018, covered deposits amounted to approximately €492 million, while uncovered deposits amounted to approximately €425 million.

A significant part of the bank's business was represented by indirect funding, which in December 2018 amounted to €1,155 million, down by approximately 24% compared to December 2017.

The loan portfolio was heavily deteriorated: in December 2018, gross non-performing exposures amounted to approximately €381 million, or about 39.4% of total loans to customers.

Shareholders' equity had declined significantly at the end of 2018 and, following the results of the due diligence carried out by Igea Banca—proposed as a partner for a business combination operation—it was negative for approximately €5.5 million. As to the capital ratios, as of 31 December 2018 Banca del Fucino presented a CET1 ratio and a Tier 1 ratio of 1.6% and a total capital ratio of 3.7%.

The economic trend in 2018 was negative. Gross operating result, which in 2017 was positive for €9.9 million, in December 2018 was negative for about €13.4 million. The cost/income ratio at the end of 2018 was 130.8% (Fig. 10).

The solution of the crisis. Since the early months of 2018, the FITD had examined the weak situation of the bank, whose problems were exacerbated by its liquidity position, as well as the difficulties encountered in finding a solution.

The bank had started to seek industrial partners on the market willing to carry out a business combination.[8] Negotiations had been initiated

[7] Banca del Fucino, *2018 Annual Report and Financial Statements*.

[8] GRUPPO BANCARIO IGEA BANCA, *Annual Report and Financial Statements—31 December 2019*.

Data as of December 2018; (€ mln; %)	
Direct funding	917
o/w: covered deposits	492
% FITD total covered deposits	*0.08%*
Total assets	1,224
NPEs ratio (GBV)	39.4%
Cost-Income ratio	130.8%
Net profit (loss)	(5.1)
ROE	neg.
CET 1 ratio	1.6%
Total capital ratio	3.7%
Employees	309
Branches	32

Fig. 10 Banca del Fucino: main data (*Source* Banca del Fucino, Annual Report on 31 December 2018)

with some Italian and foreign banking and financial parties, but reaching an agreement proved difficult, the main points of contention being the guarantees requested by the prospective investors and the coverage of the bank's restructuring costs. Some banks and financial institutions potentially interested in the transaction demanded large compensatory measures from FITD.

In this context, in September 2018 Banca del Fucino initiated contacts with Igea Banca,[9] with the aim of evaluating possible industrial synergies between the two banks—also considering the complementarity of their

[9] Igea Banca SpA was a very small bank, born in 2018 from the merger of Igea Finanziaria with Banca Popolare dell' Etna. The bank had a commercial network consisting of 4 branches located in 2 regions, which operated under a traditional banking model. The bank also had a fintech platform for carrying out transactions through the digital channel.

respective business models—not only to allow the capital strengthening of Banca del Fucino, but also to preserve and enhance its operational business, as well as its human resources and distribution network.

In order to assess the feasibility of the combination between the two banks, Igea Banca carried out an accounting, administrative and legal due diligence on Banca del Fucino.

On 6 March 2019, the Board of Directors of Igea Banca decided to present a binding offer for the acquisition of Banca del Fucino and in April 2019 submitted to the Bank of Italy an application for authorisation to acquire the controlling stake in Banca del Fucino, based on the 2019–2022 business plan prepared for this purpose.

In particular, by virtue of the recapitalisation commitments undertaken by its shareholders and other investors, Igea Banca drew up a business plan for the banking group over a four-year period (2019/2022).

The structure of the integration project was structured as follows (Fig. 11):

- capital increase in Igea Banca in the years 2019–2022 of €110 million, to be subscribed by the previous shareholders and other investors;
- capital increase in Banca del Fucino, with the exclusion of option rights, reserved for Igea Banca, for an amount of €50 million;
- sale to SGA (now AMCO) of almost all of Banca del Fucino's portfolio of non-performing exposures through a securitisation transaction. In particular, on 20 December 2018, the SGA presented a

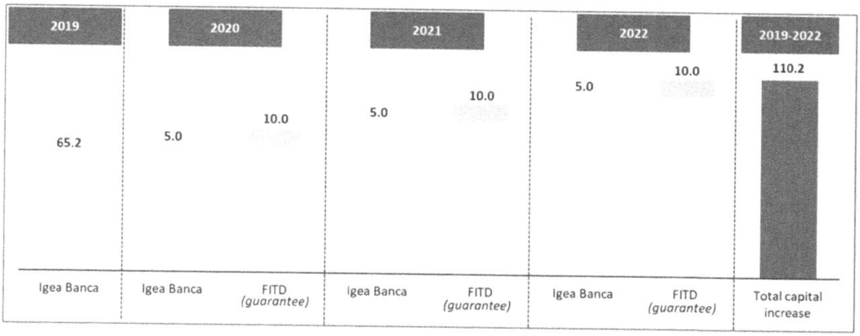

Fig. 11 Banca del Fucino: intervention structure

binding offer for the sale of NPEs for a gross value of approximately €300 million, at a price of approximately 33.4% (€100 million);
- simultaneous partial spin-off by incorporation of Banca del Fucino in favour of Igea Banca and creation of a traditional bank (the parent company) and a digital bank (the subsidiary).

In addition to the capital increases, the issue of €13.5 million of subordinated bonds by the new banking group was carried out in 2019.

On 18 July 2019, Banca del Fucino, in agreement with Igea Banca, applied to the FITD for a support measure pursuant to Article 35 of its Statutes. The FITD decided to intervene by issuing a guarantee of €30 million for the execution of capital increases (€10 million in each of the years 2020–2022).

The FITD's decision was based on the assessment that the preventive intervention was less costly than repaying the depositors in the event of compulsory liquidation. The other conditions provided for by the law and the Statutes had also been verified, including the declaration by the Bank of Italy that the bank was not in resolution and that the conditions for starting a resolution action were not met, and the fact that the bank was able to pay its extraordinary contributions to the FITD.

The agreements established that these capital increases would in any case be offered in option to the bank's shareholders and to private investors identified by Banca Igea; the FITD would intervene only if the option rights were not exercised in the amount envisaged in the business plan or if Igea Banca were unable to find investors on the market interested in supporting the business project.

On 2 August 2019, the FITD, Banca del Fucino and Igea Banca signed an agreement governing the commitments, terms and conditions relating to the issue of the FITD's guarantee. In particular, both banks agreed to provide the FITD with adequate information flows on the new group's capital increase programme and on the implementation of the business plan.

The operation carried out by the FITD was the only solution to the bank's crisis, an alternative to compulsory administrative liquidation, which would have required the reimbursement of covered deposits for an amount of approximately €492 million.

As mentioned, some proposals made by other third parties that had expressed their interest in acquiring Banca del Fucino were based on interventions by the FITD for huge amounts, not comparable with those envisaged in the transaction with Igea Banca. In particular, under the requests of the potentially interested parties, the Fund would have borne not only the entire amount necessary to cover the current and future capital needs of the Banca del Fucino, but also the costs of its restructuring.

The intervention of the Fund generated further positive effects. Specifically, it made it possible to avoid disrupting the bank's relations with its clients, both families and businesses, and to safeguard its important payment functions as well as employment levels. The operation also protected approximately €534 million of uncovered depositors and other unsecured creditors, who would otherwise have suffered the consequences of the application of the insolvency rules. In this way, traumatic effects on depositors were avoided, preserving the image and reputation of the banking system.

Based on the trend of the bank and its evolutionary prospects, in September 2020 the bank communicated to FITD its intention not to activate the guarantee for that year, since it had received subscriptions from the bank's shareholders and other investors for an amount sufficient to cover the capital requirement for 2020.[10] Consequently, the maximum commitment of the FITD was reduced to €20 million, to guarantee any unsubscribed capital shares in the years 2021–2022.

3.4 *Banca Popolare di Bari. A Case of Nationalisation Achieved with the Use of Private Resources*

Tools Applied

- Special administration of the bank.
- Restructuring plan prepared by the special administrators.
- Approval by BPB's extraordinary shareholders' meeting of the transformation of the bank into a joint-stock company and the recapitalisation operation.
- FITD support measure, pursuant to Article 35 of the Statutes, by means of an increase in capital to cover losses.

[10] BANCA DEL FUCINO S.P.A., *Il Consiglio d'Amministrazione approva il nuovo Piano Industriale*, press release, 2 November 2020.

- Contribution of capital and acquisition of control by Banca del Mezzogiorno—Mediocredito Centrale, a State-owned bank.

Main Steps

- **Mid '19:** the management of Banca Popolare di Bari starts the first contacts with FITD to request a support measure for the recapitalisation of the bank, on the basis of a business plan being drawn up.
- **Dec. '19:** the Bank of Italy decides to dissolve BPB's management and control bodies and to submit the bank to the special administration procedure, on the basis of the significant capital losses.
- **Dec. '19:** Decree-Law 142 is published, which authorises the MEF, through its own subsidiary, to confer capital to MCC up to €900 million.
- **Dec. '19:** FITD carries out a first anticipatory intervention on the capital, pursuant to Article 35 of the Statutes, to ensure compliance with the bank's minimum capital requirements as of 31 December 2019.
- **Apr. '20:** FITD makes a second anticipatory contribution of €54.3 million, as part of the future capital increase, to compliance with the minimum capital requirements as of 31.3.2020.
- **Apr. '20:** special administrators present the final assessment of the bank's situation, identifying the definitive capital requirement at €1.6 billion, necessary to comply with the maintenance of a CET1 ratio and a TCR of approximately 12% during the four-year period 2020–2024.
- **May '20:** The Commission's DG-Comp confirms that a MCC investment of up to €430 million is in accordance with the market economy investor principle. Subsequently, the ministerial decree for the recapitalisation of MCC is published for said amount.
- **May '20:** on the basis of the request of the special administrators, the FITD approves the definitive intervention in favour of BPB, for an amount of €1.17 billion, including advance payments carried out in December 2019 and April 2020.
- **June '20:** BPB's shareholders' meeting approves the transformation of the bank into a joint-stock company and the capital increase. The

shares acquired by the FITD after the intervention are transferred at a symbolic price to MCC, which takes control of the bank.

3.4.1 *The Bank: General Information and Main Data*

Banca Popolare di Bari ScpA (BPB) was a financial cooperative bank, parent company of the group of the same name.

The BPB Group was a significant banking player in the South of Italy in the field of credit intermediation and in the provision of financial, insurance and payment system services. The group mainly operated in the retail market: its products and services were mainly directed to families and small and medium-sized enterprises. On 30 June 2019, the parent bank had a commercial network of 341 branches and 2,987 employees.

For several years, the bank had been showing weaknesses in its technical, organisational and managerial structures, accentuated by potential disputes with shareholders (about 70,000), in relation to the sharp reduction in the value of the shares and the difficulty of selling them; the bank also had outstanding subordinated bonds for approximately €288 million placed with retail customers.

The bank had a significant capital need, due to a high rate of non-performing exposures and structurally negative profitability. The liquidity situation also showed weaknesses.

Direct funding (equal to approximately €10.7 billion in June 2019 at consolidated level) contracted significantly in 2019 and in the first months of 2020. In particular, from December 2018 to March 2020 the decline was of approximately 20.7%, mainly attributable to deposits.[11]

On 30 June 2019, the bank's treasury, including cash, financial assets and loans to banks, was approximately €4.8 billion, down by approximately €300 million compared to the previous half year. This decrease was mainly due to the need to face the reduction in retail deposits.

Profitability was the most important concern. Gross operating margin, which in 2018 had been positive for €20.4 million, in June 2019 was negative for about €15 million, as the revenues generated by the bank were insufficient to cover operating costs. As at 30 June 2019, the BPB Group had an operating loss of €73 million and its cost/income ratio,

[11] BANCA POPOLARE DI BARI, *Explanatory report made by the Administrators of the Bank in Temporary Administration on the Balance Sheet as at 31 March 2020 and June 2020.*

Consolidated data as of June 2019; (€ mln; %)	
Direct funding	10,719.7
o/w: covered deposits	5,065.0
% FITD total covered deposits	*0.46%*
Total assets	13,636.4
NPEs ratio (GBV)	22.9%
Cost-Income ratio	109.4%
Net profit (loss)	(73)
ROE	(17.3%)
CET 1 ratio	6.2%
Total capital ratio	8.1%
Employees	2,987
Branches	341

Fig. 12 BPB Group: the main data (*Source* Banca Popolare di Bari, Consolidated interim financial statements and management report, 30 June 2019)

which was 94% in December 2018, was significantly worse in the first half of 2019, reaching 109.4%.

The capital ratios of the banking group in June 2019 were slightly higher than the minimum CET1 ratio and Total Capital Ratio requirements provided for by Article 92 of the CRR (Fig. 12).

3.4.2 *The Special Administration and the First FITD Intervention to Cover the Capital Deficit on 31.12.2019*

In the second half of 2019, BPB first contacted the FITD to request preventive support for its recapitalisation, both to address the capital shortfall and to support the defined strategic plan.

On 13 December 2019, the Bank of Italy, in view of the losses incurred by BPB, decided to dissolve BPB's management and control bodies and to place the bank under special administration for serious capital losses. Two special administrators were appointed to manage the bank.

In the meantime, Decree-Law 142 was published (*'urgent measures to support the credit system in South Italy and to create an investment bank'*), providing that the Ministry of Finance would grant capital contributions of up to €900 million to a bank owned by it, the Banca del Mezzogiorno—Mediocredito Centrale (MCC), to be allocated—according to market logic, criteria and conditions—to develop financial activity and business investments in the South of Italy, including the acquisition of shareholdings in the banking sector.[12]

On the basis of the initial analyses carried out and the needs identified, the end-2019 projections carried out by the special administrators showed a phased-in CET1 ratio of 0.16% and a phased-in total capital ratio of 1.94%. In the light of these results, on 27 December 2019, the special administrators requested the FITD's support pursuant to Article 35 of its Statutes, to restore the capital ratios above the regulatory minimum thresholds by means of an immediate capital injection. Another reason for the request was the need to ensure access to the ECB's liquidity (approximately €1.9 billion), which the bank would lose if it did not meet the minimum capital requirements under Article 92 of the CRR.[13]

On 30 December 2019, the FITD approved an intervention in favour of BPB, pursuant to Article 35 of its Statutes, in the amount of €310 million, by way of payment towards the bank's future capital increase. This was an advance measure in the context of a broader project to strengthen and relaunch the bank, which involved the transformation of BPB into a joint-stock company and a capital increase of €1.4 billion to be carried out in 2020, in line with the provisions of Decree-Law No 142/2019.

[12] A. PERRAZZELLI, Hearing before the VI Commission (Finance) of the Chamber of Deputies, *Examination of the draft law C. 2302, converting into law Decree-Law No 142 of 2019, containing urgent measures to support the banking system in the South and to build an investment bank*, 9 January 2020.

[13] The banks' participation in monetary policy operations is subject to the ongoing maintenance of financial soundness requirements on an individual and consolidated basis. The Eurosystem may adopt discretionary measures, including of a prudential nature, aimed at suspending, excluding or limiting access to transactions by counterparties that do not comply with the capital, liquidity and debt requirements established by EU Regulation 575/2013 (for more details, see Chapter 10).

As part of the overall operation, the FITD and MCC were expected to participate in the strengthening of the bank's capital in equal parts, each for an amount of €700 million. On the basis of the guidelines of the business plan prepared by the special administrators, this amount was considered adequate to achieve the bank's recovery and relaunch objectives.

The conditions for carrying out the overall transaction were governed by a framework agreement signed on 31 December 2019 by BPB, the FITD and MCC. The agreement provided for an in-depth assessment of the bank's assets and liabilities (*confirmatory review*) and the determination of its final capital needs, on the basis of a business plan suitable to support the bank's long-term sustainability.

3.4.3 *The Final Assessment of the bank's Situation and Business Plan. The Intervention of the FITD and MCC*

Following the FITD's initial measure, dialogue continued between the parties to define, on the one hand, the results of the bank's due diligence and its business plan and, on the other hand, the timing and structure of the overall transaction, which involved the transformation of the bank into a joint-stock company and a simultaneous capital increase.

On 31 March 2020, the bank had an additional capital need of €54.3 million, to comply with a Total Capital Ratio of 8%. At the request of the special administrators, the FITD carried out a new advance payment in favour of BPB, also aimed at maintaining liquidity facilities with the European Central Bank.

In the meantime, detailed discussions were underway between the Ministry of Economy and Finance, MCC and the Commission's DG-Comp to confirm the full compatibility of MCC's intervention with the rules on State aid. According to the rules established by the Commission, the amount of the capital increase carried out by MCC had to be consistent with market logic, criteria and parameters (the so-called market economy operator principle—MEOP). In particular, under the market operator approach, the extent of MCC's intervention had to be such as to ensure a return on invested capital (IRR) higher than the cost of equity (CoE) observable on the market.

Since the proposed operation was in line with the MEOP, the Commission concluded that MCC's intervention did not constitute State aid. Consequently, the sharing of losses (burden sharing) by BPB's subordinate bondholders was avoided. In this context, the FITD's intervention allowed bondholders not to incur any losses, the bank to restore its minimum capital ratios and MCC to have the financial resources to implement the restructuring and relaunch plan of BPB.

The Rules of the Market Economy Operator Principle

The Market Economy Operator Principle (MEOP) was developed by the European Commission in a 2016 Communication[14] *to determine whether a transaction done by a public entity offers an advantage to a particular company and therefore must be classified as State aid.*

Under the EU rules on State aid, public interventions in favour of enterprises can be considered outside State aid if carried out with market logic, criteria and parameters. If this principle is not respected, public interventions involve State aid pursuant to Article 107 of the Treaty on the Functioning of the European Union (TFEU), since they confer an economic advantage on the beneficiaries, by favouring them or by distorting or threatening to distort competition.

To determine whether State intervention is in line with market conditions, an ex-ante assessment must be carried out, taking into account the information available on the date the intervention was decided. If a Member State claims to have acted as a market economy operator, it must provide evidence that the transaction was carried out on the basis of economic assessments similar to those which, in the present circumstances, an operator in a rational market economy would have carried out in order to determine the profitability or economic benefits of the transaction.

[14] EUROPEAN COMMISSION—Commission Notice on the notion of State aid as referred to Article 107 (1) of the Treaty on the Functioning of the European Union, 19 July 2016.

The compliance of a transaction with market conditions can be directly established upon the occurrence of the following circumstances, which constitute direct and specific proof of the compliance of the transaction with market conditions: (i) the transaction is carried out on equal terms (pari passu) by public entities and private operators; (ii) the transaction concerns the sale or purchase of assets, goods and services carried out through a competitive, transparent, non-discriminatory and unconditional tender procedure.

The absence of the above circumstances does not, however, imply that the transaction does not comply with market conditions. In this case, compliance with market conditions can be ascertained by benchmark analysis or by other valuation methods (i.e. internal rate of return method—IRR, net present value method—NPV).

Even the granting of loans and guarantees by public entities can constitute State aid, if not done in accordance with market conditions.

In April 2020, the special administrators presented to the other parties their final assessment of the bank's economic, financial and equity situation, with a final estimate of the capital requirement, quantified in €1.6 billion, necessary to allow the maintenance of a CET1 ratio and a total capital ratio at levels close to 12% over the entire time horizon of the business plan (2020–2024).

The final version of the business plan, which incorporated the observations formulated by DG-Comp as part of the evaluation of the MCC intervention, was based on the following main drivers: (i) de-risking, through the sale of a portfolio of NPEs equal to approximately €2 billion in gross terms; (ii) relaunch of the core business activity and development of new revenue streams, also through the potential synergies achievable from the business integration with MCC; (iii) the recovery of efficiency and the review of the bank's organisational model, by cutting approximately 881 jobs and closing approximately 91 branches; (iv) the termination of some existing contracts deemed too burdensome for the bank (relating to synthetic securitisation and the servicing of certain deteriorated loans).

Based on these actions, the Group was expected to return to value creation in 2023–2024. In particular, a ROE of 7.9% was estimated for 2024, compared to the current situation of structural loss, and a cost/income of 66%, compared to a pre-restructuring value well above 100%.[15]

With reference to MCC's intervention, in consideration of the forecasts contained in the business plan, DG-Comp gave a positive response, communicating that an investment by MCC up to €430 million would be in compliance with the market economy operator principle. Subsequently, the MEF issued a ministerial decree for MCC's recapitalisation.

On the basis of the maximum intervention of MCC of €430 million identified by DG-Comp, the special administrators requested an overall intervention by the FITD in favour of Banca Popolare di Bari of €1,170 million, including the advance support provided to cover the capital shortcomings on 31 December 2019 and 31 March 2020.

On 27 May 2020, the FITD approved the intervention in favour of BPB, within the terms envisaged by the special administrators, pursuant to Article 35 of the Statutes (Fig. 13).

The transaction as defined by BPB, the FITD and MCC was submitted to the bank's shareholders' meeting, which approved it on 30 June 2020.

In line with the objective of safeguarding the relationship between the bank and its catchment area, including its shareholder base and the customers, FITD allocated a share of its support—precisely €10 million—to restore positive equity, thus avoiding the zeroing of pre-existing shareholders, as a result of the reduction of the bank's share capital. In addition, it assigned free shares for €20 million to shareholders of the bank, on certain conditions.

Furthermore, the shares acquired by the FITD following its intervention and remaining after the coverage of losses and the free assignment of shares were acquired in full by MCC at a symbolic price.

These shares were sold to MCC to cover the absorbable losses calculated on the basis of the business plan projections, in line with the provisions of the agreements between the parties and in addition to

[15] BANCA POPOLARE DI BARI, *Explanatory Report by the Administrators of Banca Popolare di Bari S.C.p.A. in Temporary Administration on the Balance Sheet as of 31 March 2020.*

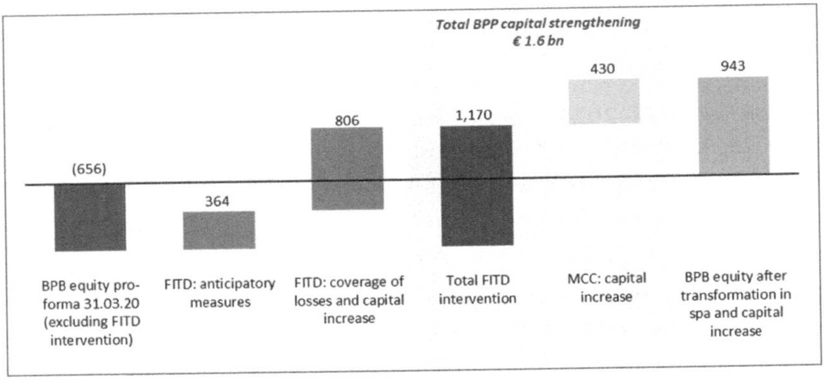

Fig. 13 BPB: the final structure of the intervention

those recorded in the pro-forma balance sheet of BPB of 31 March 2020. In this way, MCC was able to achieve the IRR target identified by DG-Comp.

At the end of this complex operation, MCC acquired 97% of the bank's capital, while the remaining 3% was held by the bank's previous shareholders. As a result, BPB is in the hands of a state-owned bank, through the decisive contribution of private financial resources provided by the FITD, which enabled the implementation of the rescue project.

On 15 October 2020, the bank's shareholders' meeting appointed the new management and control bodies. On the same date, therefore, the BPB's special administration ended.

PART II

Lessons Learned and the (Many) Open Questions

CHAPTER 8

How to Manage the Crises?

The Italian experience and the ongoing debate highlighted critical issues in the European institutional model and crisis management rules. These issues are equally evident in the Eurozone, where the Banking Union is still to be completed.

Fundamental aspects of the institutional architecture and regulation of crisis management, including some key provisions of the BRRD, should be rethought to improve the functioning of the crisis management system. Experiences outside Europe could be looked at, because they may offer useful guidance. However, any insights need to be tailored to the features of the European context.

In particular, we need to reflect on the notion of 'public interest', which guides the decision regarding the resolution or the liquidation of the insolvent bank. Depending on the size of the bank, public interest can determine the solution and the tools that can be used: resolution for large banks and liquidation for small and medium-sized ones. This framework is too simplistic and has led to major uncertainties and inconsistencies.

G. Boccuzzi, *Banking Crises in Italy*, Palgrave Studies in Financial Instability and Banking Crisis Regulation,
https://doi.org/10.1007/978-3-031-01344-7_8

We propose to go beyond the notion of public interest. We ascribe to all banks, also small and medium-sized, a general interest to be resolved in an orderly manner with all the available tools.

1 Some Preliminary Considerations

The recent banking crises in Italy tested the effectiveness of the new European legal framework for crisis management (BRRD, DGSD, SSM, SRM, Rules on State aid) and the new principles, objectives and intervention tools they introduced into national law. The European legislation meant to unify the responses to the global financial crisis of 2007–2009 and to the large number of bank insolvencies that occurred in the USA and Europe, when an unprecedented amount of public money was used to bail-out systemic intermediaries and prevent financial chaos. The European framework followed closely and adapted the international standards that had been issued by the Financial Stability Board.[1]

The new European regulatory framework was already in force[2] when Italy's banking crises began. This made Italy the first major testing ground for the new legislation. The tests revealed shortcomings, inconsistencies and procedural delays. These were duly noted by academia, operators, international institutions and regulators and brought reactions from different categories of stakeholders, even stronger than those raised during the global financial crisis. In the USA, the *Federal Deposit Insurance Corporation* (FDIC) managed 3,500 banking crises in the period

[1] FINANCIAL STABILITY BOARD, *Key Attributes of Effective Resolution Regimes for Financial Institutions*, October 2014. The Key Attributes, published in October 2011, were supplemented in October 2014 by some additional guidelines, regarding the exchange of information for the resolution. The addition mainly concerned the application of the KA to insurance companies and market infrastructures, also introducing client asset protection in resolution.

[2] During this period, in Europe there were fewer cases than during the financial crisis. Most significantly: Banco Spirito Santo in Portugal (2014); Banco Popular in Spain (2017); ABVL Bank in Latvia and ABVL Bank Luxembourg (2018); NORDLB in Germany (2020); AS PNB Banka (2019) and other smaller banks in Eastern Europe. For cases in the Eurozone since 2016, see *Single Resolution Board:* https://srb.europa.eu/en/content/resolution-cases. For Italian national cases, see https://eba.europa.eu/regulation-and-policy/recovery-and-resolution/notifications-on-resolution-cases-and-use-of-dgs-funds.

1980–2019—500 between 2018 and 2013—without facing similar reactions and requests for ex-post support similar to that offered in Italy.[3]

The reasons for these reactions are multiple. In Italy, prior to the introduction of the new EU framework, banking crises were resolved through a range of tools, including public intervention ensuring the protection of savers and almost all the parties involved, where necessary.[4] Following the application of the new rules on burden sharing, savers suffered significant losses.

Bail-in proved particularly divisive. It was introduced as the pivot of the new legal framework for allocating the losses of bank insolvency to shareholders and creditors. If the mere perception of negative consequences from banking crises—regardless of the real effects—can undermine confidence in the system, a policy measure directly impacting clientele can do so to an even greater extent. Bail-in entered the headlines and the critical literature.[5] It became a major problem, not gaining credibility and indicating poor flexibility.

From the Italian experience, together with that of other countries in which banking crises occurred, we can draw lessons and elements of reflection, which is increasingly necessary in a context of regulatory and market complexity affecting the banking sector.[6]

So far, policymakers have only made small additions and adjustments to the 2014 European reforms[7]; today they seem to be considering a

[3] FEDERAL DEPOSIT INSURANCE CORPORATION, *Crisis and Response. An FDIC History, 2008–2013*, November 2017; P. BAUDINO, A. GAGLIANO, E. RULLI, R. WALTERS, *How to Manage Failures of Non-Systemic Banks? A Review of Country Practices*, Financial Stability Institute on policy implementation, No 10, October 2018.

[4] In Italy, the protection of savings has a constitutional value. Article 47 of the Constitution states that after the introduction of BRRD, doubts have been raised on the legitimacy of bail-in, considering, *inter alia*, the low protection granted to the parties affected by this measure. On this issue, P. DE GIOIA CARABELLESE, C. PAGLIARIN, Bail-in and Italian Constitutional Rights, *LUISS Law Review*, Vol. I, Issue 40, I, 2021.

[5] P. DE GIOIA CARABELLESE, *Crisi della banca e diritti dei creditori*, Cacucci editore, 2020.

[6] For an in-depth analysis of these topics, see BOCCUZZI G., *Il Regime Speciale della Risoluzione Bancaria. Obiettivi e Strumenti*, Cacucci Editore, 2018.

[7] The changes to the BRRD were an integral part of the Banking Package proposed by the European Commission in 2016 to implement the reforms defined by the Basel Committee and the Financial Stability Board (FSB). A first amendment to the BRRD was introduced in December 2017 with Directive 2399 on the hierarchy of bail-inable instruments in the event of resolution. This directive added 'buffer' bonds (non-preferred

broader review of the current framework. A critical rethinking of the 2014 reforms is under way to design a framework that is more responsive to concrete application needs and national situations. New initiatives in this direction have been announced.[8] It remains to be seen which proposals will be made and the extent of the changes with respect to the needs that emerged from recent experiences.

It is important to highlight that the context is still changing. The COVID-19 pandemic has caused a massive unforeseen exogenous shock on the economy and society, increasing the urgency of the scramble to find damage-reducing solutions. We need a critical rethinking of our intervention model and toolbox in order to promote preventive measures over insolvency regulation and management.

Systemic crises are frequent, as demonstrated by the fact that just ten years have passed since the last global financial crisis. And between two

debt instruments) to absorb losses before ordinary bondholders and after subordinated financial instruments. The reform package was completed in June 2019 with the adoption of BRRD2 (Directive (EU) 2019/879, which entered into force on 27 June 2019, to be implemented by 28 December 2020). BRRD2 operationalised the TLAC for systemic banks, set-up a new configuration of the MREL and attributed to the Resolution Authority the power to suspend the contractual payment obligations of an institution (moratorium). Similar changes have been made to the SRM Regulation (EU Regulation 2019/877 of 20 May 2019, SRM 2).

[8] In the context of the revision of the BRRD, the EBA has recently issued three 'Opinions' to the Commission on some key aspects of the functioning of DGSs. See EUROPEAN BANKING AUTHORITY, *Opinion of the European Banking Authority on the Eligibility of Deposits, Coverage Level and Cooperation between Deposit Guarantee Schemes*, August 2019; EUROPEAN BANKING AUTHORITY, *Opinion of the European Banking Authority on Deposit Guarantee Scheme Payouts*, October 2019; EUROPEAN BANKING AUTHORITY, *Opinion of the European Banking Authority on Deposit Guarantee Scheme Funding and Uses of Deposit Guarantee Scheme Funds*, January 2020. Other initiatives, concerning the use of preventive and alternative measures and calculation of the least cost, are under way. More recently the Commission has launched a consultation on the revision of the EU's crisis management and deposit insurance framework. The consultation regards the BRRD, the SRM and the DGSD. The main purpose of the review is to: (i) assess how the current crisis management and depositor insurance framework works, (ii) find ways to make the framework more proportionate, efficient and consistent in handling the resolution or liquidation of any bank in the EU; (iii) improve the synergies between crisis management and depositor protection, including by taking steps to complete the Banking Union. See EUROPEAN COMMISSION, *Targeted Consultation on the Review of the Crisis Management and Deposit Insurance Framework*, 26 January 2021.

systemic crises there could be many more circumscribed crises that need to be addressed promptly and effectively. We must prepare in advance.

The following chapters explore the most important issues that have emerged in the regulatory and institutional set-up.

2 The Model: Competencies, Procedures and Instruments

2.1 The Institutional Framework

One of the most important lessons learned from recent experiences is that the timely detection of crisis situations and understanding of their causes are crucial. Moreover, the solutions to crises must be rapid, efficient and effective in order, respectively, to reduce the likelihood of insolvency and, when crises occur, the related costs. Does the reformed European system meet these criteria? Opinions are divided.

The current institutional set-up is characterised by uncertainties and complexities in the decision-making process, as clearly shown by the banking crises in Italy. The new institutional architecture in Europe—and even more in the Eurozone—is very complex, being based on a multi-level decision-making system that leads to an unclear distribution of duties among the authorities involved (national and European Supervisory authorities, national and European resolution authorities, EBA). The complexity increases further when the EU Commission is involved in issues of State aid and in the evaluation of banks' business plans. Therefore, the governance model for banking crisis management must be redesigned to enable a faster and more effective response to situations of instability.

The question of which model to choose is not an easy one. The FDIC (Federal Deposit Insurance Corporation) model in the United States is often taken as an example. The FDIC has regulatory, resolution and deposit insurance functions and is also the receiver in liquidation proceedings. This is a very comprehensive and effective design.[9] However, its

[9] The FDIC model has been integrated with the Dodd-Frank Act, which integrated the FSB *Key Attributes of Effective Resolution* for Financial Holding Companies. On this, see F. RESTOY, *How to Improve Crisis Management in the Banking Union: A European FDIC*, Lisbon, July 2019; J. DESLANDES, C. DIAS, M. MAGNUS, *Liquidation of Banks: Towards an FDIC for the Banking Union, Directorate-General for Internal Policies*, February 2019; G. MAJNONI D'INTIGNANO, A. DAL SANTO, M. MALTESE, *The*

model cannot be directly translated to the Eurozone, which has its own bank resolution mechanisms: the Single Resolution Mechanism (SRM) and the Single Resolution Board (SRB). Still, these mechanisms, de facto, have not been used for bank resolution; this circumstance encourages us to seek original and tailor-made solutions for Europe, depending on the objectives we want to achieve.

For example, criteria could be set to clearly allocate duties between European and national authorities, thus strengthening coordination and avoiding overlaps. Where the participation of several authorities is necessary, the primary responsibilities should be allocated *ex-ante* and the decision-making process expedited to ensure that the administrative procedure is completed in a reasonable timeframe, consistent with the severity of crisis. Crisis management is a delicate and complex matter that requires speed of action and univocal direction, with clear legal and operational procedures.

In particular, roles and responsibilities should be allocated in a clear and efficient way, aligning supervision and resolution. Decision-making responsibility should be assigned to the European authorities for significant banks and to national authorities for less significant banks. In either case, European-level funding tools should be available, including the resolution fund and the resources of the deposit guarantee systems and even a unified deposit insurance scheme.

2.2 Complexity and the Need for a Wider Toolkit

Banking crises are a complex phenomenon with diverse features, as confirmed by the Italian experience. Each banking crisis has its own peculiarities, depending on the bank's size, organisational structure, legal entity and international projection. The causes, symptoms and solutions of a crisis can be manifold. Therefore, there cannot be a one-size-fits-all approach. Intervention measures may need to be tailor-made, depending on what caused the crisis, its impact on the bank's balance sheet and the position of the bank in the market and the institutional context.

This is the approach taken in Italy, albeit with difficulties. In our country, banking crises have been resolved using all the available tools

FDIC Bank Crisis Management Experience: Lessons for the EU Banking Union, Note di stabilità finanziaria e di vigilanza, No 22, August 2020.

(precautionary recapitalisation, orderly liquidation, preventive and alternative measures carried out by the FITD). Private intervention tools have been predominant. Public intervention has been used only for larger banks and to prevent systemic impacts.

Extraordinary public and private instruments were also created ad hoc to deal with complex situations. Examples are GACS, the Atlante Fund and the FITD's Voluntary Scheme. When simultaneous banking crises occur, even concerning small and medium-sized banks, the authorities must be ready to take appropriate action, with all the tools available, even extraordinary ones.

As an example of this approach, in the cases of the Four banks and the liquidation of the Veneto banks, where burden-sharing was applied, extraordinary mechanisms and instruments were put in place. In both cases, specific legislative measures were taken to shield savers from losses, such as the Solidarity Fund, managed and funded by the FITD, which compensates subordinated bondholders, and the *Fondo Indennizzo Risparmiatori* (FIR) which uses public funds to compensate retail investors, shareholders and investors.

Bank crises occur in complex settings where many different factors interact, including regulatory, institutional, strategic, operational and market factors. This can make it difficult to apply only one tool to a given case, and may require the simultaneous application of a wider toolkit. This approach may seem 'too creative' and a way to 'work around' standard rules and the primary intent of policymakers.[10] This is not the case. All the tools used are available in the legislation or are provided by private entities, with private resources.

The most important question is whether, against the complexity and variability of real situations, the new legal framework (BRRD, DGSD, SRM) is effective, credible and coherent. Apparently, it would seem so. The framework expresses a new vision of crisis management based on the assumption that the cost of the crisis must be borne by private individuals, shareholders and creditors of the insolvent bank (internalisation of losses), and not by taxpayers, as happened during the global financial crisis (i.e. a shift from bail-out to bail-in). In addition, if external resources are necessary to cover losses and restructuring costs, the banking sector has to contribute through the resolution funds or the deposit guarantee schemes

[10] STANDARD & POOR'S, *Continued Bank Bail-Out Stretch the Credibility of Europe's Resolution Framework*, February 2020.

(bail-with).[11] All these measures are intended to reduce moral hazard: banks would not be 'private when alive' and 'public when insolvent'.

However, implementation of the new framework 'on the ground' has brought to light shortcomings and inconsistencies which have undermined its credibility and effectiveness. This has been the Italian experience. The cycle of banking crises in Italy has clearly highlighted that the new European system and the EU authorities' approach seem to favour rigidity and excessive simplification in crisis management. This framework only allows two opposing solutions: resolution or liquidation. If there is a 'public interest', the bank undergoes resolution for business restructuring or transfer; if not, the insolvent bank exits the market through liquidation.

This approach, based on standardised mechanisms, needs to be reconsidered; it appears inadequate to the specificities of banking crises and the complexities that the banking sector is facing. Indeed, the rigidity of rules has caused serious problems in those countries, such as Italy, which come from a different legal and operational framework for handling bank insolvency. The lack of flexibility poses a risk especially for small and medium-sized banks: for them, at the moment, there is no alternative to liquidation with reimbursement of depositors, given the absence of clear possibilities of intervention for the banks' restructuring or transfer, due to State aid constraints and other limiting factors.

What is needed is a system able to ensure—to the maximum extent possible—the orderly exit from the market of small and medium-sized banks, avoiding the disruptive effects of insolvency. The options for intervention can be manifold: recapitalisation, restructuring, the sale of the bank or of the business, or—as appropriate—a combination of several tools. Accordingly, in the light of the objective of protecting the general interests related to banking activity, the bank's resolvability should be assessed with a different methodological approach: the possibility of using recovery tools (in the broad sense)[12] should be examined first and, only

[11] P. DE GIOIA CARABELLESE, Bail-in: Do Italians Do It Better (or Worst or Not at All)?: Case Studies and a Reflection on the Italian Approach to the BRRD: The Bail-with, *European Business Law Review*, Vol. 32, No 1, 2021.

[12] The concept of recovery outlined here implies the general principle that the insolvent bank must exit the market. But the exit from the market does not necessarily imply the liquidation of the bank, since this can be done through other instruments suitable for achieving the same final results. The orderly exit, whatever its method, should in any case take place through a profound change in the bank's capital and ownership composition, structure and organisation, management and strategic guidelines.

where the outcome of this evaluation is negative, should liquidation be considered.

Moreover, even in the case of liquidation, the transfer of the assets and liabilities of the bank in liquidation to another bank should always be preferred, since the insolvent bank exits the market and the transfer limits the impacts on creditors and ensures the continuity of essential relationships.

Thus, the European framework fails to give the necessary importance to preventive and alternative measures for small and medium-sized banks, which serve a general interest and deserve protection as well. A change in the culture of crisis management must be considered. Today, the international debate seems to be moving in that direction.[13]

The existence of a general interest in the banking sector, which is the basis for the proper functioning of the banking and financial systems is widely recognised in the literature.[14] Hence the peculiar nature of banking and its special regulation, from the constitution of the bank to its operation, and to the exit from the market when insolvent. Obviously, in a crisis, such general interest is made more evident and concrete. When a bank fails, its capital is reduced by losses or even zeroed out and it becomes inevitable to establish a priority scale among the many interests at stake and the extent of their protection.

[13] P. BAUDINO, A. GAGLIANO, E. RULLI, R. WALTERS, *How to Manage Failures of Non-systemic Banks? A Review of Country Practices, Financial Stability Institute Insights on Policy Implementation*, No 10, October 2018.

[14] A. KERN, *Principle of Banking Regulation*, University Press, Cambridge, May 2019; M. ONADO, *La Banca come impresa, Manuale di gestione Bancaria*, il Mulino, October 1996; G. BAZOLI, *La banca, un'impresa 'speciale'*, Lectio Magistralis, Cerimonia di chiusura del Master in Giuristi, Consulenti e Professionisti d'Impresa A.A. 2015/2016 Scuola di Specializzazione in Studi sull'Amministrazione Pubblica (SP.I.S.A.), Bologna, June 2017; D.W. DIAMOND, P.H. DYBVIG, Bank Runs, Deposit Insurance, and Liquidity, *Journal of Political Economy*, June 1983; C. GOODHART, P. HARTMANN, D. LLEWELLYN, L. ROJAS-SUAREZ, S. WEISBROD, *Financial Regulation: Why, How and Where Now?*, Routledge, May 1998; D. LLEWELLYN, *The Economic Rationale for Financial Regulation*, FSA, 1999; E.H. HUPKES, *Insolvency. Why a Special Regime for Banks? Current Developments in Monetary and Financial Law*, Vol. 3, IMF, 2005; D. KIM, A.M. SANTOMERO, Risk in Banking and Capital Regulation, *The Journal of Finance*, Vol. 43, No 5, December 1988; A. SIRONI, *The Evolution of Banking Regulation Since the Financial Crisis: A Critical Assessment, Baffi Carefin Centre Research*, Paper No 2018-103, November 2018.

The question is whether this general interest is correlated to the size of the bank or is served by any bank, regardless of its size, as the legislation on banking activities suggests. This is a crucial issue, which must be addressed in the debate on the possible ways of resolving banking crises.

2.3 *'Public Interest' Between Resolution and Liquidation: A Dichotomy to Be Reconsidered?*

The EU and Italian legal systems aim to preserve business value and prevent the insolvency of both banks and commercial enterprises.[15]

The need to preserve the value of banks should be greater, given the sector's features and sheer number of interests at stake. However, the new European Union legislation and its implementing measures seem to have taken a different approach: failing or likely to fail banks (FOLTF) are placed under resolution or liquidation according to whether or not they are deemed to be of 'public interest'.[16]

[15] Commission Recommendation No 135 of 12 March 2014 and Regulation (EU) 2015/848 of the European Parliament and of the Council of 20 May 2015 on insolvency proceedings, which replaced Regulation (EC) No 1346/2000. These new regulatory guidelines emphasise the need for early notice and timely intervention to avoid insolvency, inasmuch as the likelihood of saving the enterprise decreases as the time for the intervention increase. In Italy, bankruptcy law was already moving in this direction in 2005–2007, when agreements between debtors and creditors were made part of the legislation. With the new reform of 2019, a preventive 'alert' phase was also introduced to facilitate the reorganisation of the company to prevent the state of insolvency and the timely activation of negotiation tools for crisis management. In this sense, Legislative Decree No 14 of 12 January 2019, which amended Article 2086 of the Italian Civil Code, introduced the duty of the entrepreneur and corporate bodies to establish 'adequate structures for the timely detection of crisis and loss of business continuity'. Therefore, adequate organisational, administrative and accounting structures should be set-up in any enterprise by its administrative bodies.

[16] Both procedures have common triggers, as stated in Article 17 of Legislative Decree No 180/2015 and BRRD. These are: (i) the bank is failing or likely to fail; (ii) it is not possible to envisage alternative measures to prevent the failure or risk of failure in an adequate timeframe, including the intervention of one or more private parties or institutional protection scheme, or supervision measures, such as early intervention or special administration measures according to the Consolidated Banking Act. Pursuant to Article 20(2) of the decree, the third condition for resolution is the existence of a 'public interest', which occurs where resolution is deemed necessary and proportionate to pursue one or more of its objectives (continuity of essential banking services, impacts on financial stability, protection of depositors and investors), which forced liquidation would not guarantee.

'Public Interest' is not an easy concept. How is it defined? Is it adequate? How is it applied? Some clarifications are needed. The notion of public interest and its role in the application of resolution or liquidation requires further investigation. This aspect is fundamental in the management of banking crises.

The BRRD states that resolution is considered to be of public interest if it is necessary to achieve one or more resolution objectives which liquidation would not accomplish. These objectives, which are listed in Article 31 of the directive (transposed by Article 21 of Legislative Decree No 180/2015) are: to ensure the continuity of critical functions, to avoid negative effects on financial stability, to prevent contagion, minimise the use of public funds and protect depositors and investors. From this definition, it has been inferred that 'public interest' can be identified only for banks having systemic implications.[17]

This means that only the larger banks can undergo resolution, i.e. can be restructured or transferred to ensure the continuity of their critical functions.[18] In line with this approach, the authorities conduct a Public Interest Assessment (PIA) predetermining for each bank whether it would be subjected to liquidation or resolution should it become failing or likely to fail. According to this criterion, small and medium-sized banks are not of 'public interest'. They would be liquidated and their depositors reimbursed by deposit guarantee systems.

Thus, PIA is designed to give preference to liquidation in the solution of banking crises. The BRRD provides that resolution authorities, in the context of the resolution plan, must assess the bank's resolvability by first determining the feasibility of liquidation according to the ordinary insolvency procedures. Only in the case of a negative assessment, would a resolution strategy be identified and evaluated.[19]

[17] E. KÖNIG., *Developments in the SRB: Setting MREL and Safeguarding Operational Continuity, Speech to the BPFI in Dublin*, January 2019.

[18] In collaboration with some national resolution authorities, the SRB Resolution Committee has recently started an investigation of shared methodologies to quantify the effects of the liquidation of a bank on the real economy.

[19] A possible classification of the issues and criteria for the assessment: (i) criteria for assessing the feasibility and credibility of liquidation; (ii) criteria for identifying the appropriate resolution strategy; (iii) criteria for assessing the feasibility of a resolution strategy, with reference to structure and operations, financial resources, information, cross-border issues, legal aspects; (iv) criteria for assessing the credibility of a resolution strategy. See EBA, *Final Draft Regulatory Technical Standards on the Content of Resolution Plans*

In the European regulatory framework, therefore, liquidation is the only option for small and medium-sized banks, since there seems to be no 'public interest' in preserving their business and minimising costs and negative impacts on the various categories of their stakeholders. However, this approach is clearly unsatisfactory, since it does not consider that small and medium-sized banks too, and not only the larger ones, may play a fundamental role in the economy of regional areas and, in some circumstances, may have wider effects on the financial system.[20]

In our perspective, to improve the crisis management system, we need to investigate further the legal basis of the Public Interest principle, which seems very simplistic and unsuitable for our purposes. Its basic idea is that small and medium-sized banks can exit the market through liquidation without causing disruption to the financial system and the economy. Conversely, the damage caused by the liquidation of systemic banks would be too substantial, hence the need for resolution (Fig. 1).

Is this really the case? We propose to look deeper into whether the definition of 'public interest' is narrow enough to exclude small and medium-sized banks from resolution (or quasi-resolution) and the application of resolution tools. Furthermore, we must decide what is the main priority when making decisions about liquidation and resolution.

and the Assessment of Resolvability, EBA/RTS/2014/15, December 2014); EUROPEAN COMMISSION, *Delegated Regulation 2016/1075*, March 2016 (Article 23, Section II, Assessment of resolvability).

20 M.C. DOBLER, E. EMRE, A. GULLO, D. KALE, *The Case for Depositor Preference*, IMF, Technical notes and manuals, December 2020, p. 13. According to the authors, in conditions of severe stress and higher contagion risk, even relatively small banks may contribute to systemic risk. A wider range of options and powers can allow resolution authorities to modulate resolution actions according to the specific characteristics of the crisis, improving the trade-off between financial stability risks—associated with losses for creditors—and the tax costs and moral hazard associated with the bail-out. Resolution regimes that can effectively allocate losses to stakeholders and, at the same time, preserve financial stability can have certain positive effects: (i) stakeholders potentially exposed to losses may impose greater discipline on the administrative bodies of the bank, reducing excessive risk and, in turn, the likelihood of a bank crisis; (ii) the risk of systemic crisis spillovers can be reduced by recognising the possibility of losses for stakeholders and requiring adequate absorption capacity by the bank; (iii) by decreasing the probability of a crisis and the direct tax costs associated with it, resolution regimes can also weaken the effects associated with the link between banks and public balance sheets (the 'sovereign-bank nexus'); (iv) resolution regimes can ensure a level playing field by reducing the 'too-important-to-fail discount' which systemic banks benefit from, through lower funding costs than smaller banks.

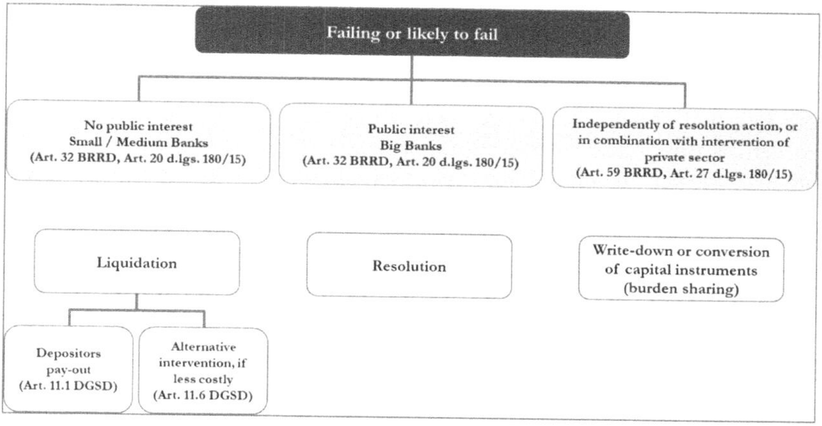

Fig. 1 The approach of European legislation in the event of failing or likely to fail

Lastly, we will consider what could be the right approach for applying the resolution tools to small and medium-sized banks as well.

Starting from the first point, the legislation does not provide a clear definition of public interest; this gives rise to application problems. In Italy, the two Veneto banks exemplify the issue (Chapter 5). Having failed the public interest test for the implementation of resolution, they were placed by the authorities[21] in 'orderly liquidation', with the granting

[21] On 23 June 2017 the Single Resolution Board decided not to implement resolution for Veneto Banca and Banca Popolare di Vicenza, stating that they lacked the necessary precondition under Article 18(1)(c) of Regulation (EU) No 806/2014 (public interest). In particular, the SRB's conclusion was based on the following reasons: (1) the functions performed by the two banks, e.g. deposit taking, lending activities and payment services, were not critical functions, as they were provided to a limited number of customers and could be replaced within a reasonable timeframe; (2) The failure of the banks was unlikely to produce any significant adverse impact on financial stability, given their low financial and operational interconnections with other financial institutions; (3) The normal Italian insolvency procedure would have achieved the same objectives as resolution, achieving the same level of protection for depositors, investors, other clients, funds and client assets. See SINGLE RESOLUTION BOARD, *Summary of the Srb's Decision in Relation to Banca Popolare di Vicenza*, June 2017.

of State aid to protect financial stability, which is also a 'public interest'.[22] Two different definitions of public interest were applied in the same instance: the first to exclude resolution, the second to apply orderly liquidation.[23] Luckily, however, creditors enjoyed a higher degree of protection under the orderly liquidation, through the transfer of assets and liabilities to another bank instead of bail-in. In the new European framework consistency problems arise, as in this case.

From another approach, the definition of public interest, as said, refers only to the resolution objectives as listed in Article 31 of the BRRD. This narrower definition seems inappropriate, since the same objectives can be applicable to banks of all sizes and complexity, not only to larger banks having systemic relevance. For example, the protection of depositors and investors and the continuity of critical functions are crucial for small and medium-sized banks, especially when these are rooted in certain territories or economic contexts.

In terms of priority, the conceptual approach that relies on this legal principle is inadequate to deal with the multiplicity of problems and interests that come into play in banking crises. The process might merit a U-turn: a bank's resolvability assessment should first consider the possibility of recapitalisation, merger or transfer of the business to another bank. Liquidation would be implemented only when these instruments are deemed unfeasible. Even then, the transfer of the assets and liabilities of the bank in liquidation to another bank should always be the preferred

[22] EUROPEAN COMMISION, *Communication from the Commission on the Application, from 1 August 2013, of State Aid Rules to Support Measures in Favour of Banks in the Context of the Financial Crisis ('Banking Communication')*, paragraph 6 'Specific considerations in relation to liquidation aid'. In particular, to allow State measures in support of liquidation, burden sharing must be applied (point 44 of the Communication, according to which 'State aid must not be granted before equity, hybrid capital and subordinated debt have fully contributed to offset any losses').

[23] A. ENRIA, *Audizione al Senato della Repubblica Italiana, Commissione Finanze e Tesoro su Il 'pacchetto bancario' CRD 5/ CRR 2/ BRRD 2*, July 2017: 'A key principle for resolution is the 'no creditor worse off', i.e., no creditor must be in worse conditions in resolution than liquidation. In my view, this implies that no creditor can benefit from a better treatment in liquidation than the resolution, since resolution activates several public safeguards to preserve the continuity of critical functions. This was not the case for Veneto banks. It seems that public interest is valued differently at European and national (or regional) level, with the risk that different preferences emerge at the national level on the use of public support mechanisms. This can have negative effects on the level playing field within the single market, also by differentiating the costs of funding for banks of different Member States in relation to their fiscal capacity'.

solution, given that the exit from the market of the insolvent bank should be accompanied by measures aimed at limiting the negative impacts on creditors and ensuring continuity of essential operations.

Italy has always followed this strategy. Liquidation, with the reimbursement of depositors, has been applied in only two cases concerning banks of very small size. In this approach, atomistic liquidation with the reimbursement of depositors would be the last resort, applied only where there are no other options.

2.4 *Public Interest and General Interest*

We need to definitively clarify the difference between the 'general interest' featuring the banking activity in itself, given all types of stakeholders involved and interests at stake, and the 'public interest', which justifies the application of resolution proceedings. This clarification is of utmost importance in deciding the resolution strategy and the tools that can be activated to preserve the value of the insolvent bank.

Hence, the underlying problem to be addressed is whether the choice between resolution and liquidation is appropriate and credible or other solutions could be explored, as has been the case, generally, in Italy and some other countries. The idea is to apply resolution measures (quasi-resolution) also to small and medium size banks, for which these measures may consist of restructuring and/or business transfer outside formal resolution proceedings; another option could be transactions for the sale of the business in a context of liquidation. These too can be considered resolution measures, even though financed by a DGS and not by a Resolution Fund.

This distinction merits further clarification. In Europe, resolution is a formal procedure for failing or likely-to-fail banks, which is governed by the rules on insolvency. In other jurisdictions, however, the term 'resolution' does not necessarily imply formal proceedings but refers, more in general, to the solution of a bank's crisis with tools such as restructuring or transfer of the bank, thus avoiding liquidation and repayment of depositors. This broader definition of resolution gives jurisdictions more room to operate in banking crises.

In this sense, it is only a matter of implementing resolution tools (sale of business, good bank-bad bank separation, bridge bank, recapitalisation on a going concern basis) for small and medium-sized banks, outside the resolution procedure. This already happens in Italy with preventive and alternative interventions of deposit guarantee systems, pursuant to Article 11(3) and (6) of the DGSD and Italian Legislative Decree No 180/2015. In accordance with these provisions, when a bank is deemed failing or likely to fail, reduction or conversion of equity instruments can be applied together with the intervention of a private sector actor, including the DGS. Other European countries have introduced these tools into domestic law but have yet to use them (Fig. 2).

How can we remove the inconsistencies of the current framework and improve the functioning of the system in the future? An optimal, albeit radical, solution would be to eliminate the notion of public interest for bank resolution. The resolution objectives, applicable to all banking crises, should embrace the idea that even small and medium-sized banks can be 'resolved' (in a broad sense, with all alternative instruments to liquidation and reimbursement of depositors).

This is the governing principle of the US FDIC, which does not consider the size of the banks in crisis. The FDIC Act, which regulates deposit-taking institutions, accounts for resolution and liquidation under the least cost principle. The Dodd-Frank Act widened the mandate of the FDIC by implementing the FSB Key Attributes for systemic financial holding companies. If these companies fail the financial stability test, meaning that they might hamper financial stability under the Bankruptcy Code framework, the FDIC will intervene.

The FDIC framework has also been discussed at European level. The authorities have looked at implementing the FDIC model in Europe. This

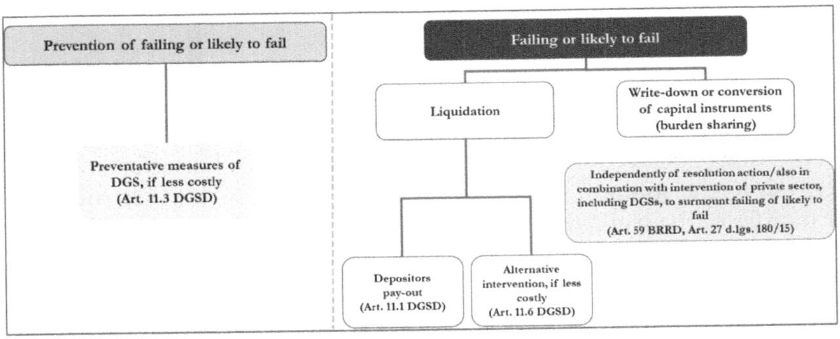

Fig. 2 The approach to be followed for small/medium-sized banks

would change the European framework for crisis management and deposit insurance.[24]

The governing principle should be that all banks, regardless of size, imply general interests to be protected and are worthy of specific treatment in case of insolvency, in order to avoid disruptive effects on various categories of stakeholders. The application of resolution measures could lead to a different configuration of the crisis financing system, particularly of the resolution fund and the deposit guarantee fund. Ultimately, this approach might promote a new design for the funding of banking insolvency in the Eurozone, since these two funds have essentially the same function, despite one being centralised and the other nationalised. And the EDIS would be set-up.

[24] On this: G. MAJNONI D'INTIGNANO, A. DAL SANTO, M. MALTESE, *The FDIC Bank Crisis Management Experience: Lessons for the EU Banking Union*, No 22, August 2020. See also I. VISCO, *L'economia italiana e le banche: implicazioni della pandemia e prospettive*, September 2020: 'The experience in crisis management gained in jurisdictions such as the United States appears useful. The comparison with the related regulatory framework, and in particular with the modus operandi of the Federal Deposit Insurance Corporation, suggests a series of possible regulatory interventions capable of reducing the fragmentation and rigidity of the European approach. These are measures closely related to the regulation and use of the deposit guarantee fund, as part of the implementation of the 'third pillar' of the Banking Union. Among these interventions, we can see those aimed at decreasing the functional dispersion between institutions, achieving the gradual convergence of national liquidation procedures, adopting the 'least cost' as a guiding principle in intervention and for promoting the convergence of national procedures'.

CHAPTER 9

The Debate on the Harmonisation of the Insolvency Framework in Europe

There is no single European insolvency framework. Only national bankruptcy rules apply to the resolution or liquidation of banks. And these are very different.

Therefore, distortions in crises management may arise, especially for cross-border banking groups.

There is currently a debate on the establishment of a harmonised insolvency framework in Europe, according to a special administrative model, which could lead to an EU liquidation procedure, similar to the FDIC's model.

This far-reaching project is very challenging and deserves further investigation and impact analysis, considering that it requires other innovations in the Banking Union's institutional set-up and in crisis management rules.

1 What Is a Harmonised Insolvency Framework?

The introduction of a harmonised insolvency framework to improve the current crisis management processes in Europe has been at the centre of the debate for the resolution-liquidation of banks declared failing or likely to fail. The issue is key, inasmuch as the lack of such a framework could

G. Boccuzzi, *Banking Crises in Italy*, Palgrave Studies in Financial Instability and Banking Crisis Regulation,
https://doi.org/10.1007/978-3-031-01344-7_9

seriously aggravate cross-border banking crises, which are regulated by national rules, in case of application of resolution and liquidation.

Indeed, both procedures make reference to the national laws of the countries in which the two proceedings are open. This is the case, for example, when applying priority rules for creditors in the distribution of the proceeds of liquidation or participation in resolution losses.

But what is a harmonised insolvency regime and why is it important? It should be noted that insolvency rules apply to the liquidation of failed firms; they establish principles, procedural and substantive rules, rights and safeguards for all the parties involved in a crisis with the aim of realising the assets (estate) and distributing the proceeds among creditors according to the priority rules established by law. They are thus aimed at maximising recoveries for the creditors.

In many legal systems, the insolvency regime applicable to banks is court-based (the general model, applied in Canada, Ireland, United Kingdom); in other jurisdictions (Italy, United States, Brazil), special administrative procedures apply, in which public authorities—generally, resolution authorities—are responsible for their direction and coordination. In yet other countries, hybrid procedures are applicable, with the administrative and judicial authorities co-managing the liquidation of banks.

Nonetheless, the special regime incorporates the basic features of the general model, having as a common objective the realisation and distribution of the assets of insolvent banks, in accordance with bankruptcy rules. Banking-specific functions can also be added to this more general objective, depending on national laws. Special rules may enable the pursuit of other objectives, such as:

1. the protection of certain categories of stakeholders, for example, depositors, through depositor preference, or deposit guarantee schemes that subrogate the rights of depositors in liquidation;
2. the realisation of the assets, through the immediate bulk sale of deposits, liabilities and assets, in whole or in part, to another financial institution, often associated with the provisional continuation of the activity of the insolvent bank to ensure the orderly transfer of the business;
3. internal procedures aimed at speeding up the liquidation process.

In these cases, the administrative authority plays a central role in the direction and management of the procedure compared to the courts' normal power in standard procedures.

The issue of a single European insolvency framework has been debated for decades, but no clear path has been defined, mainly due to insufficient political will. Countries push for maintaining their own insolvency frameworks, which are closely linked to other important sectors of their national law, including civil and commercial law, labour law and competition law.[1]

Since the global financial crisis, however, the debate on a harmonised insolvency framework has acquired new momentum. Regulators and international organisations are undertaking various initiatives to define an effective and coherent set-up.[2]

In particular, the introduction of the BRRD and its resolution framework has reignited the debate by highlighting how, in resolution, when it comes to the application of insolvency rules (e.g. bail-in, No Creditor Worse Off—NCWO), the legislation refers to the national insolvency regimes due to the lack of a harmonised framework. Consequently, liquidation and resolution procedures are regulated only by national insolvency laws.

Therefore, while resolution is regulated at European level, insolvency is a purely national matter. Since even resolution, in some aspects, may require the implementation of insolvency rules, the reference to national

[1] The first attempts to design a European framework for banking crises date back to the 1980s. It took many years of work—and various drafts—to draw up Directive No 2001/24/EC on the reorganisation and winding up of credit institutions. The directive was minimalist, in that it was still strongly centred on national laws, without any convergence towards a harmonised system of rules. Each country would retain its institutional structure and crisis management procedures according to national laws. This restricted the scope of the directive to just identifying the country responsible for opening a reorganisation or liquidation procedure and the applicable law. In particular, national procedures were mutually recognised, becoming fully effective throughout the European Community, extending their effects to all branches of the credit institution in the Community.

[2] For an in-depth analysis of the issue, also from a comparative perspective, we refer, among others, to P. BAUDINO, A. GAGLIANO, E. RULLI, R. WALTERS, *How to Manage Failures of Non-Systemic Banks? A Review of Country Practices, Financial Stability Institute Insights on Policy Implementation*, No 10, October 2018; EUROPEAN PARLIAMENT, *Liquidation of Banks: Towards an FDIC for the Banking Union?*, Economic Governance Support Unit (EGSU), February 2019.

insolvency laws is inevitable. This causes distortions and inconsistencies between the various States where a cross-border group operates.

The topic is extremely complex, since it is often unclear what should be harmonised: whether the procedures (authority to open the procedure, management of the liquidation and rules for the realisation of assets) or the substantive rules of insolvency (the creditors' rights and priority rules in the distribution of assets, the protection of rights and judicial appeals). As mentioned, the rules on insolvency are important not only for the liquidation of banks, but also for their resolution. Since in both situations banks are failing or likely to fail, it is of the utmost importance to regulate the participation of the various stakeholders in the losses generated by insolvency.

2 The Starting Point. Insolvency Regimes in EU Countries

National insolvency laws vary immensely across Europe. There is no area as diverse as banking insolvency when it comes to European legal frameworks. A harmonised insolvency framework at European level would ensure that the same rules—and the same effects—would apply in the event of cross-border resolution or liquidation.

In order to understand where to intervene to best achieve this objective, it is important to take a quick look at the main differences among the model:

1. **Diversity of the insolvency models applicable to banks**. There are several ways in which such diversity may be problematic for the coherent management of cross-border crises. For instance:
   a. the consequences that can derive from having different triggers on the opening of the procedure and decision-making powers, since normally the conditions for the opening of an administrative procedure are broader in scope than judicial conditions due to the need to intervene earlier in bank liquidations as opposed to ordinary enterprises. For banks, the status of failing or likely to fail is very different from that of ordinary bankruptcy procedures. Consequently, even the triggers are different for the individual companies of a cross-border group, depending on where they are located;

b. the different objectives (maximise value for creditors, protect depositors, according to the specific rules on depositor priority over other creditors, maintain the business on a temporary basis);
c. the different role of the administrative authorities in the management of liquidation proceedings; and
d. the involvement of creditors in decisions regarding the liquidation process;

2. **Diversity in approaches to liquidation management.** Liquidation may be aimed only at closing an enterprise and realising its assets (piecemeal liquidation), or at other objectives too, such as the temporary continuation of all or some of its legal relationships and the en-bloc sale of the business (including the bank's assets and liabilities);
3. **Diversity in the substantive rules on insolvency.** There may be differences in the rules on the priority of claims in asset distribution, on the preparation of the statement of liabilities, on the method for realising assets, as well as on judicial safeguards, the criminal consequences of the failure and other rights and protections granted to different stakeholders;
4. **Absence of a group insolvency framework.** In many countries, there are currently no insolvency guidelines for groups. Consequently, resolution authorities cannot resolve a banking group as a whole under an integrated framework.

Currently, resolution tools are applicable only to legal entities, according to national insolvency law (territorial approach). But different national insolvency laws may entail different treatment for creditors. This issue is especially evident in the application of the NCWO principle in resolution, especially when a bank has subsidiaries in different Member States which apply their own insolvency regimes.

In the current debate, also among European authorities, proposals have already been made to move towards a more integrated approach, which deals with the crises of banking groups.[3]

This is another thorny issue that should be carefully studied and regulated, given the diversity of situations that may arise and the different

[3] G. BOCCUZZI, *Il Regime Speciale della Risoluzione Bancaria. Obiettivi e Strumenti*, Cacucci Editore, 2018, cap. 6.

solutions that may be implemented for the various members of the group. This often happens when, within the group, there are solvent entities for which non-insolvency solutions are needed, such as the transfer at market conditions.

What is important is to have unitary and integrated management, rather than to apply the same procedure to the parent company and to all group members. The ABVL case in Latvia is often quoted as an example of what can happen in the absence of harmonised insolvency rules. In this case, the Court of Luxemburg refused to place the bank's Luxembourg subsidiary in liquidation. However, this different assessment was not caused by the lack of a harmonised insolvency framework, but instead by the fact that the bank had been deemed solvent in a different evaluation.

3 The 'No Creditor Worse Off' Principle

A solid and harmonised European insolvency framework is necessary for the implementation not only of resolution tools, but also of the No Creditor Worse-Off (NCWO) principle, whenever national insolvency rules are to be applied for the resolution of cross-border groups.

Regulated by Article 32 of the BRRD, the NCWO principle is a crucial element of the resolution framework.[4] According to NCWO, the losses suffered by the creditors of a bank in resolution cannot be greater than those that would have occurred if the bank had been liquidated under national insolvency rules. This principle, to some extent, reflects the application in the resolution framework of the 'equal treatment of creditors' enforced in national insolvency laws.

The issue, however, is that in a resolution losses are estimated at the beginning of the procedure, when not all valuation information may be available. According to the BRRD, fully implemented in Italian law (Article 23 of Legislative Decree No 180/2015), the Bank of Italy must delegate to an independent expert[5] a fair, prudent and realistic valuation of the assets and liabilities of the bank before initiating the resolution

[4] G. DAVIES, M. DOBLER, *Bank Resolution and Safeguarding the Creditors Left Behind*, Bank of England, London, Quarterly Bulletin, September 2011.

[5] On the independency prerequisites of experts, the EBA has issued the Regulatory Technical Standards, which later became part of the Commission Delegated Regulation (EU) 2018/345 of 14 November 2017: EUROPEAN BANKING AUTHORITY,

procedure or applying the write-down or conversion of shares or other capital instruments. This valuation would determine any consequences on the bank's stakeholders.

The main objective of the valuation is to verify the conditions for resolution or for the reduction/conversion of capital instruments. If these conditions are met, the valuation will guide the decision-making process and help to quantify the capital reduction or conversion necessary to cover losses and comply with capital requirements.

If a bail-in is envisaged within the resolution actions, the valuation serves to quantify the extent of the reduction and conversion of eligible liabilities; in the case of a sale of business, it helps to identify the assets and legal relationships to be transferred to the bridge institution or to the vehicle created for the management of assets, determining any compensation to be paid to the bank in resolution or to holders of shares or other capital instruments, depending on the object and the modalities of the transfer.

In cases of urgency, the Bank of Italy or the special administrators appointed pursuant to Article 71 TUB can carry out a provisional valuation (Article 25), to determine the initiation of a resolution action or the reduction or conversion of shares, other equity investments and capital instruments. This provisional valuation is carried out, where possible, according to the principles set out in Articles 23 (1) and (3), and Article 24(1), (4) and (5). The provisional valuation must be followed by a final valuation as soon as possible.[6]

Since in the provisional valuation the amounts of the reduction or conversion may be higher or lower than those actually necessary to cover the losses and ensure compliance with the bank's capital requirements, the final valuation must account for all losses and provide the actual

Final Draft Regulatory Technical Standards on Valuation for the Purposes of Resolution and on Valuation to Determine Difference in Treatment Following Resolution Under Directive 2014/59/EU on Recovery and Resolution of Credit Institutions and Investment Firms, EBA/RTS/2017/05—Final draft RTS on valuation before resolution, May 2017; EUROPEAN BANKING AUTHORITY, *Final Draft Regulatory Technical Standards on Independent Valuers Under Article 36(14) of Directive 2014/59/EU, EBA/RTS/2015/07*, July 2015.

[6] The provisional valuation, if carried out together with the assessment of the difference in shareholders' and creditors' treatment pursuant to Article 88, must remain separate (Article 25(3)).

amount of reduction/conversion and of the instruments subject to bail-in, and, if necessary, indicate any difference in amounts, thus correcting any distortions in the provisional valuation.

The matter of valuation is at the centre of an ongoing debate, considering its effects on the bank's shareholders and creditors. Only practical experience, however, can help us to verify the ability of the European regulatory framework to face any problems arising from the resolution valuation, also considering the difficulties in determining the 'correct' amount of a bank's assets and liabilities. Professionals and specialists can contribute to refining the methodologies and strengthening the credibility of the mechanisms provided for by law.

The difference between liquidation and resolution is evident. While in liquidation the losses suffered by shareholders and creditors are determined at the end of the liquidation process, that is, after the realisation and distribution of the assets to creditors, in resolution the amount and distribution of losses depend on the valuation made at the beginning of the procedure. The NCWO principle, therefore, acts as the '*ex-post* remedy' to the valuation carried out *ex-ante*.

The resolution authority carries out this *ex-post* valuation on the basis of an independent expert valuation. In this sense, the NCWO principle safeguards creditors during a resolution procedure, ensuring that they will not be worse off than they would be in liquidation. The NCWO is applicable to all resolution tools (bail-in, bridge bank, sale of business, asset separation) if creditors argue that they were subjected to worse treatment than they would have if the bank had been liquidated. If the *ex-post* valuation supports their claim, creditors have the legal right to claim compensation via the Resolution Fund.

Given the subjectivity of the assessment and the difficulty in guaranteeing that the rule is correctly applied, the NCWO could pose a legal risk for resolution authorities, especially when applied to the various legal entities of a cross-border banking group.

At this stage, it is difficult to argue for or against the effectiveness of the NCWO principle. NCWO still requires a clearer and more solid regulatory definition because there is still no evidence that the principle and *ex-post* compensation measures are effective in national or cross-border resolutions. Ultimately, we do not know whether this rule can protect creditors affected by the valuations made at the start of a resolution procedure. Neither do we know whether it works across borders, since differences in insolvency regulations among Member States can determine different results for creditors of different entities of the same group located in different jurisdictions.

4 A European Liquidation Regime. The Adoption of the 'FDIC' Model

Developments in the ongoing discussion about the need to harmonise insolvency rules in Europe have led to the idea of introducing a single European liquidation regime in parallel to the European resolution regime. This idea, too, requires careful consideration.

The issue is whether we are aiming for a single European liquidation framework, with harmonised insolvency rules, or for something slightly different. Some of the proposals put forward, in fact, go beyond mere regulatory harmonisation and towards a revision of the institutional set-up for banking crisis management in the Eurozone. Some proposals, based on the FDIC model, contemplate the centralisation of bank liquidation procedures in the hands of the SRB, which would administratively manage the procedures. This was the idea proposed by the Committee on Economic and Monetary Affairs (Econ) of the European Parliament.[7]

This option would require the creation of an administrative regulatory framework for European bank insolvency (the harmonisation effect), to be accompanied by an expansion of the SRB's crisis management functions (the centralisation effect). The FDIC model would ultimately be set up

[7] EUROPEAN PARLIAMENT, *Liquidation of Banks: Towards an FDIC for the Banking Union?*, Economic Governance Support Unit (EGSU), February 2019. In particular, the document reiterates the position expressed by the International Monetary Fund as part of its 2018 valuation on the Eurozone, in which the IMF recommended that the SRB take over the administrative side of liquidation procedures. On this, INTERNATIONAL MONETARY FUND, *Resolution Funding: Who Pays When Financial Institutions Fail?*, August 2018: "This tool would allow the resolution authority to appoint a liquidator and commence proceedings. The SRB would be able to apply this tool to all banks within its remit and banks considered systemic at the time of failure, by itself or in combination with other resolution tools, including an effective sale-of-business tool. Such a tool should be underpinned by a harmonised creditor hierarchy (applicable also for purposes of the 'no creditor worse off' safeguard) and would be especially useful for ensuring that cases involving cross-border banks are dealt with at a euro area level, facilitating needed coordination. Meanwhile, creditor hierarchies (where progress has been made following the 2017 BRRD amendment) and the availability of resolution tools (which differs widely) under national bank insolvency frameworks should be further harmonised'.

in the Eurozone, as recommended by many parties. However, this is a complex issue, requiring further discussion.

In fact, these possible changes are far-reaching and would require significant innovations in the current crisis management model, with a different allocation of supervisory and resolution responsibilities between European and national authorities. In a centralised regime, the SRB would also be responsible for the liquidation of small and medium-sized banks, which, in the current design of the SSM and the SRM, are managed by the national supervisory and resolution authorities under national insolvency rules: a set-up which, in itself, is fully consistent.

How can these different needs be combined into an efficient and effective banking crisis management model? And how do we solve the issues concerning the current SSM and SRM-based model of the Banking Union?

First of all, it must be assessed whether the FDIC model, which many claim is the ideal model, can work in Europe, since obviously each legal system has its own distinctive features. It is not possible to just mechanically transfer models that may be valid and justifiable in certain institutional and legal contexts from one system to another, each having different characteristics. Before making such decisions, it would first be necessary to carry out an analysis of the history, legal systems, core principles, banking systems structure, traditions and experiences of individual countries, and to analyse the impact of such a transposition, which would modify principles and long-established balances. Figure 1 shows the different European and US crisis management models.

We must not repeat the same mistakes made with the BRRD, when significant innovations (recovery and resolution plans, burden sharing, bail-in, Minimum Requirement for own funds and Eligible Liabilities—MREL) were introduced in the legal systems of European countries when they were still unprepared and without an adequate transitional period. Innovation is important, but its scope and timing must be well calibrated. Dangerous leaps forward must be avoided.

The Banking Union is very recent; many of its fundamental elements have yet to be introduced, and some of those that have been introduced have yet to be applied. Without the experience to evaluate existing provisions, it seems unwise to plan further changes that would extend the powers and responsibilities of an institution that is still in its early stages. The question is how to harmonise the European powers and responsibilities in bank crisis management with the local dimension of banks.

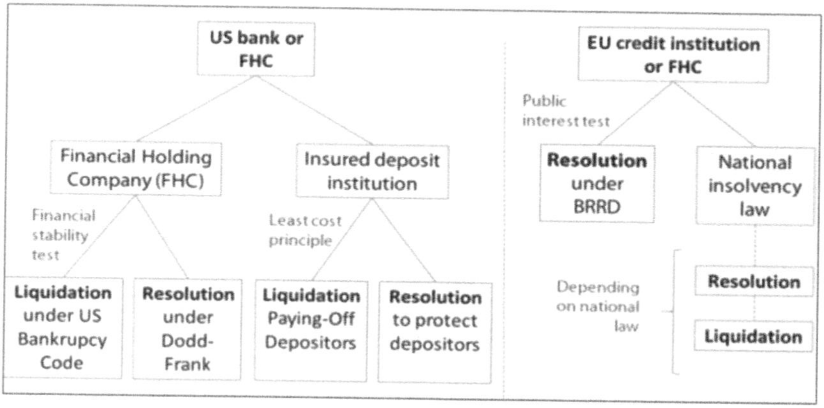

Fig. 1 US and EU insolvency framework (*Source* EGOV)

The SRM was designed to manage crises of systemic banks at European level and it is not clear how it could take on the crises of small and medium-sized banks, too.

The liquidation of small and medium-sized banks has always been managed by national authorities, according to national insolvency rules and in combination with national deposit guarantee schemes. How, then, can the national dimension of DGSs be combined with the centralisation of liquidation? This harkens back to the creation of the EDIS for applying liquidation at European level. You cannot have one without the other.

Furthermore, we must consider that many bank insolvency tools in Europe have already been harmonised, such as the ranking of creditors (depositor preference, albeit with different configurations in the various countries, and the treatment of non-preferred senior debt).

Thus, at this stage, it is necessary to carefully evaluate what the Banking Union needs in order to pursue financial stability and improve the crisis management framework. A gradual approach is certainly in order.

The first necessary step would be to harmonise insolvency regimes at European level, based on a careful analysis of the existing regimes and their differences. This first step is already ambitious in itself and not easy to take, as shown by similar attempts made in the past. It is the precondition for standardising the application of insolvency rules in the resolution and liquidation of cross-border groups. There seems to be a degree of consensus on the need for a European bank insolvency regime.

The bank insolvency regime should be separate from the ordinary bankruptcy procedures applicable to other commercial enterprises, and should consist of an administrative procedure for the liquidation of banks. This already exists in many jurisdictions, including Italy, where the compulsory administrative liquidation of banks was introduced by the Banking Law of 1936/1938, if not even earlier, considering that a special liquidation procedure was envisaged for savings banks as early as the end of the 1800s.

Harmonisation remains, however, a mandatory step, before launching any impact analyses to gauge the effects of the possible centralisation of liquidation management at European level. Centralisation, in any case, should be accompanied by other substantial changes in the existing crisis management systems. This is a whole other and much more ambitious goal than a simple harmonisation of rules.

CHAPTER 10

Who Gets the Bill in a Crisis?

The financing for a banking crisis depends essentially on the availability of banks' internal and external resources to cover losses and carry out restructuring operations or transfer the insolvent bank. Financial needs may vary according to whether the aim of the intervention is to re-establish the bank's liquidity or its solvency position.

In solvency funding, the legislation provides for the participation of shareholders and creditors in covering costs by implementing bail-in and, in some circumstances, a more limited burden sharing (write-down and conversion of capital instruments). In resolution proceedings, external resources are provided by the Resolution Fund and, in the case of liquidation, by deposit guarantee schemes. The latter, depending on their institutional mandate, may intervene in liquidation or in other circumstances. As a last resort, the legislation also allows public intervention.

Liquidity funding, which is crucial for banks in pre-resolution and resolution, is more problematic. The available instruments are clearly insufficient and the search for new solutions is the key objective, through a new role of central banks in banking crises and new

G. Boccuzzi, *Banking Crises in Italy*, Palgrave Studies in Financial Instability and Banking Crisis Regulation,
https://doi.org/10.1007/978-3-031-01344-7_10

instruments in close coordination with supervisory and resolution authorities.

1 The Contribution of Shareholders and Creditors

In the new crisis management system, as a general principle, the costs of insolvency primarily fall on the shareholders and creditors of the insolvent bank (the burden-sharing principle, Article 34 BRRD; Point 44 Banking Communication[1]), when it is necessary to apply measures involving the use of the Resolution Fund or State aid.

The implementation of burden sharing in Italy proved to be very burdensome. It was applied in the resolution of the 'four banks' and the liquidation of the two Veneto banks, with the zeroing of the capital and subordinated bonds previously issued by the banks. This measure was problematic since a large part of the bonds was held by retail customers. In addition, as discussed previously,[2] the BRRD made no allowance for a transitional period to protect securities issued before the new rules.

The enormous costs of this unprecedented event led Italian legislators to intervene by creating an ad hoc safety mechanism to protect retail investors. The savers were granted *ex-post* protection through the establishment of the Solidarity Fund (Article 1(855)-(861) of Law No 208 of 28 December 2015, known as the 2016 Stability Law). This Fund aims to protect investors with limited income flows and movable assets.

The Interbank Deposit Protection Fund was entrusted with managing the Solidarity Fund, which deployed resources from the banking sector. Through the Solidarity Fund, the holders of subordinated bonds of the

[1] EUROPEAN COMMISSION, *Communication of 31 July 2013 on the Application of the Rules on State Aid Applicable to the Banking System in the Context of the Financial Crisis from 1 August 2013* (Banking Communication).

[2] G. BOCCUZZI, *Il Regime Speciale della Risoluzione Bancaria. Obiettivi e Strumenti*, Cacucci Editore, 2018. On this topic, see I. VISCO, *The Governor's Concluding Remarks*, Annual Report 2015, May 2016: 'Contrary to what was proposed by the Italian delegation in official fora, an adequate transitional period was not provided to give all the parties involved time to acquire a full understanding of the new regime, nor has the application of the new system to debt instruments already marketed, even to retail investors, been ruled out'. See also V. CALANDRA BUONAURA, *La disciplina del risanamento e della risoluzione delle banche. Aspetti critici*, in Orizzonti del Diritto Commerciale, anno V, No 2, February 2017.

four banks placed under resolution and the two Veneto banks put into liquidation were compensated for their losses. The overall burden of compensation paid by the Interbank Deposit Protection Fund—and by the banking system—was approximately €280 million.

The 2019 Stability Law introduced a further layer of protection for savers affected by banking crises. The Stability Law established the Savers Compensation Fund (Fondo Indennizzo Risparmiatori—FIR) to partially compensate savers of banks and subsidiaries put in compulsory administrative liquidation after 16 November 2015 and before 1 January 2018. The compensation could be enacted when it was ascertained that savers were affected by misleading information, as well as lack of diligence, correctness and transparency, as required by the Consolidated Finance Law (Testo Unico della Finanza—TUF). The Ministry of the Economy and Finance (MEF) delegated the management of the FIR to a public institution. Investors in subordinated bonds who have not already accessed the Solidarity Fund can access the FIR.

The aforementioned crisis events and the application of the burden-sharing principle have highlighted the problems that can arise when bail-inable assets are held by retail investors, who are not always able to assess the riskiness of investments, often due to the mis-selling of financial products by banks. Furthermore, these events raised the question of whether the protection of public savings was enough to justify the burden placed on the FITD and the banking sector.

1.1 Is Bail-In Feasible?

When we talk about resolution, we immediately—and somewhat negatively—think of bail-in. Bail-in implies that if a bank is 'failing or likely to fail' (and there is public interest in its resolution), the coverage of losses and the capital increase must be borne by the shareholders and other capital instruments holders. When their contribution is not sufficient, the creditors of the bank must contribute proportionally according to the national insolvency rules. Only depositors protected by the DGSs are exempt from bail-in (Article 44(2)(a) of the BRRD, implemented by Article 49(1)(a)of Legislative Decree No 180/2015).[3]

[3] P. DE GIOIA CARABELLESE, *La ricapitalizzazione bancaria interna*, Studium edizioni, 2020.

However, although allocating the cost of insolvencies to shareholders and creditors is justifiable in principle, it can have destabilising effects in some situations. The transfer of the costs of an insolvent bank to those who invested in the bank's financial instruments may give rise to contagion effects. Therefore, bail-in should be applied with caution, to avoid the risk that 'an instrument devised to reduce the impact of a crisis [might] create the premises to make one more likely'.[4]

The same BRRD (Article 44(3)(c)) allows for some flexibility as regards bail-in. It establishes that resolution authorities can decide to apply bail-in only partially should its impact on financial stability have effects contrary to the general interest of the Member State and the EU. Precisely, the provision states that, under exceptional circumstances, resolution authorities can exclude certain liabilities from being bailed-in to avoid the risk of contagion or disruption to the economy. However, these flexibility mechanisms should be enhanced and the cases in which they can be applied should be clarified.

Further reflection is required on bail-in for systemic banks, to verify whether it works effectively in the light of the risk of contagion to other major financial institutions holding bail-inable securities. In addition, sustainability for the balance sheets of banks issuing bail-inable securities (the cost of MREL) must be carefully analysed given the high cost of these securities correlated with their inherent risk. The result could be that the advantages in terms of major loss absorbency capacity are less than the costs in balance sheets. This is especially true for medium-sized banks, which may encounter difficulties in accessing capital markets to place MREL securities; normally, these banks are not listed and have a business model mainly focused on retail banking.[5]

Bail-in, which was initially celebrated as the silver bullet to solve banking crises and also to avoid the recourse to public interventions, does not seem to match up to expectations, perhaps not even in the eyes of the regulators themselves. In fact, bail-in has never been applied in Europe

[4] I. VISCO, *Workshop on Stability of the Banking System*, Keynote Speech by the Governor of the Bank of Italy, European University Institute – The State of the Union, Florence, May 2016.

[5] The solution considered is to exclude bail-in for small and medium-sized banks, even though this could raise an issue of unequal treatment between small and medium-sized banks on the one hand, and large banks on the other. Such a rule could be justified by the proportionality principle.

for bank resolution, due to the fear that it might compromise trust in the banking system. The Italian experience has shown this clearly, albeit with respect to the narrower burden-sharing tool.[6]

Many questions are still open. What financial instruments should be subject to bail-in? What categories of investors should be involved? What would the effects on the issuing banks be? The high risk associated with bail-inable financial instruments requires that the rules and limitations applicable be clearly defined and that consumer protection be maximised. Rules for the allocation of these instruments to retail customers have to be precisely stated. For instance, the issue of bail-inable assets could be limited to qualified financial institutions (pension funds, insurance companies and other asset managers).

EBA and ESMA are moving in this direction as shown by their joint 2018 Communication.[7] They highlight the issues of bail-inable securities held by retail customers for both consumer protection and the effectiveness of the resolution process. In particular, when preparing resolution plans, resolution authorities are required to assess the feasibility of bail-in with retail investors and the existence of the conditions for the exemptions from bail-in under Article 44(3) of the BRRD. For the first time in an official regulatory act, the problems of bail-in and the need for greater flexibility are emphasised.

In the same direction, Directive 2017/2399/EU of 12 December 2017 introduced a new category of securities, the 'Non-preferred debt instruments', which are somewhere between senior bonds and subordinated financial instruments. In Italy, this category was introduced by the 2018 Stability Law (Law No 205 of 27 December 2017),

[6] The US and European frameworks differ in the application of bail-in and the establishment of buffers for its implementation. In Europe, bail-in is part of the tools introduced by the BRRD and is subject to specific requirements in terms of MREL (and TLAC for systemic banks). Both the national authorities and the SRB can use these instruments for resolution. Differently, the Dodd Frank Act does not overtly allow for the implementation of bail-in. On this, see European Parliament (2019); IMF (2015, page 58).

[7] EUROPEAN BANKING AUTHORITY - EUROPEAN SECURITIES AND MARKETS AUTHORITY, *Statement of the Eba and Esma on the Treatment of Retail Holdings of Debt Financial Instruments Subject to the Bank Recovery and Resolution Directive*, Eba/Op/2018/03, May 2018.

incorporating the new category of 'second-level unsecured instruments' in the Consolidated Banking Act (TUB).[8]

Therefore, the applicability of bail-in should be carefully assessed. Various options can be considered. For example, the object and the scope of bail-in could be restricted to certain categories of liabilities, on a contractual basis (contractual bail-in), in order to give *ex-ante* certainty to creditors and reduce the risk of a general reduction in funding. This approach, however, would hinder the financing of resolution through bail-in and would require additional resources from other sources (the resolution fund and even public support).

1.2 Reasons for the Failure to Apply Bail-In

The bail-in rule was introduced without a phasing-in process and without considering the types of holders of bonds or subordinated debts. As a result, the main tool of the new framework was too complicated to apply. Ultimately, Europe was unprepared for bail-in.

Applying bail-in is a challenge. This tool requires banks to be prepared and equipped. However, doing this is expensive and time-consuming. The general opinion is that the banking system was not ready to implement this complex tool. And it still is not. The preparation process is complex and involves multiple aspects, including internal assessment tools and procedures, specific skills and adequate technological infrastructures to allow immediate access to information and assessments on bail-inable tools. A bail-in also requires the involvement of external counterparties in the process, including independent entities to carry out the valuation process, and market infrastructures (paying agents, central counterparties) for the write-down of the securities and the issuing and placement of shares.

Project management involves experts from different areas and levels of seniority within the banks and requires a close relationship with resolution authorities.[9]

[8] Article 12a regarding second-level unsecured instruments was introduced; paragraph c-bis was also added to Article 91(1a).

[9] Recently, the Single Resolution Board published a set of documents describing operational guidelines for the application of bail-in. The documents include guidelines for defining the bail-in playbook and instructions on the bail-in data set. The bail-in playbook is drawn up by the bank for carrying out the reduction and/or conversion pursuant

The approach of the new resolution framework was based on the 'Bail-in first, MREL later' principle, but it should have been the other way around: 'MREL first, Bail-in later'. This would have given time to build adequate capacity for banks to absorb losses (Loss Absorbency Capacity) through the application of the MREL requirements.

The effectiveness of bail-in as a resolution tool has been questioned in the literature, with many authors highlighting its possible side effects.[10] In Italy, for example, the case of the four banks under resolution was subjected to constant media scrutiny, mostly focused on the issue of the retail investors in subordinated securities issued by the banks in resolution; this damaged the image of the national banking system.[11]

to Article 21 of the SRMR and for implementing bail-in as part of the resolution. The bail-in playbook should describe all internal and external actions that must be taken by or on behalf of the banks to effectively enforce the bail-in. The guidelines provide operational indications on preparing the playbook. The bail-in data set provides information on the data needed by the Resolution Authority for the application of the bail-in. It provides, inter alia, indications regarding the data on liabilities that a bank under resolution should provide to the resolution authorities, specifying the required level of data quality and any additional requirement to ensure legal certainty in the implementation of the bail-in tool. See SINGLE RESOLUTION BOARD, *Operational Guidance on Bail-in Implementation*, August 2020.

[10] C. GOODHART, E. AVGOULEAS, *A Critical Evaluation on Bail-ins as Bank Recapitalisation Mechanism*, Centre for Economic Policy Research, Discussion Paper 10065, August 2014. The authors argue that in case of systemic instability 'bail-in regimes will fail to eradicate the need for an injection of public funds where there is a threat of systemic collapse'. On the other hand, bail-in tends to be effective when failure is idiosyncratic. Thus, the impact of the bail-in process is likely to be in terms of triggering capital flight and rising funding costs. PERSAUD A.D., *Why Bail-In Securities Are Fool's Gold*, Peterson Institute for International Economics, No PB14-23, November 2014. He argues that bail-in works well in idiosyncratic bank failures, but in the presence of systemic crises it might actually make matters even worse. HADJEMMANUIL C., *Limits on State-funded bailouts in the EU Bank Resolution regime*, European Economy, No 2, December 2016. The author formulates similar arguments. He points out that in a context of widespread distress, the application of bail-in in a single (failing) bank may push creditors of other banks to reconsider their positions, thus 'precipitating an across-the-board flight to quality'. A.C. HUSER, G. HALAJ, C. KOK, C. PERALES, A. VAN DE KRAAIJ, *The Systemic Implications of Bail-in: A Multi Layered Network Approach*, Working Paper Series, European Central bank, No 2010, February 2017. The authors investigate the possible contagion effects of bail-in.

[11] In this regard, A. GRAZIANO, V. FRANCESCA, S. FONTANA, M.R. DELLA PERUTA, *Look Who's Talking: Banking Crisis, Bail-in and Mass Media*, 9th Annual Conference of the EuroMed Academy of Business, Warsaw, Poland, September 2016.

An analysis of the behaviour of bank creditors and depositors[12] showed a decline in deposits placed in the four banks since the beginning of the special administration. This trend increased near the start of the resolution, especially for deposits not covered by the deposit guarantee scheme. The size and speed of the phenomenon hinted at the emergence of 'panic' situations, closely connected to the perceived uncertainty of the new regulatory framework. Creditors and depositors were reacting to the fear of being subjected to bail-in. A similar trend was observed in deposits in solvent banks affected by capital shortages.

On the basis of these negative considerations, we have to ask ourselves whether bail-in is really to be considered the 'silver bullet' and bail-out should be definitively excluded. This does not seem to be the case, at least not yet.

2 External Financing of the Crisis

2.1 *Solvency Funding*

Overall, crisis management requires access to external resources to restore the bank's solvency or to cover losses before the sale of the bank in crisis. In the new European crisis management framework, two funding channels have been established in addition to bail-in: the Resolution Fund and the Deposit Guarantee Fund, applicable in different situations and on the basis of different conditions.

The resources of the Resolution Fund are to be used exclusively for financing resolution measures and ensuring the effective application of resolution tools. In particular, they can be used to support any resolution action for absorbing losses, compensating creditors and supporting liquidity.[13]

[12] G. BOCCUZZI-R. DE LISA, Does Bail-in Definitely Rule Out Bailout?, *The Journal of Financial Management, Markets and Institutions (JFMI)*, January 2017.

[13] The interventions can be carried out with various methods and technical forms: the issue of guarantees against assets and liabilities of the bank in resolution, its subsidiaries, a bridge bank or an asset management vehicle; the granting of loans to the same parties; contributions to the capital of a bridge bank or an asset management vehicle company; the purchase of assets of the bank under resolution; the payment of indemnities to shareholders and creditors under the safeguards regime provided for in Article 89 (Legislative Decree No 180/2015); the disbursement to the bank in resolution of a contribution in lieu of what it would have obtained from the reduction or conversion of liabilities of certain creditors, if the bail-in is applied and the resolution authority has ordered optional

However, the Resolution Fund cannot be used directly to cover losses or to recapitalise a bank, except for ensuring the effectiveness of the other resolution measures (Article 79(2) of Legislative Decree No 180/2015).[14] More specifically, the provision serves to avoid direct coverage of losses, except under specific conditions, which are the same as those regarding the optional exclusions of certain liabilities from bail-in. Bail-in must be applied first to no less than 8% of the total liabilities (including own funds) of the bank in resolution. In this circumstance, the contribution of the resolution fund cannot exceed 5% of the bank's total liabilities, including own funds.

In the case of liquidation, deposit guarantee funds are used to repay depositors, while in resolution they help to cover losses without involving protected deposits, which are excluded from bail-in. The total amount would be up to the losses the DGSs would have incurred in the event of liquidation of the bank (loss absorber). DGSs can also carry out preventive or alternative interventions other than depositor reimbursement.

In contrast, outside Europe both functions are usually carried out by a single fund, which intervenes in the financing of resolution and in the repayment of depositors in liquidation. Thus, the single fund has a solvency funding function. This framework has also been suggested for implementation in Italy.[15]

As we have seen, a key element of the European framework is that the resolution financing system is essentially based on the use of private resources. But to what extent can private resources alone take on large-scale insolvencies? Is there a limit to private intervention? It would be necessary to assess how sustainable the transfer of losses to the private sector truly is, especially in the case of more vulnerable banks with income

exclusions from the bail-in measure; the provision of loans on a voluntary basis to other resolution funds.

[14] Moreover, where the resolution financing mechanism has to indirectly bear the losses, the principles governing the use of resolution funds in the context of bail-in pursuant to Article 49(6) (Legislative Decree No 180/2015), including the use of the bail-in for at least 8% of the bank's total liabilities and the capping of the resolution fund's contribution at 5% of total liabilities. However, notwithstanding this provision, the resolution fund can intervene if the bail-in has already been applied to 20% of the total liabilities, if it has ordinary contributions equal to at least 3% of the protected deposits and if the group in resolution has consolidated assets of less than €900 billion.

[15] G. MAJNONI D'INTIGNANO, A. DAL SANTO, M. MALTESE, *The FDIC Bank Crisis Management Experience: Lessons for the EU Banking Union*, No 22, August 2020.

problems. The limits to the use of private resources should be identified to avoid the risk that the costs of bank failures be transferred from bad banks to healthy banks, thereby causing financial instability. A question inevitably arises: why not introduce a public measure that can be applied in exceptional circumstances to protect financial stability? After all, the BRRD allows it as a last resort solution, to avoid negative impacts on financial stability and to protect public interest, after all the other resolution tools have been assessed (Articles 56-58 BRRD).

Any public measure should operate outside resolution as well, to carry out open-bank assistance operations, in the presence of a general interest to rescue the bank in crisis.

2.2 *Liquidity Funding. The Need for New Tools to Support Liquidity in Resolution and Pre-Resolution*

The new legal framework for resolution is focused mostly on solvency funding (MREL, bail-in, Resolution Fund), while little or no consideration has been given to liquidity funding. The same occurs in the case of preventive measures by DGSs (open-bank assistance), as was the case recently in Italy. What if the bank undergoing resolution or restructuring outside the resolution runs out of the necessary liquid funds or lacks sufficient assets to give as collateral?

Liquidity funding is central to the banking crisis management system. The European discussion is finally addressing the issue of liquidity in the pre-resolution and post-resolution phases.[16] This complex issue involves different authorities (governments, central banks, supervision or resolution authorities.), with a wide-ranging problem: illiquidity could trigger insolvency and thus undermine the restoring of a bank.

The objective of policymakers is to design new prudential rules to strengthen banks' liquidity *ex-ante*, as was the case with the introduction of new ratios in the framework of Basel III (Liquidity Coverage Ratio—LCR and Net Stable Funding Ratio—NSFR), and at the same time to ensure that the bank in crisis can have recourse to extraordinary liquidity in both pre-resolution and resolution.

[16] For an in-depth analysis, see EUROPEAN PARLIAMENT, *How to Provide Liquidity to banks After Resolution in Europe's Banking Union*, Demertzis M., Gonsalves Raposo I., Hutti P., Wolff G. (External Authors), November 2018.

In the early stage of a crisis, preserving the bank's liquidity is fundamental. A bank in trouble, but still viable, can incur a liquidity shortage, caused by different factors: illiquidity may be a consequence of a more serious deteriorating business or be a separate and temporary problem. In this phase, it is crucial to cover the bank's liquidity needs, in order to have the time to take corrective actions and prevent illiquidity situations from leading to insolvency.

Liquidity needs can be met by the market itself, provided there is confidence in the bank. Where this is not possible, resources can be provided by the central bank. In the Eurozone, following the Bagehot rule, the central bank—the ECB together with the other 19 Eurozone central banks—acts as the lender of last resort. It can 'lend only to solvent banks with liquidity problems, but not to insolvent banks'. These loans can only be made on a collateralised basis.

A liquidity shortfall may also arise after a bank has become distressed and, for example, has been placed in special administration. In this case, the market may be reluctant to trust the bank.

Special administration procedures require time to analyse the bank's situation, draw up a business plan and assess capital needs. These procedures are also extremely complex and delicate: it is necessary to find investors willing to provide the necessary capital for the re-establishment of the bank's prudential requirements and long-term viability. Over that period, the bank must have the necessary liquidity. The same happens in resolution procedures: while the conditions for recapitalisation and the covering of losses are clearly set out through the bail-in and the Resolution Fund, who meets the liquidity needs?

The banking crises in Italy (the four banks in resolution, the interventions of the Voluntary Intervention Scheme in favour of the three Casse di Risparmio, and the FITD's recent interventions for Banca Carige and Banca Popolare di Bari) exemplify this issue. The Italian experience has shown that, while a restructuring plan had been properly set up and approved, liquidity support was difficult to find. Without clear rules on liquidity support, it is hardly possible to engage in the restructuring of a bank, because it is unlikely that the market will provide liquidity funding to a bank in crisis. In these cases, only one possibility remains—the central bank, which provides liquidity as a lender of last resort. However, here too the rules on central bank interventions in crisis management have not proven adequate.

In the current regulatory framework of the European System of central banks, there are two possible options for banks to obtain liquidity:

a. Eurosystem monetary policy operations, carried out by the European Central Bank. These include ordinary operations (MROs and LTROs) and non-standard monetary policy operations (e.g. TLTROs).[17] For these operations to be implemented, the ECB Guidelines on the implementation of the monetary policy framework must be met. First, the bank must be considered financially sound.[18] Second, adequate collateral must be provided to avoid any losses for the Central Bank. The latter situation could go against Article 123 of the TFUE, which forbids central banks to carry out monetary financing, since this is a specific task of governments.[19] The ECB has often argued in favour of this position, stating that

[17] Conventional open market operations, whose function is to inject or drain liquidity from the System, include: (i) main refinancing operations (MRO), with weekly frequency and maturity; (ii) longer-term refinancing operations (LTRO), with a duration of three months. Non-conventional operations include: (i) three-year LTROs, which in recent years have been a complement to ordinary operations; (ii) TLTRO (targeted longer-term refinancing operations), transactions that provide financing to banks for periods of up to four years at advantageous conditions to facilitate credit conditions to the private sector and stimulate banks to finance the real economy; (iii) APP (asset purchases programmes), additional programmes introduced in 2009 to support growth in the euro area in line with the goal of keeping inflation below, but close to, 2%; (iv) PELTROs (pandemic emergency longer-term refinancing operations), seven operations decided on 30 April 2020 to provide liquidity support to the financial system of the euro area and ensure favourable market conditions during the pandemic period; (v) PEPP (pandemic emergency purchase programme), a temporary programme announced on 18 March 2020 in the amount of €750 billion, lasting until 31 December 2020 and designed in response to the unprecedented health emergency for the monetary union.

[18] Eligibility criteria must be met by all counterparties submitting offers for monetary policy operations and are defined in Article 55 of the 'Guideline (EU) 2015/510 of the ECB of 19 December 2014 on the implementation of the Eurosystem monetary policy framework'. The participation of banks in monetary policy operations is subject to the maintenance, on an ongoing basis, of financial strength requirements on an individual and consolidated basis. The Eurosystem may adopt discretionary—and prudential—measures aimed at suspending, excluding or limiting access to the operations of counterparties that do not comply with the capital, liquidity and debt requirements set by EU Regulation 575/2013 (Article 158 of the ECB Guideline).

[19] Article 123(1) of the Treaty prohibits overdraft facilities or any other type of credit facility with the ECB or with the NCBs in favour of EU institutions, bodies, offices or agencies, central governments, regional, local or other public authorities, other bodies governed by public law, or public undertakings of Member States. It also prohibits the

central banks should not be concerned with providing liquidity for resolution, but should only be involved in the management of resolution measures.[20]

b. In addition to ordinary operations, emergency liquidity assistance (ELA) can be granted by national central banks under strict conditions, such as haircuts and applicable interest rates. ELA can be granted to solvent banks with temporary liquidity shortages, outside the framework of the single monetary policy.[21]

Through these transactions, the Central Bank can provide, on a discretionary basis, credit of last resort in the form of temporary loans under adequate guarantees. The extraordinary loans can be either liquidity disbursement or guaranteed securities lending.

Although ELA is regulated and paid for by central banks, it is not unconditional. The ECB can limit ELA if it deems it to interfere with its monetary policy or the objectives of the Eurosystem. Furthermore, central banks do not seem willing to supply ELA to problematic banks, as recent experiences have shown.

According to ordinary rules, when the bank being restructured already benefits from central bank lines of credit, its access to the monetary policy of the Eurosystem could be frozen at a certain level and it may be unable to resort to the central bank whenever its capital is deemed insufficient. This was the case for the recent banking crises in Italy, when the banks did not meet their minimum capital requirements, even if temporarily. And this happened despite the fact that the restructuring plan had already been approved, which would have allowed the bank to comply with regulatory capital requirements at the end of the restructuring process. Therefore, if

purchase by the ECB or NCBs of debt instruments directly from these public-sector entities.

[20] See Y. MERSCH, *The Limits of Central Bank Financing in Resolution*, IMFS Distinguished Lecture Series Goethe University Frankfurt, January 2018: 'Liquidity provision by central banks in the event of resolution must not be assumed *ex-ante*, even though the possibility is not excluded provided the specific rules and objectives of the Eurosystem are followed. The provision of central bank liquidity will be the independent and ad hoc decision of the Eurosystem under the respective frameworks for monetary policy and potential emergency lending not interfering with monetary policy'. On this, see also EUROPEAN CENTRAL BANK, Convergence Report, June 2020.

[21] EUROPEAN CENTRAL BANK, *Agreement on Emergency Liquidity Assistance*, May 2017.

a bank does not meet its capital requirements, even if for a short time, it may be considered insolvent and unworthy of central bank liquidity support.

For example, in the recent cases of Banca Carige and Banca Popolare di Bari, the FITD had to carry out advance interventions to replenish the temporary capital shortfalls before the governing bodies of the banks had formally approved the capital increase. This was necessary to prevent the bank being declared insolvent and losing access to central bank liquidity support.

Clear inconsistencies exist. The FITD can carry out preventive measures, after the resolution and supervision authorities have declared that the bank is not in resolution and that the conditions for resolution do not apply (Article 11(3)(a) and (4) DGSD). The same rule is not applicable for accessing central bank liquidity support. It is therefore difficult for banks undergoing restructuring to access emergency liquidity. This could accelerate the deterioration of a bank towards insolvency. It seems that central banks' money is not available just when it is most needed.

From the picture provided, it follows that the issue of liquidity funding is vital and yet not adequately addressed in the European banking crisis management framework. Uncertainty is widespread. To solve this problem, we would need to assume that, by definition, the bank in resolution is solvent after resolution measures are applied as part of a feasible resolution programme. The assessment of the financial soundness of the bank would be implicitly made by the supervisory or resolution authorities when they approve the resolution measures. The same approach would have to be implemented for DGS preventive interventions, following the supervisory statement, in agreement with the resolution authority, that the bank is not in resolution and that the conditions for resolution are not met.

Therefore, a bank which has been or is being recapitalised following a resolution action should be considered a typical 'Bagehot case', because the bank, although solvent, can still be illiquid and in need for financial resources.

In addition to the central bank's last resort lines of credit, a bank in resolution could also use the resolution fund. Pursuant to Article 101(1)(b) of the BRRD (Article 79 of Legislative Decree No 180/2015), the fund can provide loans to the bank in resolution, its subsidiaries, a bridge bank or an asset management vehicle, or it can grant guarantees on assets and liabilities. However, this source of liquidity is limited, since the Single Resolution Fund alone cannot cover all liquidity needs. Once its revision is finalised, the ESM should contribute.[22] Alternatively, national governments should guarantee a public backstop mechanism for ELA operations carried out by central banks.[23] Likewise, it does not seem feasible that, outside resolution, liquidity support could be provided by deposit guarantee schemes, when they carry out preventive intervention, given that their primary function is to protect depositors (see Chapter 12).

The ongoing debate in the Eurozone has again brought to the fore the issue of liquidity funding. A recent proposal is to establish a Eurosystem Resolution Liquidity facility, which would be tasked with providing the necessary liquidity in resolution. The centralisation in the ECB of this emergency liquidity tool could be useful.[24]

[22] EUROPEAN COMMISSION, *How to Provide Liquidity to Banks After Resolution in Europe's Banking Union*, Econ, November 2018: 'Only the ECB is able to provide liquidity credibly to large banks after resolution. A scheme solely relying on the Single Resolution Fund, even if it could draw on the European Stability Mechanism (ESM), would not be credible as it has limited firing power. But in the absence of appropriate collateral, the ECB would need to get a public guarantee against possible fiscal risks'. To this regard, see European Commission (2018). This Paper proposes a solution to meet the liquidity needs of banks in resolution through the use of the SRF. In this sense, it is observed that 'There are several solutions under consideration for addressing the liquidity needs of banks that have just been through resolution and need to regain market confidence'. This Paper proposes to introduce a Transitional Liquidity Assistance (TLA). This would provide ECB liquidity support for resolved banks based on an SRF guarantee. This SRF guarantee would be based on potential further commitments from banks to the fund. These commitments would be maximum 0.125% of covered deposits per year. Such annual contributions are similar to the current contributions during the build-up of the fund and would only be required at the moment that the guarantees are called on. The TLA should only be provided under strict conditions to lower the risk of the funds being called on. TLA returns the lender of last resort function to the ECB. See also S. FERNANDEZ DE LIS, J. GARCIA, *Funding Before and in Resolution. A Proposal for a Funding in Resolution Mechanism*, May 2018.

[23] The topic is now to the attention of the European authorities. In the Eurogroup meeting of 3 November 2020, some options were presented to secure the liquidity needs of banks under resolution. One option is the issuance of securities by the SRB, which could be used by banks in resolution as collateral for loans granted by the ECB. Another option is the issue of a guarantee by the SRB on the liabilities of the bank under resolution. A further option provides for the joint intervention of the ESM and the SRB in the provision of liquidity. All these possible solutions will be again examined by the Eurogroup during the meetings scheduled for 2021.

[24] EUROPEAN PARLIAMENT, *The Financing of Bank Resolution—Who Should Provide the Required Liquidity?*, Economic Governance Support Unit (EGOV) Directorate-General for Internal Policies PE 624.420, June 2018. This document shows

Diverging opinions have been expressed. Many believe that governments should provide liquidity in resolution. It is interesting to note that in the United States and the United Kingdom, central banks can access Treasury guarantees to provide liquidity to banks under resolution. However, to be effective, this instrument should be applicable for all types of intervention for the restructuring of the insolvent bank, including preventive and alternative interventions by DGSs.

Another interesting proposal that has been put forward is the 'Pawnbroker For All Seasons' (PFAS).[25] With the PFAS, the central bank (the *pawnbroker*) would pledge liquidity support to banks, at any time (any *season*), against the provision of adequate collateral. This form of financing would be available regardless of the conditions of the banks and would contribute to eliminating the stigma of resorting to emergency liquidity. The basic idea of this proposal is to allow each bank to pledge a certain amount of assets as collateral to the central bank and, based on a haircut, to know in advance how much liquidity it can obtain from the central bank in case of need.

Therefore, awareness is increasing in Europe on the importance of liquidity funding in crisis situations. Many interesting proposals have been made in support of the new crisis management framework, in order to make the whole resolution toolkit more feasible and credible.

Rules and procedures must be clear and simple. To this end, close cooperation and communication between governments, central banks, supervisory and resolution authorities is crucial in the delicate pre- and post-resolution phases. Cooperation is needed for central banks to quickly gather all the information about the bank's current and projected situation, the instruments that have been implemented and the availability of collateral or other forms of guarantees.

that the centralisation of the ELA in the ECB would not require amendments to the Treaty but would still require a backstop mechanism outside the ECB, which cannot provide monetary financing. The paper also investigates the problem of liquidity in resolution, analysing whether the current mechanisms need to be redesigned to provide adequate resolution support. The question is being analysed by the Eurogroup and private actors. Among these, the Association for Financial Markets in Europe (AFME) advocates for the introduction of a European instrument for the financing of resolution with the involvement of the ECB and SRF (which would also handle the backstop).

[25] M. KING, *The End of Alchemy, Money, Banking, and the End of the Global Economy*, March 2016.

The primary role of supervisory and resolution authorities is to determine whether the bank is viable during and after a resolution. They should confirm the credibility, feasibility and effectiveness of the resolution programme. Next, the central bank should decide if and when to intervene by providing emergency liquidity assistance to the bank.

Liquidity support is undoubtedly crucial in banking crisis management. The central banks should play a central role in pre-resolution and resolution by providing lines of credit. Specific legislation, based on more flexible conditions, should be adopted to provide for such a support.

CHAPTER 11

Public Intervention in Crises

History has taught us that sometimes, when financial stability is at risk, public intervention is unavoidable because the private sector (shareholders, creditors, banks) cannot bear the costs alone.

Financial stability is a public good and a priority for governments.

The Italian experience has shown that the regulatory framework for public interventions in banking crises is still incomplete, not fully effective and hampered by concerns relating to competition rules.

1 The Role of Public Intervention

The transition from bail-out to bail-in seems to have been an abrupt innovation in the banking crisis management system. That is why the use of public resources for the resolution of banks has come under wide criticism and is seen as a substantial departure from the BRRD.[1]

[1] Among others, see STANDARD & POOR'S, *Continued Bank Bail-outs Stretch The Credibility of Europe's Resolution Framework*, February 2020; T. PHILIPPON, A. SALORD, *Bail-ins and Bank Resolution in Europe: A Progress Report*, Geneva Reports on the World Economy Special Report 4, CEPR, ICMB International Center for Monetary and Banking Studies, March 2017.

G. Boccuzzi, *Banking Crises in Italy*, Palgrave Studies in Financial Instability and Banking Crisis Regulation,
https://doi.org/10.1007/978-3-031-01344-7_11

But things are different, because governments may be legally justified in resorting to public resources when this is necessary to avoid disruptive effects on the financial system and the economy. This approach has always been followed in financial history, from the twentieth century until the 2007–2009 global financial crisis. The same happened in the recent banking crises in Italy. Financial stability is a public good because it underpins economic growth and social stability.

However, financial stability comes at a cost. If stability is threatened, someone has to pay the cost of preserving it: shareholders and creditors and, in extreme conditions, taxpayers are called upon to pay. But the sacrifice of creditors is not always better than that of taxpayers. Indeed, past crises have shown that it is the State that is the 'last resort' when creditors have to be sheltered from the worst effects of banking crises. Only the State has the resources and a stretchable balance sheet. So, the principle of public responsibility is key.

The BRRD allows for public intervention under special conditions. The directive states that, in the extraordinary scenario of systemic crisis, the resolution authority can use 'government financial stabilisation tools' as a last resort for the financing of resolution (Articles 56-58 BRRD). The BRRD allows for some flexibility. Specific State interventions can also be carried out outside the resolution procedure. Figure 1 lists the numerous tools that can be used within—and outside—a resolution procedure.

Government financial stabilisation tools can be implemented as part of resolution and are added to the resolution authority's standard toolkit. In accordance with State aid rules, they provide extraordinary public financial support to help resolve a bank and avoid the disruptive effects of liquidation.[2]

These tools are applicable under certain conditions. A bail-in of at least 8% of the bank's total liabilities, including own funds,[3] must be applied and approval under the rules on State aid must be obtained

[2] Based on the definition provided by Article 1(1)(28) of the BRRD, '"extraordinary public financial support" means State aid within the meaning of Article 107(1) TFEU, or any other public financial support at supra-national level, which, if provided for at national level, would constitute State aid, that is provided in order to preserve or restore the viability, liquidity or solvency of an institution [...] or of a group of which such an institution or entity forms part'.

[3] It was argued that the bail-in level (8% of liabilities) was set at a high value, in order to minimise the use of public intervention, considering that during the financial crisis, on average, the losses suffered by banks insolvent were far below that level. On the subject, V.

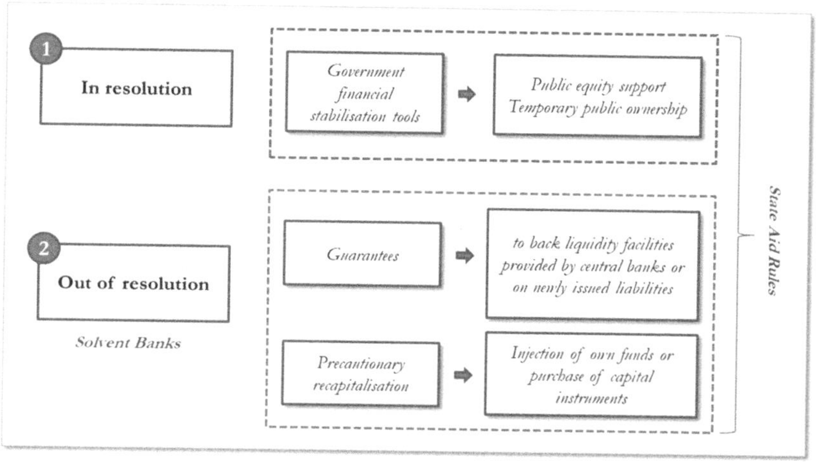

Fig. 1 Public intervention in the BRRD

(Article 37(10) BRRD). Only the government, in collaboration with the resolution authority, can activate public measures.

Public intervention can be done in two ways:

i. Public equity support;
ii. Temporary public ownership.

Both forms are last resort solutions to maintain financial stability when other resolution tools have been exhausted.

Public equity support can be used only if the conditions for resolution are met and if the authorities determine that: (1) standard resolution tools are ineffective in avoiding negative effects on financial stability; (2) standard resolution tools would not protect public interest, if the institution has previously received extraordinary liquidity assistance from the central bank.

Temporary public ownership can be applied if the authority establishes that the application of resolution tools would not be sufficient to

COSTANCIO, *Challenges for the European Banking industry*, Lecture at the Conference on *European Banking Industry: What's Next?*, University of Navarra, Madrid, July 2016.

protect public interest, **where** the institution has already benefited from public equity support. In these cases, authorities may transfer shares to a nominee of the Member State or to a wholly State-owned company (Article 58 of the BRRD).

Member States may participate in the recapitalisation of an institution through Common Equity Tier 1 instruments or through Additional Tier 1 or Tier 2 instruments.

Italian legislation (Legislative Decree No 180/2015) has not yet incorporated the extraordinary public support tools provided for by the Directive.

The only form of extraordinary public financial intervention in Italy is precautionary recapitalisation under Article 32(4(d)) of the directive, which is applicable outside resolution in certain situations and under specific conditions (Article 18 of Legislative Decree No 180/2015). This would apply only to solvent banks and only if burden sharing is applied before the intervention of the State. In Italy, Banca MPS was the only case in which precautionary recapitalisation was applied (see Chapter 5).

Some uncertainties in the legislation and subsequent interpretative issues have sparked an ongoing debate on precautionary recapitalisation.[4] The most controversial issue is the application of the reduction and/or conversion of capital instruments (burden sharing).

In the BRRD, precautionary recapitalisation is an exception to the principle that public intervention in itself entails that the bank is failing or likely to fail (Article 32(4)(d), Article 18 of Legislative Decree No 180/2015), because it is applicable only to solvent banks having a capital shortfall and under specific conditions. This measure is meant to prevent or remedy serious disturbances to the economy and financial stability.

[4] For more details on the legislation, see W.P. DE GROPEN, *Precautionary Recapitalisation: Time for a review*, Centre for European Policy Studies (CEPS), June 2017. The paper notes that precautionary recapitalisation was limited to two Greek banks and to MPS in Italy. It is also argued that: 'While precautionary recapitalisation is a legitimate instrument for bank crisis management, the conditions set for it by BRRD are restrictive and have so far been effective to prevent its inappropriate use on insolvent banks. Nevertheless, the European Stability Mechanism should be empowered to participate in future precautionary recapitalisations'.

However, if the bank is not failing or likely to fail, how would the reduction or conversion of capital (burden sharing)[5] actually be applied, as provided for in point 43 of the 2013 Communication on State aid? Furthermore, the decision-making process and powers need further clarification with regard to the assessment of solvency conditions, the amount of losses and recapitalisation and the prospective dangers to financial stability. Supervisory authorities and governments are entrusted with these assessments. They interact with the European Commission which is responsible for applying the State aid rules. To this end, clearer interaction processes should be defined to increase the legal certainty of the administrative procedures.

Pre-determined and formalised procedures would help to expedite decision-making and increase the credibility of the whole crisis management system put in place for the effective solutions of banking crises.

Article 105 of the BRRD allows the national Resolution Fund to receive financial support from third parties should its resources be insufficient. The State itself may grant loans to the Resolution Fund, although the legislation does not expressly state this. With the Single Resolution Mechanism (SRM), the national compartments operating within the Single Resolution Fund (SRF)[6] are supported in the transitional phase by bridge financing arrangements such as lines of credit granted by the State to the respective national compartment, as agreed with the Single Resolution Board (SRB).[7] It is a last resort mechanism which, together with the

[5] The disbursement of public funds automatically determines the application of the rules on State aid and, consequently, of the rules on burden sharing provided for in the 2013 Commission Communication. In this regard, point 43 provides that, if the bank that has the capital shortfall has a capital ratio above the regulatory minimum, 'the bank should normally be able to restore the capital position on its own, in particular through capital raising measures as set out in point 35'. If there are no other possibilities, including any other supervisory action such as early intervention measures or other remedial actions to overcome the shortfall as confirmed by the competent supervisory or resolution authority, then subordinated debt must be converted into equity, in principle before State aid is granted.

[6] The national compartments, into which the resources to be transferred to the central level flow, are destined to disappear at the end of the transitional period foreseen for the achievement of the target level of the SRF.

[7] The SRB completed the procedures for signing the framework agreements with the Eurozone countries in February 2017. In Italy, the 2016 Stability Law (Article 1(880-881) provided for the provision of bridging loans up to a maximum total amount of €5,753 million.

transfers between national compartments, is meant to provide resources for resolution in case of need.

The debate on the SRF emergency resources is centred on the 'common backstop', as part of the reform of the European Stability Mechanism (ESM). The 'common backstop' would help to strengthen the credibility and intervention potential of the Single Resolution Fund by providing additional support whenever resources would be insufficient for an intervention mandated by the SRB. The ESM reform and the introduction of the common backstop in 2022 were agreed in November 2020.

Box 1: The European Stability Mechanism (ESM)

The European Stability Mechanism (ESM) is the permanent crisis management fund in Europe, introduced in October 2012 to replace the temporary European Financial Stability Facility (EFSF). The establishment of the ESM took place through an intergovernmental treaty, signed by the EU countries on 2 February 2012.

The ESM is ruled by the Board of Governors, made up of the finance ministers of the euro area States; the Commission's Commissioner for Economic Affairs also takes part as an observer.

The financing method of the ESM is based on the issuance of debt securities, with a maturity of 1 to 30 years, placed with institutional investors through syndicated loans, auctions or private placement. The functions of the ESM have evolved over the years and can be summarised as follows.

1. **Support to Member States**. The fundamental function of the ESM is to provide financial assistance, subject to specific conditions, to those Member States which—despite having a sustainable public debt—are in temporary difficulties in raising finance on the market;
2. **Bank recapitalisation instrument**. With the launch of the SSM in November 2014, the mandate of the ESM was extended to the direct and indirect recapitalisation of failing or likely-to-fail banks. On 9 September 2019, a proposal to amend the founding Treaty aimed at renewing the governance,

stabilisation functions and operational capabilities of the ESM was presented. The reform focuses on the following points:

- **common backstop of the Single Resolution Fund**: The ESM is given the function of common backstop to the SRF (Single Resolution Fund), through the provision of a credit line intended to enter into force at the latest on 1 January 2024 (end of the transitional period for the establishment of the SRF). The common backstop will act as lender of last resort, if the SRF does not have the necessary resources and the Single Resolution Board is not able to collect sufficient ex-post contributions or fails to activate loans at affordable rates. At the end of 2019, the maximum amount of the loan was agreed (€68 billion), together with the operating procedures and the decision-making procedures for the activation of the backstop[8]. This agreement provides for the possibility of early backstop introduction by political decision of the Eurogroup and the European Council during 2020, in the light of a risk reduction assessment conducted by the competent authorities in accordance with agreed guidelines, with regard to progress in the establishment of the MREL requirement and the reduction of NPEs;
- **Precautional credit lines**: the aim of the reform is to make the ESM's precautionary credit lines more effective, through the introduction of: (i) the PCCL (Precautionary Conditioned Credit Line); (ii) the ECCL (Enhanced Conditions Credit Line). The eligibility criteria for the PCCL would be the government deficit (no more than 3% of GDP) a budget equal to or above the minimum benchmark of the country and a deficit/GDP ratio of less than 60%; otherwise, the ECCL

[8] EUROGROUP, *Letter of the President of the Eurogroup to the President of the Euro Summit*, 5 December 2019; EU COUNCIL, *Remarks by Mário Centeno Following the Eurogroup meeting of 4 December 2019*; EUROPEAN STABILITY MECHANISM, *The reform of the European Stability Mechanism, Discussion Paper No 14*, September 2020. See also *Terms of reference of the common backstop to the Single Resolution Fund*, 4 December 2018.

credit line would be open to countries not aligned with the PCCL criteria;

- **bank assistance**: the review concerns the more significant role of the ESM in the preparation and supervision of bank assistance programmes. In addition, each future Memorandum of Understanding will be signed by both the ESM and the Commission and both will monitor the risks for financial stability and debt sustainability;

3. **Pandemic Crisis Support.** In response to the Covid-19 pandemic, a credit line called 'Pandemic Crisis Support' was activated, aimed at financing direct and indirect health care at zero rate. It is made available to all euro area countries for an amount equal to 2% of the national GDP at the end of 2019.

On 30 November 2020, the Eurogroup voted in favour of the reform and the early introduction of the backstop mechanism in 2022. The ESM Treaty amendment agreements were signed on 27 January 2021, initiating the ratification process by Member States.

In addition to such measures, as required by the European directive, it would be appropriate to consider introducing a national public intervention tool, to be applied in extreme situations. We should always be ready to face up to all types of pathological phenomena, not resolvable only with ordinary instruments and private resources. Preparing the intervention tool while the crisis is ongoing is difficult and risky, also because it requires political consensus, which in itself is hard to achieve. The measures adopted for banks in response to the Covid-19 crisis are a good example, marked by excessive shyness with respect to the prospective complexity that such a situation can determine.

This leads us to a simple conclusion: a more flexible national public intervention instrument is necessary.

Finally, some recent crisis events, in Italy and abroad, require us to reflect more on a specific case of public intervention: when a capital injection by the State is not considered State aid. This happens when the State—or a designated public institution—intervenes in accordance with the market investor rule, that is, when any disbursement would guarantee a return in line with market conditions. This was the case in Italy for the intervention by the State-controlled Mediocredito Centrale in support of Banca Popolare di Bari.[9]

That case was unique in that the possibility of State support was not ruled out per se but was dependent upon certain conditions established by a Commission Communication and not by primary legislation. Hence, although real State resources were deployed, they cannot be truly considered 'State' aid, inasmuch as the State acted like a private investor.

In particular, in order to determine whether the investment by a public entity cannot be considered State aid, we must evaluate whether a private investor, in similar circumstances, would have made the same investment.

The difference with the Tercas case is evident. The resources used for Banca Tercas were private since they came from the banking sector. However, they became 'public' because FITD's activity was typical of institutions with public mandates.

Public intervention is a complex issue. The legislation has four types of public intervention, each having its own set of rules. Although this allows flexibility, it also leaves ample room for uncertainty. The framework for public intervention remains ambiguous and those areas should be reviewed to design a solid regulatory basis and unequivocal procedures.

[9] Similar cases have recently been recorded in Europe, including the German bank Norddeutsche Landesbank (NordLb), the Portuguese Caixa Geral de Depósitos (Cgd) and the Romanian Cec Bank. NordLb is a commercial bank located in Lower Saxony, Saxony-AnhalteeMecklenburg-Western Pomerania. It performs the functions of a central bank and provides compensation for savings banks (Sparkassen). As such, in 2011 NordLb received around €500 million from Lower Saxony and around €100 million from the Associations of Savings banks. In 2019, the European Commission concluded that the business plan developed by the German public authorities to strengthen the equity position of NordLb did not constitute State aid, as the plan would be implemented under market conditions. An investment of approximately €2.8 billion of public funds was envisaged. Caixa Geral de Depósitos (Cgd) was the largest bank in Portugal and was wholly State-owned. In 2012, due to Cgd's solvency problems, Portugal implemented recapitalisation measures with the subscription of newly issued ordinary shares of Cgd for €750 million, and the subscription of Cgd convertible instruments for €900 million. Private investors also participated in the recapitalisation. The Commission considered these measures to be State aid compatible with the internal market based on the restructuring plan. In 2016, Portugal informed the Commission that Cgd was unlikely to reach all the targets of the 2013 plan and notified the Commission of further recapitalisation measures and an updated business plan. Cec Bank was the seventh largest bank in Romania, owned by the State since 1864. In 2019, the European Commission declared that the recapitalisation of €200 million proposed by the State in Cec Bank did not constitute State aid, on the ground that it would be performed under market conditions.

2 Public Intervention During the Covid-19 Crisis

The need for a public intervention toolkit has become evident with the outbreak of the Covid-19 pandemic. The Commission updated the guidelines on State aid in the Temporary Framework by introducing greater flexibility for public intervention in favour of families and businesses.[10] These measures are very far-reaching and all countries are now using them.

Before the pandemic, such increased flexibility would have been unthinkable.

The Temporary Framework has also concerned the banking sector, though to a lesser degree. It introduced public intervention to support those banks that have been highly impacted by the pandemic. The Temporary Framework, especially paragraph 7, states that if banks need public support in the form of liquidity, recapitalisation or impaired assets, they can receive it without being considered failing or likely to fail. This is an exception to the already mentioned general BRRD rule which states that when a bank needs extraordinary public support it should be considered failing or likely to fail—without the need for further evaluation by the authorities—and undergo resolution or compulsory administrative liquidation.

However, the BRRD too (Article 32(4)(d)(i), (ii) and (iii)) provides that the condition of failing or likely to fail is not triggered if the extraordinary public intervention is carried out in favour of banks deemed solvent 'in order to remedy a serious disturbance in the economy of a Member State and preserve financial stability'. In this case, public intervention must be in the form of:

i. A State guarantee to back liquidity facilities provided by central banks;
ii. A State guarantee on newly issued liabilities; or
iii. A precautionary recapitalisation under specific conditions.[11]

[10] EUROPEAN COMMISSION, *Communication from the Commission Temporary Framework for State aid Measures to Support the Economy in the Current COVID-19 Outbreak*, 2020/C 91 I/01, March 2020.

[11] Transactions limited to injections necessary to address capital shortfalls established in stress tests at national, EU or Member State level, asset quality reviews or similar exercises conducted by the European Central Bank, EBA or national authorities, and confirmed by the competent authority.

In short, the framework considers Covid-19 to be a 'serious disturbance in the economy' and, as such, to justify the exception provided for by the BRRD. Paragraph 45 of the 2013 Communication on State aid to the banking sector also applies in this case, allowing for an exception to the burden-sharing principle if financial stability is at risk.

The framework adopted in response to the Covid-19 emergency was an important signal from the European authorities. It introduced necessary exceptions to the general rules. But it was a weak signal for the banking sector, because it did not take into account the potential extent of systemic events, particularly with regard to the deterioration of loans granted to firms and households.[12] In fact, the new framework added an emergency measure to an act (the 2013 Communication) whose rigidity makes it ill-equipped to deal with the possible serious impacts of macroeconomic changes on the banking sector. In any case, it remains to be seen how the European authorities would have applied the new guidelines, especially precautionary recapitalisations or other preventive measures, without burden sharing.

3 What Strategies for Putting Nationalised Banks Back on the Market?

One of the most important issues connected to public intervention is the timing and modalities for the exit of the State after having acquired banks in crisis. Recent Italian experiences showed how complex it can be to sell nationalised banks on the market as part of the crisis resolution process. The same goes for banks sold to bridge banks in resolution and banks acquired by deposit guarantee schemes in preventive interventions. These measures, which focus on the bank's capital, have the common trait of temporariness, since the acquisition is destined to last only for the time it takes to restructure the bank in view of its return to the market.

[12] For a forecast of the impact of the Covid-19 pandemic on NPEs, see MALINCONICO (2020). The issue on how to deal with the possible increase of NPEs is at the centre of the political, economic and regulatory debate. It would be important to establish Asset Management Companies (AMCs) to acquire deteriorated loans at fair prices that would not diminish their value and safeguard the assets of the bank. On this, see A. ENRIA, *Public Hearing at the Committee on Economic and Monetary Affairs*, Brussels, October 2020. He stressed the need for a European initiative to set up a network of national AMCs through common funding mechanisms and prices.

This is the approach of the BRRD. The directive states that the banks under temporary public ownership are to be managed on a commercial and professional basis and sold to the private sector as soon as commercial and financial circumstances allow it. Since the bank's restructuring plan is subject to the approval of the European Commission with regard to State aid rules, it is for the EC to determine the timing and manner of the exit of the government or the public institution from the bank. In the absence of a specific provision, the same rule applies to precautionary recapitalisation measures.

As concerns bridge banks, Articles 40-41 of the BRRD state that they can be wholly or partially owned by one or more public authorities. This may include the resolution authority or the resolution fund which acquires control of the bank.[13] The resolution authority should terminate the operation of the bridge bank as soon as possible and, in any case, within two years from the last transaction by the bank in resolution. This is what happened in Italy in the case of the four banks in resolution, when the European Commission asked the Bank of Italy, as resolution authority, to sell the bridge banks within a short timeframe.

The FITD's Statute is also clear about the temporary nature of the Fund's acquisition of a shareholding in a bank. It states that the Fund must be involved in the bank's operation only for the time necessary to conclude its divestment in favourable economic conditions.

But recent experience has shown that it takes time to prop up a bank, restore its long-term viability and search for any potential buyers. Especially after the financial crisis, returning banks to the market was difficult due to the low profitability of the banking sector and the non-attractiveness of the business model for investors who are aware of the higher risks in a bank that has been or is being restructured. The purchase conditions might be penalising for the seller, with potential buyers often demanding safeguards for equity-neutral operations and against potential risks.

[13] The resolution authority decides that a bridge bank is no longer such if: (a) the bridge bank merges with another entity; (b) the bridge bank ceases to meet the requirements of Article 40(2); (c) all or substantially all the assets, rights and liabilities of the bridge bank are sold to a third party; (d) the period referred to in paragraph 5 or, if applicable, in paragraph 6 expires; e. the bridge bank's assets are completely liquidated and its liabilities are completely discharged.

In such a context, imposing a short time limit for the sale can be counterproductive. If the restructuring process is still ongoing and its effects are not yet fully visible, the seller might incur significant losses.

Therefore, the need arises to review the BRRD as regards temporary ownership, precautionary recapitalisation and transfer to bridge banks. Flexibility mechanisms should be introduced to choose how and when to place back on the market recovered banks and guarantee the best outcome of public intervention. As a consequence, whenever there is a shortage of potential buyers or excessively penalising sale conditions, it would make sense for the bank to remain longer in public hands. The case of Banca MPS exemplifies this, inasmuch as short deadlines were imposed for its sale—at very penalising conditions if compared to the high costs of the recapitalisation—while the bank was still undergoing restructuring.

In other words, the State should take all the time necessary for the reorganisation of the bank to best prepare its return to the market. It must be able to operate as a private investor in deciding, solely on economic considerations, how and when to sell off its share.

The situation is different for banks acquired by the DGSs through preventive interventions or by bridge banks through resolution processes with resources of the resolution fund. In both cases, the sale of the bank on the market is standard practice. Deposit guarantee systems or the resolution fund are not long-term investors, but entities called upon to resolve crises. If restructuring measures require equity investments, it is therefore reasonable to believe that these will be sold to a third party when and how established by the DGS or the resolution authority. Both entities would retain full decision-making autonomy and act with a view to minimising costs.

CHAPTER 12

Deposit Guarantee Schemes: Role and Functioning in Banking Crises

There are many open issues when it comes to deposit insurance. Therefore, the European legislation regarding deposit guarantee schemes needs to be reviewed to clarify their role and functioning.

The new legal framework confers on DGSs a primary function in the financial safety net. However, uncertainties and inconsistencies remain with regard to the delicate institutional mechanisms and operations of DGSs, in particular with reference to their legal nature, mandate, the types of interventions they can carry out in crisis situations, and the conditions to which they are subjected.

The adequacy and credibility of the funding of DGSs are another critical issue, exacerbated by the lack of establishment of the third pillar of the Banking Union, i.e. EDIS, the Single European Deposit Insurance scheme.

1 Is the Legal Nature of DGSs Relevant? Or just Their Mandate?

A first critical aspect that emerged in Europe and Italy concerns the legal nature—public or private—of deposit guarantee schemes (DGSs). The problem lies in the fact that the insurance of bank deposits is a public

G. Boccuzzi, *Banking Crises in Italy*, Palgrave Studies in Financial Instability and Banking Crisis Regulation,
https://doi.org/10.1007/978-3-031-01344-7_12

function; it is an instrument set up by States to guarantee depositors, within certain limits, in the event of bank insolvency. This tool is instrumental to financial stability, a public good of primary importance. Hence, deposit guarantee systems are fundamental in the safety nets and public policies in place in the various jurisdictions to strengthen confidence in the banking sector.

In the theoretical debate and in the opinions expressed by international bodies, the issue of the legal nature of the DGSs has arisen with reference to the compatibility of a private entity with its public function. Particular attention is focused on the fact that DGSs are part of a system in which the other components of the financial safety net (banking supervision, resolution, lending of last resort) are carried out by public entities; this may impose limits on the exchange of information, which is crucial for the prevention of financial instability, and especially in the case of interventions in favour of banks in crisis, which involve access to confidential information.

It should be noted that, internationally, there is not just one model, as both public and private DGSs exist. While the majority of DGSs are public, there are also several private ones. According to a recent survey conducted by IADI (International Association of Deposit Insurers) on the legal nature of its member deposit guarantee schemes (overall 87, as of 2020), 66% are public (56% are government legislated and administered, and 10% are central bank administered).[1] This heterogeneity depends on a variety of factors, attributable to the specific choices made by individual legal systems, linked to historical and political reasons, as well as the peculiarity of the financial system and other institutional variables. As a matter of fact, there is ample evidence of the compatibility of the private nature of DGSs with the public function they exercise.

The IADI international standards do not prioritise any legal configuration of DGSs, focusing instead on governance, meaning the way the systems should be managed and governed in order to ensure their autonomy and independence. The Core Principles, in particular Core Principle 3, state that DGSs must be operationally independent, transparent, and free from any political or industry interference.

[1] INTERNATIONAL ASSOCIATION OF DEPOSIT INSURERS, *Chart Pack Research Unit*, June 2020.

In this framework of neutrality regarding the legal nature of DGSs, the position expressed by the IMF (International Monetary Fund) in the context of the FSAP[2] is clearly in favour of public systems, as evidenced by its observations and recommendations of recent years relating to private DGSs. Why is it important for the IMF that deposit insurers be public? What are the benefits in terms of stronger crisis management capacity?

On governance, the IMF emphasises the risk of possible conflicts of interest that may arise in the management of private DGSs, which normally have bank representatives participating in decision-making bodies. Hence, the suggestion to exclude active bankers from the management bodies, to strengthen the independence of DGSs. The IMF also emphasises other benefits of the transition of private DGSs to public status, in terms of: exchange of supervisory information; full participation of the system in the contingency planning framework; access to public backstops; legal protection for management and staff.

The issue is very delicate and not easy to solve, since it involves changing long-established legal and organisational set-ups of DGSs that have ensured the protection of depositors, including by carrying out alternative interventions to the reimbursement of depositors. Ultimately, there is no concrete evidence of conflicts of interest when it comes to carrying out interventions in favour of banks in crisis.

After all, in many jurisdictions—including Italy—there are numerous examples of private entities carrying out public functions. Furthermore, it is possible to mitigate—if not eliminate—any potential conflict of interest connected to the presence of bank representatives in the bodies of the DGS through clear corporate governance rules aimed at strengthening independence and autonomy, as well as through the introduction of statutory constraints in the decision-making processes of the governing bodies, adequate control systems and rigorous rules of conduct.

The Italian experience has moved in this direction, introducing in the FITD's Statute specific rules to manage potential conflicts of interest, through specific governance provisions, effective internal control systems

[2] The FSAP (Financial Sector Assessment Program) is an in-depth analysis of a country's financial sector carried out by the International Monetary Fund for developed economies and by the International Monetary Fund and the World Bank for emerging economies. See International Monetary Fund (2019).

and the affirmation of shared values, included in the Code of Ethics and Conduct.

It follows that the composition of the bodies, and therefore the presence of bankers in the governing bodies of private DGSs, does not necessarily cause undue interference in decision-making on institutional interventions. In fact, for reimbursement of depositors and resolution, the decisions of the DGS are bound by law, which confers on the Supervisory and Resolution authorities the decision-making powers regarding the liquidation or the resolution of the bank. Therefore, the discretionary scope of the DGS regarding when, how and to what extent to intervene for the reimbursement of depositors and for the contribution to resolution funding is minimal or null.

For all other types of interventions, namely preventive and alternative, which are carried out on a voluntary basis, the least cost principle applies. Therefore, the choice of carrying out these interventions stems from the consideration that they would be less costly than the reimbursement of depositors. Even the access to confidential information about the bank can be carefully handled through clear and effective internal governance rules and procedures.

Furthermore, the private nature of a DGS should not be relevant when it comes to the role of deposit guarantee systems within the safety net, as there should be no obstacles to establishing a formalised framework of collaboration and information exchange, to be defined in a Memorandum of Understanding signed by all safety net participants. In this context, the role of the DGS—regardless of its legal nature—in the institutional framework for the prevention and management of systemic crises and participation to simulation exercises should be defined.

Finally, similar considerations apply with regard to the DGSs' access to emergency financing, since what matters is their institutional function. The repayment of loans is based on the power of the DGSs, including private ones, to collect resources from the banking sector, on a mandatory basis. In this regard, it is important to note that the effective financial capacity of intervention of DGSs is, by definition, limited. The international experience, as also authoritatively highlighted in the literature, shows that deposit guarantee systems, by nature, can only manage crises of smaller banks, where they are limited in number. Therefore, to manage large-scale interventions, or in the event of the simultaneous crisis of many small and medium-sized banks, the DGS cannot have sufficient existing resources or readily obtain them from the banks. Hence, it is necessary to seek effective forms of emergency financing.

We have shown that in the current European regulatory context, the role of deposit guarantee schemes is not linked to their legal nature, but to their public policy objective, enshrined in law and/or their statutes. Their mission is the pursuit of financial stability and the protection of depositors. However, the issue must be carefully investigated, because it may have multiple regulatory implications regarding the role and the functioning of DGSs. Looking ahead, the matter will need to be weighed and regulated consistently with the establishment of the single European Deposit Guarantee Scheme (EDIS), also considering the functions that will be attributed to the national DGSs in the regulatory framework of the Banking Union.

2 Institutional Mandates and Operational Scope

International classifications identify various models of deposit guarantee schemes, depending on the functions they perform. IADI international standards identify four official mandates for DGSs: pay-box, pay-box plus, loss-minimiser and risk-minimiser.[3]

In Europe, the DGSD is in line with international standards in allowing DGSs to carry out a variety of functions. As a matter of fact, the European directive extends the mandate of DGSs beyond mandatory interventions, which are the reimbursement of depositors (Article 11(1)) and interventions in resolution processes (Article 11(2) and Article 109 BRRD) (Table 1).[4]

[3] INTERNATIONAL ASSOCIATION OF DEPOSIT INSURERS, *Core Principles for Effective Deposit Insurance System* (CPs), October 2014.

[4] Whereas recitals (3) and (16) of Directive No 2014/49/EU on Deposit Guarantee Schemes state the following principles: (3) 'In view of the costs of the failure of a credit institution to the economy as a whole and its adverse impact on financial stability and the confidence of depositors, it is desirable not only to make provision for reimbursing depositors but also to allow Member States sufficient flexibility to enable DGSs to carry out measures to reduce the likelihood of future claims against DGSs. Those measures should always comply with the State aid rules. (16): It should also be possible, where permitted under national law, for a DGS to go beyond a pure reimbursement function and to use the available financial means in order to prevent the failure of a credit institution with

Table 1 Deposit guarantee schemes and institutional mandates

Typology of guarantee scheme	*Institutional mandates*
Paybox	A mandate where the deposit insurer is only responsible for the reimbursement of insured deposits
Paybox plus	A mandate where the deposit insurer has additional responsibilities, such as certain resolution functions (e.g. financial support)
Loss minimiser	A mandate where the deposit insurer actively engages in a selection from a range of least cost resolution strategies
Risk minimiser	A mandate where a deposit insurer has comprehensive risk minimisation functions, including risk assessment/management, a full suite of early intervention and resolution powers, and in some cases prudential oversight responsibilities

Source IADI Glossary

The directive states that DGSs can also carry out preventive and alternative interventions on a voluntary basis (respectively, Article 11(3) and (6)). These are not mandatory and can be carried out only if the Member States incorporate them into national laws.

In Italy, banking law regulates this wider operational scope of DGSs, which has been applied since the creation of the DGSs themselves. Preventive interventions allow the 'resolution' of small and medium-sized banks, which do not meet the 'public interest' requirement. The legislation also introduced the least cost principle, according to which a DGS can carry out preventive and alternative interventions only if the cost of the measure is lower than the reimbursement of the depositors of the bank in liquidation.

a view to avoiding the costs of reimbursing depositors and other adverse impacts. Those measures should, however, be carried out within a clearly defined framework and should in any event comply with State aid rules. DGSs should, inter alia, have appropriate systems and procedures in place for selecting and implementing such measures and monitoring affiliated risks. Implementing such measures should be subject to the imposition of conditions on the credit institution involving at least more stringent risk-monitoring and greater verification rights for the DGSs. The costs of the measures taken to prevent the failure of a credit institution should not exceed the costs of fulfilling the statutory or contractual mandates of the respective DGS with regard to protecting covered deposits at the credit institution or the institution itself'.

The situation at the European level is more complex. There is no single framework on measures other than the reimbursement of depositors. Most national systems do not consider preventive interventions; some allow alternative interventions, in various forms, including the bulk sale of the assets and liabilities of a bank in liquidation.

The latest surveys at the European level showed that 10 out of 27 European countries have introduced in their legal frameworks the possibility of interventions in support of the en-bloc sale of the assets and liabilities of a bank in liquidation, instead of the reimbursement of depositors.[5] As for preventive interventions, the survey showed that 9 EU countries allow them and have even defined the intervention methods; however, only a few countries actually apply these operations, also in the light of the position of the Commission, which, by classifying preventive interventions as State aid measures, states that the bank is deemed failing or likely to fail, and thus resolution or liquidation should apply.

It is important to note that the prudence in applying these measures can be explained by the possible greater riskiness of preventive interventions for DGSs compared to alternative interventions.

In fact, in alternative interventions, through the sale of the assets and liabilities of the bank in liquidation, the loss for the DGS is certain and limited to the amount necessary to cover the transfer deficit. In exiting the market, the liquidated bank does not pose any further risk to the DGS, which, through least cost, reduces its burden compared to the reimbursement of depositors.

On the contrary, preventive measures imply the risk—even though not material—of a double intervention, inasmuch as the bank benefiting from the support remains on the market and the DGS may be called upon to intervene again to reimburse its depositors—or to carry out another preventive or alternative measure—if the bank's recovery plan is unsuccessful. Therefore, the DGS would have to bear the cost of repaying depositors or, possibly, of a further reorganisation operation. To this, we must add the burden for the DGS to secure adequate skills and highly specialised instruments to assess the inherent risks of carrying out such operations and monitor them afterwards.

[5] CEPS, *Options and National Discretions Under the Deposit Guarantee Scheme Directive*, November 2019.

This justifies the attention and tight constraints required by the directive for carrying out preventive interventions (see Chapter 7).

A last issue concerning preventive interventions is whether or not they should include liquidity funding. The matter is very complex since, in principle, the provision of liquidity to banks in crisis is beyond the mandate of DGSs, whose primary function is the repayment of the depositors of the insolvent bank, whereas liquidity support, in the form of the ELA, pertains the central bank (see Chapter 8).

It should also be noted that liquidity interventions normally involve the disbursement of significant amounts compared to solvency funding, which is normally linked to the coverage of losses and the replenishment of capital of the restructured or sold bank. Consequently, there might be high uses of the DGS's financial endowment (with significant effects on its availability), which may impact on the target levels established *ex-ante* by the DGS or legislation.

Furthermore, providing liquidity to banks in crisis involves the risk that these resources might be used to counteract the withdrawal of unprotected deposits, which are the first to 'run' when a crisis is looming,[6] in contrast with the institutional function of the DGS to protect deposits within the limits set.

These risks are essentially the reasons why the IMF recommends that DGSs avoid preventive measures to support solvency and liquidity in open bank assistance operations.[7] For example, in the United States, where about 500 banks were 'resolved' during the 2008–2013 financial crisis, also thanks to the FDIC's support to solvent banks, the legislator

[6] G. BOCCUZZI, R. DE LISA, *The Changing Face of Deposit Insurance in Europe: From the DGSD to the EDIS Proposal*, XXI Rapporto sul Sistema Finanziario, *The Changing Face of Banking*, Ass. Rosselli, July 2016.

[7] M.C. DOBLER, M. MORETTI, A. PIRIS, *Managing Systemic Banking Crises, New Lessons and Lessons Relearned*, IMF, 2020: 'Allocating deposit insurance funds in a way that would expose the scheme to significant uncertainty and risk, and erode depositor confidence in the scheme, for example, providing solvency or liquidity support to an open bank outside of resolution (so-called open bank assistance) should be ruled out. Deposit insurers are typically not well placed to judge the risk of such operations, which are likely to be highly risky; especially, for example, if the bank remains in the hands of the original shareholders and managers responsible for its failing'.

intervened to limit the discretion of the FDIC operations, excluding the possibility of providing preventive assistance.[8]

This general picture clearly shows the need for a uniform framework of DGS operations, with reference to preventive and alternative interventions. These measures constitute essential instruments in the toolkit for the management of banking crises, especially of small and medium-sized banks, whenever liquidation—not resolution—applies due to the lack of public interest. The EU Directive, as already underlined, allows ample operational possibilities, which, however, are subject to various uncertainties, constraints and limitations, which need to be carefully evaluated, and possibly removed, to improve the overall functioning of the system.

The two main issues are:

1. The application of State aid rules to DGSs, when these carry out preventive and alternative interventions;
2. Operational difficulties in applying the least cost principle established by law.

2.1 The State Aid Rules

The rules on State aid (as issued by the European Commission in the 2013 Banking Communication) state that DGS interventions different from the reimbursement of depositors may constitute State aid if the decision to deploy resources is attributable to the State and the resources themselves are under State control.

As seen in some cases in Italy (Banca Tercas, the four banks in resolution), the extensive application of the State aid rules had negative consequences on the intervention policy of the FITD, which the Commission considered to be 'public' when it carried out alternative and preventive interventions, despite being managed and funded privately.[9]

The Commission's position limited the operational scope of the FITD primarily, if not exclusively, to the reimbursement of deposits of banks in compulsory administrative liquidation, where State aid rules did not

[8] G. MAJNONI D'INTIGNANO, A. DAL SANTO, M. MALTESE, *The FDIC Bank Crisis Management Experience: Lessons for the EU Banking Union*, No 22, August 2020.

[9] The Commission concluded that the FITD's intervention in support of Banca Tercas was of a public nature and declared it incompatible with internal market rules, as per Article 108(3) of TFEU, ordering its recovery.

apply. This approach not only prevented the FITD from performing preventive interventions in contrast with the provisions of the DGSD, but also prevented the use of a fundamental tool for the management of banking crises, aimed at the reorganisation and restructuring of banks in crisis—even small ones—over the more costly and disruptive liquidation.

The approach followed by the Commission is unique in the international arena, where DGS interventions are never classified as State aid, and where systemic stability prevails over competition rules.

This situation changed in the aftermath of the EU General Court ruling on the Tercas case on 19 March 2019, which overrode the Commission decision of 23 December 2015. The judgement, albeit referring to a case that had occurred before the implementation of the DGSD, and hence under the previous regulatory framework, assumes great importance even after the application of the DGSD. After this ruling, the FITD resumed its preventive interventions. The final decision of the Court of Justice, on the appeal brought by the EU Commission, has definitely settled the case in the favour of the Italian parties, but it cannot solve all the problems raised by this issue, which require regulatory intervention.

We need a clear legislative change reflecting a new strategic vision of banking crisis management. Both the DGSD and the State aid rules should be reviewed, since both have shortcomings and incoherencies in their interaction. Such revision would require setting a priority scale among the objectives of competition and financial stability rules.

Profound and radical changes are needed to overcome this dichotomy. We should go beyond the Tercas case and the Court of Justice ruling. Interventions of the deposit guarantee schemes should never constitute State aid, since their resources belong to banks, and the decision to intervene is not attributable to the State. This has been the case in many countries outside the EU, where State aid is not envisaged. Furthermore, the resources used by the DGS for preventive and alternative interventions must be restored by the DGS themselves through additional contributions. Therefore, any resources used for these interventions do not affect the financial endowment of DGSs, equal to 0.8% of the protected deposits, which, in any case, must be brought back to target.

2.2 Least Cost and Depositor Preference Application Issues

The second problematic aspect is the application of the least cost criterion, according to which a DGS can carry out preventive and alternative interventions only if their cost is lower than the reimbursement of the depositors of the bank in liquidation.

The objective, therefore, is to minimise the financial burden for the DGS compared to the reimbursement of depositors, and to reduce any disruptive effects of the 'piecemeal' liquidation of the bank's assets.

The least cost principle is established by the DGSD. According to the DGSD (Article 11(3)(c)), least cost is a condition for carrying out preventive measures, whose cost must be compared with that 'for fulfilling the statutory or contractual mandate' of the DGS. Article 11(6), which deals with alternative measures, states that interventions can be carried out if costs for the DGS do not exceed 'the net amount of compensating covered depositors at the credit institution concerned'. This means that the cost of a payout equals the difference between the amount of covered deposits and the estimated recoveries from the liquidation proceedings.

Although least cost is recognised internationally (IADI Core Principle 14), it still needs to be clearly defined at regulatory level, including its application methods. Therefore, currently, the implementation of least cost is in the hands of the DGS alone.

In Italy, the Consolidated Banking Act (TUB) has implemented least cost for both preventive and alternative interventions, leaving further specifications to the DGSs (Article 96a(1a)(c) and (d)). When transposing the DGSD and the TUB, the FITD's Statute confirmed the least cost principle as a condition for alternative (Article 34) and preventive (Article 35) interventions.

Two main factors can influence the implementation of least cost:

1. the level of depositor protection (the higher the amount, the higher the cost of a reimbursement operation);
2. The depositor preference rule and the priority given to DGS in the liquidation over other unsecured creditors (super depositor preference).

The depositor preference rule is crucial in resolution and liquidation because it determines how to allocate losses among creditors in the case of insolvency. There are different configurations of the rule, namely:

1. *Covered depositor preference*, when protected deposits have priority in the allotment of liquidation over all unprotected depositors and other unsecured creditors; it may give similar priority to the DGS, which subrogates to the repaid depositors in receiving the proceeds of liquidation.[10] In this case, a DGS participates in full to the liquidation distribution and has a greater chance of recovering the amount paid for the reimbursement of depositors compared to the remaining unsecured creditors. Thus, the net cost of repaying depositors for the DGS tends to be minimised;
2. *Tiered depositor preference*. In the case of a two-tiered depositor preference, protected deposits have priority over non-protected deposits; furthermore, for the amount exceeding the limit of protection, some categories of depositors[11] have priority over other unsecured depositors. Here too the DGS, which subrogates to protected depositors, takes priority in the distribution of the proceeds of liquidation;
3. *General depositor preference*, when all depositors—protected and unprotected—have priority over all unsecured creditors. In this case, the DGS, which subrogates to the protected depositors, participates in the distribution of liquidation recoveries *pari passu* with non-protected depositors. The cost for a DGS would be higher than in (1) or (2).

In Italy, protected deposits and DGSs have priority by law. They are granted the highest protection and are first in receiving any proceeds of liquidation (after pre-deduction of liquidation costs and preferred creditors). Article 91(1a) of the TUB, introduced when the BRRD was

[10] For a detailed analysis of the depositor preference types in various jurisdictions, see FINANCIAL STABILITY INSTITUTE, *How to Manage Failures of Non-systemic Banks? A Review of Country Practices*, October 2018.

[11] Article 108 of the BRRD states that unsecured deposits of certain types of companies (micro, small and medium-sized enterprises) have priority over other unsecured creditors. An additional residual category has been introduced into the Italian legal system, 'other deposits', which has priority over other unsecured securities.

implemented by Legislative Decree No 181/2015, establishes that, in the distribution of the bank's assets in liquidation:

a. the following have higher priority ranking than other unsecured claims: (1) deposits of natural persons, micro, small and medium-sized enterprises eligible for reimbursement and greater than €100,000; (2) the same deposits indicated in point (1), at non-EU branches of banks with registered offices in Italy;
b. the following have higher priority ranking than the claims indicated in point (a): (1) protected deposits; (2) the claims of deposit guarantee systems following their subrogation in the rights of protected depositors;
c. the other deposits within the bank have higher priority ranking than other unsecured claims but lower than the claims indicated in point (a) and (b).

We must ask ourselves what the best configurations of the depositor preference rule could be in order to incentivise alternative and preventive interventions of DGSs, through the application of the least cost criterion. The current priority rule established by the BRRD and TUB is such that the DGSs are likely to receive a high percentage of reimbursed deposits, if not the full amount, in case of liquidation. In this way, the losses of liquidation would be borne by the other unsecured creditors. Thus, depositor preference reduces the estimated costs of liquidation for a DGS when compared to alternative or preventive measures, making such measures unlikely to pass the least cost test and hence difficult to apply.

In Europe, the ongoing debate on depositor preference revolves around the revision of creditor hierarchy and of the DGSs' right to subrogate to depositors' rights in the liquidation procedure. To this end it has been proposed to eliminate the super priority for DGSs like in the US model—and to increase deposit protection above the current limit of €100,000.[12]

[12] G. MAJNONI D'INTIGNANO, A. DAL SANTO, M. MALTESE, *The FDIC Bank Crisis Management Experience: Lessons for the EU Banking Union*, Notes on Financial Stability and Supervision, No 22, August 2020.

The issue is very complex and needs to be looked at in detail. On one hand, the priority given to depositors ensures the stable presence of small deposits in a bank before a crisis, since the risk of loss in case of insolvency is less perceived. On the other, super depositor preference reduces the possibility for DGSs to intervene in any way other than payout. Both needs should be further evaluated in the light of the ultimate objectives to be achieved. A change in legislation could give the same priority to all depositors, so that the DGSs that in the liquidation procedure subrogated to reimbursed protected depositors within the reimbursement limits, would share the proceeds of liquidation *pari passu* with non-protected depositors. But there are multiple options.[13]

The cost of liquidation is another important aspect of the least cost assessment. The costs of an atomistic liquidation vary depending on the size of the insolvent bank and its role in the banking system. In the case of a large bank, the costs cannot be limited to the difference between the amount of covered deposits and the estimated recoveries (direct costs), since indirect costs may also accrue in the event of contagion triggered by the bank's liquidation.

Since 2016, the FITD's Statute has allowed the computation of any indirect costs for the banking sector together with the direct costs of liquidation. Since its establishment (1987), the FITD has applied the least cost principle in all cases of preventive and alternative interventions. Most recently, the principle was implemented in alternative interventions in favour of BPPC and Banca Base, and preventive intervention in favour of Banca del Fucino, Banca Carige and Banca Popolare di Bari.[14]

In some countries, including the US, Canada and Japan, whenever stability is at risk, the systemic risk exemption is applied instead of least cost. This exemption could be considered as an alternative to least cost

[13] M.C. DOBLER, E. EMRE, A. GULLO, D. KALE, *The Case for Depositor Preference*, IMF, Technical notes and manuals, December 2020.

[14] The method of calculation of least cost is now being discussed at the European level. With regard to the costs that must be included in the total cost of an atomistic liquidation of a bank with reimbursement of depositors, the EBA stressed the need for greater clarity, also through the introduction of an adequate legal framework, to give greater certainty to the DGSs that apply preventive and alternative measures to the reimbursement of depositors. See EUROPEAN BANKING AUTHORITY, *Opinion of the European Banking Authority on Deposit Guarantee Scheme Funding and Uses of Deposit Guarantee Scheme Funds*, January 2020.

with the consideration of the indirect effects of a bank liquidation on the banking system.[15]

Least cost is very complex in that it is difficult to choose a single quantitative methodology, considering the different situations that may arise whose risks are not always measurable.

Box 1: Least Cost Calculation Methodology

Least cost is calculated by comparing the cost of reimbursement of depositors and the cost of the alternative or preventive intervention of the DGS.

This assessment requires the DGS to have comprehensive information on the bank's economic, financial and equity situation, based on a complete set of data provided by the bank itself.

The first step is to estimate the overall cost for the DGS in the liquidation scenario (atomistic liquidation). The valuation is based on the value of the bank's assets (recoverable assets). In this context, the 'quick sale' value of the various types of assets is considered and analytically estimated through 'desktop' valuations, based on market practices and benchmarks, also taking into account the valuations made by the special administrators or the liquidators.

The recoveries attributable to the DGS are estimated by subtracting, from the liquidation value of the bank's assets, the amount of: i) costs relating to the insolvency procedure (pre-deductible costs); ii) claims of preferred creditors under national bank insolvency laws.

[15] INTERNATIONAL MONETARY FUND, *Euro Area Policies—Financial System Stability Assessment*, July 2018, page 11: 'Some countries (e.g. Canada, Japan, and the United States) allow Difs to depart from least cost principles where adherence to them could have a severe adverse impact on financial stability. Any exception should be subject to strict governance safeguards to minimise moral hazard and to ensure it is only deployed in extremis in a way that would not undermine confidence in the scheme or propagate contagion. If a separate resolution fund is available for systemic cases, it may reduce the need for such an exemption'.

The cost of reimbursement of depositors (payout) is given by the difference between the amount of protected deposits and the estimated recoveries attributable to the DGS according to the depositor preference rule.

The cost of the payout can also include indirect costs; i.e. the effects that the compulsory liquidation of the bank could have on other banks in crisis and on the banking system in general.

The cost of the payout is finally compared with the cost of the alternative or preventive intervention.

In the current European regulatory framework, there is serious uncertainty about whether deposit guarantee schemes can carry out preventive or alternative interventions to the reimbursement of depositors, as the FITD has been doing since its establishment in 1987.

It is difficult to understand how, after such a massive reform in Europe, difficulties remain at the national level in applying instruments that have always been used, and which have prevented the disruptive effects of a bank liquidation and depositor reimbursement. Arguably, instead of expanding the intervention capacity of a DGS, European legislation seems to have reduced it.

These considerations are strongly supported by empirical evidence. They unequivocally point to the need for urgent reflection on how to best allow preventive and alternative interventions by DGS, overcoming, once and for all, the issues of State aid and any other legislative obstacle.

3 The Funding of Deposit Guarantee Schemes Must Be Made More Credible. The Lack of Emergency Financing

A Deposit guarantee scheme must be credible, meaning that it must be able to fulfil its institutional mandate to reimburse depositors, operationally and financially.

Measuring the financial capacity of a DGS to manage crises is a complex task. This capacity generally depends on the financial resources available or readily collectible and on the likelihood of crisis events in a specific period.

In Europe, the DGSD assigns to DGSs the task of ensuring that their funding is proportionate to potential liabilities. This implies that DGSs can estimate the banks' insolvency risk through a specific system. Nonetheless, the DGSD sets a minimum target level for DGSs (0.8% of protected deposits) to be reached by 3 July 2024.

The directive (Article10(9)) also requires DGSs to have in place alternative funding arrangements for short-term financing in the event of an intervention as well as to exchange voluntary loans between DGS within the Union (Article 12, borrowing between DGSs).

In line with these requirements, the TUB provides that the target level be calculated based on the total amount of protected deposits on 31 December of the preceding year. It also requires that member banks make periodic payments to the DGS to ensure achievement of the target level (Article 96.1(1) and (2) of the TUB).

The periodic contributions constitute the financial endowment of the DGS, which is an autonomous capital base, separate from the capital of the guarantee system, of member banks, and of any other fund set up within the same DGS. The DGS uses its financial endowment to meet the obligations contracted in the interventions and financing. To protect the destination of the DGS's resources, the financial endowment cannot be claimed by third parties, i.e. by creditors of the guarantee system or in their interest, or by creditors of the individual members or of any other funds established within the same guarantee system (Article 96.1(4)).

The collection of ordinary contributions from member banks is carried out at least annually, taking into account the economic cycle and procyclical effects (Article 96.2(1) and (2) of the TUB).

An additional form of financing (Article 96.2(3) of the TUB) is extraordinary contributions, which can be raised 'on demand', should the available financial means be insufficient for reimbursing depositors. Extraordinary contributions must not exceed 0.5% of covered deposits per calendar year; only in exceptional cases can the DGS require higher contributions.

The TUB (Article 96.2(5)) also allows DGSs access to alternative short-term funding and additional funding from other sources. Under Article 27 of the FITD's Statute, the FITD may also take short-term loans or use other sources and methods of financing, even in the medium and long term, to carry out its interventions.

Articles 24–27 of the FITD's Statute regulate DGS funding. With regard to alternative funding, the FITD agreed to receive additional funds from a pool of member banks in case of insufficient resources during a payout, without having to resort directly to extraordinary contributions under Article 26 of the Statute. This strategy helps to avoid negative impacts on the liquidity and P&L of the member banks, with possible pro-cyclical effects.

In the case of severe crises, however, even such articulate funding system might still prove to be insufficient. In the case of bigger crises, placing additional burdens on the banking system beyond 0.5% of protected deposits—also considering the other contributions requested of banks (i.e. the Resolution Fund)—could lead to a transfer of losses from the banks in crisis to the healthy banks, with the possible consequent contagion and destabilisation of the banking sector.

While the actual financial capacity of the FITD and, more generally, of all DGSs, is substantial and in line with the legal requirements, it is nevertheless limited. International examples and the academic literature have shown that deposit guarantee Schemes can only face the crises of smaller banks and with limited amounts.

Therefore, to manage larger interventions, such as the simultaneous crises of several small and medium-sized banks, ad hoc tools must be developed to allow the DGS to quickly access the liquidity necessary for the payout, to the extent that it cannot have pre-established resources or readily available from banks. This is why emergency financing is crucial.

The current regulatory framework does not provide for emergency financing to support the DGS in carrying out interventions above its financial capacity. These situations can also be excessively burdensome on the banking system, since they require adequate guarantees, which may be difficult to provide in a financial crisis situation.

The International Monetary Fund (IMF) highlighted criticalities in the funding of Italian DGSs in the 2013 FSAP.[16] In addition to recommending the transition from *ex-post* to *ex-ante* funding, the IMF underlined the need for backup funding, recommending the opening of unsecured lines of credit at market rates with the Ministry of the Economy and Finance.

16 INTERNATIONAL MONETARY FUND, *Staff Report for the 2013 Article IV Consultation*, September 2013.

In the 2018 FSAP, published in March 2020,[17] the IMF again recommended measures to facilitate the access of deposit guarantee systems to public backstop mechanisms to further increase compliance with international standards.

The recommendations made by the IMF are based on the IADI Core Principles for Effective Deposit Insurance Systems.[18] According to CP 9 'Sources and Uses of funds', DGSs should have adequate and readily available financial resources even when the financial system is under stress; these include emergency lines of credit with the Ministry of Finance or with the Central Bank.

In Italy, emergency financing mechanisms are yet to be implemented. Setting them up would require establishing lines of credit in favour of DGSs, which would operate as liquidity support, since the *super depositor preference* could allow DGSs to extinguish these lines of credit with the proceeds of liquidation.

A recent survey[19] has shown that, globally, most DGSs have access to public emergency funding or lines of credit with their central bank, even backed up by a public guarantee. This is the case in many European countries, such as Norway, Poland, Russia and Serbia.

Access to a public backup funding mechanism would allow a DGS to effectively fulfil its institutional mandate. In this way, an effective framework would be in place to carry out all kinds of intervention in case of insolvency, with the participation of all components of the safety net. This would be a crucial step forward, as the European Deposit Insurance Scheme (EDIS) is still far off on the horizon.

[17] M.C. DOBLER, E. EMRE, A. GULLO, D. KALE, *The Case for Depositor Preference*, IMF, Technical notes and manuals, December 2020.

[18] INTERNATIONAL ASSOCIATION OF DEPOSIT INSURERS, *Core Principles for Effective Deposit Insurance System* (CPs), October 2014.

[19] FINANCIAL STABILITY INSTITUTE, *Bank Failure Management. The Role of Deposit Insurance*, FSI Insights on policy implementation, No 17, August 2019. As regards the US, a credit line with the Treasury is also envisaged for $100 million to cover the losses of the *Deposit Insurance Fund (DIF)*. FDIC would have to finance reimbursement with the contribution of its member banks.

4 Failure to Implement the European Deposit Insurance Scheme (EDIS)

The European Deposit Insurance Scheme (EDIS) is intended to be the third pillar of the Banking Union together with the Single Supervisory Mechanism (SSM) and the Single Resolution Mechanism (SRM). The Banking Union is the way for Eurozone countries to build a common, centralised and harmonised institutional framework on supervision, resolution and deposit insurance, as part of the completion of the Economic and Monetary Union and the internal market.[20]

However, it seems unlikely that the EDIS can be established in the short term due to the differing views of various EU countries. The debate has been going on for five years, but the completion of the Banking Union, and thus a strengthened and credible financial capacity of deposit insurance, still seems far away.

It is worth remembering that the Commission's first proposal to set up an EDIS dates back to 2015. Based on the proposal, the EDIS would be introduced in three steps to progressively centralise decision-making processes and mutualise resources at European level.[21] Managed by the Single Resolution Board (SRB), the EDIS would carry out the reimbursement of depositors and the financing of resolutions, while the DGSD

[20] G. BOCCUZZI, *The European Banking Union. Supervision and Resolution*, Palgrave Macmillan Studies in Banking and Financial Institutions, 2016.

[21] In the proposed Regulation, the EDIS would be implemented in three phases (reinsurance, co-insurance and full insurance) with limitations and safeguards for transitioning between phases. Resources and risks would progressively be transferred to the European level. At the end of 2016, the Committee on Economic and Monetary Affairs (ECON) proposed a new, two-phased EDIS to the European Parliament, whose implementation would be divided into reinsurance (with different contents and a longer duration) and insurance (applicable only after risk containment and reduction in the banking sector). Responsibilities and management of resources would be shared equally between EDIS and national DGSs. In October 2017, the European Commission (Communication to the European Parliament, the Council, the European Central Bank, the European Economic and Social Committee and the Committee of the Regions on completing the Banking Union, COM (2017) 0592), proposed that the EDIS implementation process be divided into reinsurance and co-insurance only. However, it would initially be limited to support the liquidity needs of national DGSs in the event of a payout. In co-insurance, which would be implemented only after significant risk reduction (on NPLs and other risky assets highlighted by an Asset Quality Review), EDIS would also gradually provide the DGSs with resources to cover losses.

envisages a wider operational scope for the DGS, including preventive and alternative interventions.

Since then, no real steps forward have been taken. The political debate revolves around the introduction of measures to contain risks in the banking sector before sharing those risks among Eurozone countries; so, some countries are asking to reduce risks in the banking sector before actually building the EDIS (risk sharing vs risk reduction).

However, the debate on EDIS is still open. EDIS will presumably be set up once the right balance between risk sharing and risk reduction is agreed upon. To this end, the ECB conducted an analysis on cross-subsidisation to study risk transmission among States under a single deposit guarantee system.[22] This study concluded that there would not be unjustifiable and systematic cross-subsidisation within the EDIS, thus disproving the theory that some banking systems would contribute more than they would get from the DIF.

We have come to a stalemate. The sharing of resources, which was supposed to be a pillar of the European project, is being constantly delayed.

Despite these difficulties, in December 2018, the Eurogroup set up a team of experts (High-Level Working Group on EDIS—HLWG) to conduct an in-depth analysis of the EDIS introduction phases, the conditions for transitioning from one phase to another, and the regulation of public debt securities.[23] The HLWG stressed the importance of

[22] EUROPEAN CENTRAL BANK, *Completing the Banking Union with a European Deposit Insurance Scheme: Who Is Afraid of Cross-Subsidisation?*, Occasional Paper Series, No 208, April 2018. This work analyses the potential impact of EDIS based on the various proposals currently under discussion. Five main points emerge: (i) a fully funded DIF would be sufficient for the repayment of depositors even in a severe banking crisis; (ii) risk-based contributions should be adequately calibrated to the specificities of banks and individual national banking systems: this would facilitate the managing of moral hazard and the completion of the Banking Union with the implementation of both risk sharing and risk reduction; (iii) banks, from the smallest to the largest, would not excessively contribute to EDIS in relation to their protected deposits; (iv) there would not be an unjustified and systematic effect of cross-subsidisation within the EDIS, i.e. that some banking systems would contribute more than they would benefit from the DIF, also in the case of simulation of country-specific shocks; (v) a mixed system, whereby the national DGSs would intervene first in a payout before the DIF, would lead to greater cross-subsidisation than a full mutualisation (fully fledged EDIS).

[23] In June 2019, the group of experts studied four thematic areas relating to: (i) implementation of the 'NPL Action Plan' of the EU Council (ii) implementation of the banking package (CRDV/CRR2), including the MREL liability accumulation process;

completing the Banking Union to increase its resilience to shocks and limit public intervention. The roadmap for political negotiations was drawn up in December 2019. However, it is safe to assume that the work on the EDIS will continue for quite some time.[24]

The HLWG is encouraging member States to continue working on EDIS, in particular, on the succession between liquidity and loss coverage measures. It has also proposed a hybrid model, whereby national DGSs would be supported by a common European fund. At first, the EDIS would provide liquidity support to the DGSs—with limits still to be defined—and then add loss coverage functions. However, to implement such a model, many criteria would need to be agreed upon, such as the mandate of EDIS, its size and that of the national funds, their mutual relationships, the governance of EDIS and the reimbursement to national systems of any resources used. Only once these aspects are agreed upon, negotiations on a legislative framework can begin and impact assessment can be carried out.

It is difficult to give a clear picture of the consequences of so many uncertainties on the EDIS. As a matter of fact, the fragmentation and uneven risk distribution of the European banking system is aggravated by the absence of a public backstop.[25] The market relies on the implicit guarantee of the State to ensure that DGSs are able to repay depositors as required and, as said, in many countries DGSs have access to emergency public support or central bank liquidity lines, including those with public guarantees.

Debate is also ongoing on the adequacy of the Single Resolution Fund and EDIS to deal with insolvencies of systemic banks. A European

(iii) achievement of the target level by national DGSs; (iv) completion of the anti-money laundering (AML) Action Plan.

[24] Letter by the High-Level Working Group on a European Deposit Insurance Scheme (EDIS) Chair to the President of the Eurogroup—Further strengthening the Banking Union, including EDIS: A roadmap for political negotiations, 3 December 2019. The HLWG argued that: 'Ideally, the further work set out in the roadmap should, at the European level, be carried out within the current institutional cycle (2019–2024), taking into account the legislative processes involved, implementation, including at the national level, could go beyond this period'.

[25] G. BOCCUZZI, R. DE LISA, *The Changing Face of Deposit Insurance in Europe: From the DGSD to the EDIS Proposal*, XXI Rapporto sul Sistema Finanziario, *The Changing Face of Banking*, Ass. Rosselli, July 2016.

backstop system is necessary to ensure the availability of adequate financial resources, should bank contributions be insufficient. This backstop would boost depositor confidence in countries with weaker public finance systems. It would also strengthen the credibility of EDIS by offering external support to national authorities, which, otherwise, would be alone in supporting their banks. The vicious cycle of banking risk-sovereign risk is ready made. In its Opinion on EDIS, even the European Central Bank also supported the idea of a 'fiscally neutral public backstop', questioning the sustainability of a system that relies exclusively on national resources.[26]

[26] See, EUROPEAN CENTRAL BANK, *Opinion on a Proposal for a Regulation of the European Parliament and of the Council Amending regulation (EU) No 806/2014 in Order to Establish a European Deposit Scheme* (CON/2016/26), April 2016. The proposed regulation does not provide for a fiscally neutral public European backstop to the EDIS in the event of one or several payouts exceeding the EDIS's available financial resources, and *ex-post* contributions or alternative financing cannot be tapped quickly enough to ensure a timely depositor payout or the timely involvement of the EDIS in a resolution case. This implies that any payment obligation in relation to depositors in excess of the resources provided by the EDIS reverts in principle to the relevant DGS. Therefore, the efficiency of the whole system ultimately rests on the credibility of national backstops.

'The ECB is of the view that a fiscally neutral common public backstop for the EDIS at the latest as of the full insurance stage is necessary to ensure a uniformly high level of confidence in deposit protection under all circumstances and to effectively weaken the bank/sovereign link at the national level. Ultimately, relying on national backstops defeats the purpose of the proposed regulation of reinforcing the Banking Union by [... establishing EDIS.] However, in the absence of a common backstop, the EDIS would fail to eliminate a factor that could have a negative impact on depositor confidence as a result of doubts regarding the credibility of purely national backstops'.

CHAPTER 13

Conclusion: A Long List of Open Issues

Our study has analysed the banking crises in Italy in the years 2014 to 2020. We have grouped the events according to the solutions and tools applied. Five categories have been identified. In total, sixteen cases have been analysed. What lessons can be drawn and what can be done to improve the European framework for banking crisis management?

The first lesson is that banking crises are inherently complex events. They require a wide and diversified toolkit, capable of dealing with crises with different characteristics and of varying size and complexity.

In the cycle of Italian banking crises, all the tools available in the European framework were drawn on (resolution, liquidation, DGS interventions). Where necessary, additional instruments were activated, within the boundaries of the legislation, with the use of public funds, such as precautionary recapitalisation and orderly liquidation. In other cases, specific solutions were adopted, outside the boundaries of the legislation, such as the FITD's Voluntary Scheme, GACS, the Atlante Fund and AMCO, the asset management company specifically created to remove non-performing loans from the banks' balance sheets.

These instruments avoided liquidation procedures for the banks involved, as well as serious losses for their stakeholders, thus ensuring continuity of critical functions. An appropriate mix of private and public resources allowed these results to be achieved. This is what went right.

G. Boccuzzi, *Banking Crises in Italy*, Palgrave Studies in Financial Instability and Banking Crisis Regulation,
https://doi.org/10.1007/978-3-031-01344-7_13

By contrast, our analysis indicates that the current European regulatory framework is still not complete and lacks flexibility and adaptability in its application.

Certainly, with the reforms of the institutional and regulatory framework in Europe, new principles, objectives and tools for the management of banking crises were hastily put in place, to respond to the serious problems raised by the global financial crisis. However, many critical issues remained to be addressed. Experience must be scrutinised and all essential lessons heeded in order to achieve a crisis management framework that is fit for an increasingly complex and diverse financial system, marked by uncertainty and a variable economic environment. In particular, the Italian experience can provide many lessons and useful insights for a revision of the institutional set-up and rules for the future.

The debate opened by the Italian experience has recently also extended to the European level, triggering a process of revision of the crisis management legislation, as shown by the consultation process carried out by the European Commission.[1] This is certainly an important initiative, which signals growing awareness of the need to review a framework that has concretely revealed weaknesses in its theoretical assumptions, design of institutional structures, tools and application.

The Banking Union and its rules for crisis management deserve further consideration. We have identified areas for improvement in the institutional architecture, in aspects of the general design, in the completeness of the toolkit and in the scope for flexibility. A central issue is the treatment of small and medium-sized banks, whose regulation is clearly insufficient.

The institutional model. Which crisis management model should the Banking Union adopt? The FDIC's model seems to attract the most support in the ongoing debate in Europe, as explained in the previous chapters. However, it is necessary to also look at other solutions better suited to the Eurozone, where a new system has just entered into force but is still largely untested. The model should envision a clearer allocation of responsibilities between national and European authorities to ensure that policies and rules are unambiguous and uniform. The decision-making process must be fast: timeliness of interventions and decisions is crucial.

[1] EUROPEAN COMMISSION, *Banking Union—Review of the Bank Crisis Management and Deposit Insurance Framework (DGSD Review). Public Consultation, European Union Website.*

Rules and guidelines for crisis management, especially for small and medium-sized banks. Current legislation is based on the resolution-liquidation dualism. It states that, in the absence of public interest, the insolvent bank will exit the market through liquidation. Public interest would justify a resolution procedure for restructuring and transferring the business to ensure continuity of critical functions. This approach should be reconsidered, since it is too simplistic in the light of the complexity of today's banking crises and their consequences for banking and the wider social environment. Accordingly, the concept of 'public interest' could be revised by extending it to small and medium-sized banks. Or it could simply be eliminated, considering that the whole banking system and banking activity are inherently based on 'general interest', independently from the size of the banks.

Winding down small and medium-sized banks can be disruptive. Is public interest not also served by preserving their business and enabling continuity of critical functions? Past experience could be a useful guide here.

An improved framework should be aimed at avoiding insolvency and its harmful impacts. It should place greater emphasis on preventive measures—under specific conditions—to rescue small and medium-sized banks, applying to them too 'quasi resolution' measures.

We should design a system able to ensure—to the maximum extent possible—the orderly exit of small and medium-sized banks from the market, avoiding the disruptive effects of insolvency. The options for intervention can be manifold: recapitalisation, restructuring, sale of the bank or business, or—where appropriate—a combination of these tools. The methodological approach should be different: first, verification of the possible use of recovery tools (in a broad sense) and then liquidation.

However, if liquidation is inevitable, P&A transactions should be the preferred resolution measures, providing forms of support to the acquiring bank. Atomistic liquidations and reimbursement of depositors should be the very last resort.

Who pays the costs? Internalisation vs. externalisation. A crucial question is: who carries insolvency losses? The methods for covering losses and replenishing capital for a bank's restructuring or sale require far-reaching considerations.

In resolution, recourse to bail-in, albeit perfectly appropriate from a conceptual and legal point of view, may not be the right answer. It can have destabilising effects and should be applied with caution, otherwise

'[A] tool devised to reduce the impact of a crisis [might] create the conditions to make it more likely'.[2]

BRRD (Article 44(3)(c)) grants some flexibility. It allows resolution authorities to apply bail-in only partially where its impact on financial stability could produce effects contrary to the general interest of the Member State and the EU. Even under exceptional circumstances, resolution authorities can exclude certain liabilities from being bailed-in to avoid the risk of contagion or disruption to the economy. Such flexibility should be further enhanced through effective solutions.

Furthermore, bail-in implies MREL (or TLAC for systemic banks), meaning that banks should *ex-ante* have a certain amount of liabilities available to be converted or written down to cover losses (Loss Absorbency Capacity) and increase capital. MREL securities are costly and may have a considerable impact on banks' profitability. Given this, can we apply MREL to small/medium-sized banks? This is doubtful, given the difficulty and cost of raising capital on the market.

Another source of solvency funding is represented by the external resources provided by the Resolution Fund and the Deposit Guarantee Fund, to be applied respectively in resolution and liquidation. Both funds come from the banking system.

As a result, solvency funding is based on internal resources (bail-in) and external resources of the banking system. These are all private resources.

We must clarify the boundaries of private and public intervention. Private intervention cannot solve all bank insolvencies, as would seem to be suggested by the new European framework.

A national public tool. The history of the Italian banking crises points to the importance of having a national public intervention tool until other solutions are found at European level. The role of public intervention is to foster financial stability and economic growth. The transition from bail-out to bail-in alone is not sustainable. Both instruments should remain viable options, to be chosen case by case. In any case, bail-in would not be effective without practicable plans for restructuring the insolvent bank and restoring its long-term viability. Market investors would then guide the recovery process, taking on the burdens and gains of the investment.

[2] I. VISCO, *Fact-Finding Inquiry on the Italian Banking and Financial System and the Protection of Savings, also Regarding Supervision, Crisis Resolution and European Deposit Insurance*, Testimony before The Italian Senate, 6th Standing Committee (Finance and Treasury), April 2016.

States should equip themselves with a rigorous but flexible public intervention mechanism to be used only as a last resort. The 'Constructive ambiguity' principle, often mentioned when discussing public intervention, should refer to the timing and methods of the intervention, not to the existence and feasibility of a public intervention tool per se. The framework of public intervention cannot be assembled as the crisis occurs, since it requires time to be implemented and gain political consensus. The timing of politics is not compatible with the urgent need to resolve crises.

A pre-established toolkit—as envisaged by the BRRD—and a structured activation procedure should be in place. In an emergency, time is of the essence. The risk of 'opportunistic' behaviour is high and may result in a crisis management process based on the search for the most feasible solution, which may not be the best solution.

Governments must be ready to face crisis phenomena that cannot be solved with ordinary tools and private resources. Public responsibility should also be retained, since the sacrifice of savers is not always better than the sacrifice of taxpayers.

State aid regulation. The State aid framework should be reconsidered with a more solid legal foundation. The current framework is inconsistent with the particularities and implications of financial instability. A more balanced approach between the objectives of financial stability and competition needs to be established, obviously in favour of the first, since financial instability is very damaging.

Furthermore, the scope and application of the State aid rules must be limited to situations where State resources are used, not those of DGSs and private banks. In addition, internal and decision-making procedures should be simplified to avoid overlaps with supervisory and resolution authorities and to emphasise transparency and accountability. The State aid framework is also currently under scrutiny by the EU Commission, which has recently launched a public consultation to collect comments on a possible revision of the 2013 Communication.

A European backstop. A common backstop mechanism at European level has recently been introduced, as part of the reform of the European Stability Mechanism (ESM). After a long debate, specific initiatives have been taken to strengthen the ESM by expanding its scope and application. The ESM reform and the anticipated introduction of the common backstop in 2022 were agreed in November 2020. The reformed ESM Treaty has been approved in early 2021 and a ratification process by Member States is currently under way.

In this function as common backstop, the ESM should help to strengthen the credibility and the potential for intervention of the Single Resolution Fund by providing additional support whenever resources are insufficient for an intervention mandated by the SRB. The same approach should be followed in the case of EDIS.

Liquidity funding. Liquidity is of the utmost importance in managing banking crises. It is complementary to solvency funding.

The framework on liquidity funding is clearly insufficient, as also shown by the Italian experience. The European framework needs to be strengthened with a new role for central banks, with specific tools aimed at ensuring the supply of liquidity to banks in pre-resolution and in resolution.

This requires the close coordination of the central bank with the supervisory and the resolution authorities in the assessment of bank solvency, which is a prerequisite for ordinary and emergency financial support by the central bank.

Deposit Guarantee Schemes. Deposit insurance is another key issue. Many aspects need to be clarified, especially as regards the interventions that they can carry out in banking crises. Internationally, their institutional mandate is far-reaching, not limited to the simple pay-box function (reimbursement of depositors).

In Europe, the situation varies. There is no single model. The biggest differences are in preventive and alternative measures, in particular for small and medium banks, which are excluded from resolution.

In Italy, we follow a broader model, in line with the European Directive. However, preventive and alternative measures are hindered by some constraints and limitations, in particular relating to State aid rules and the least cost principle.

As concerns State aid rules, it should be considered that DGS funds are external resources, but not State resources. Recent judicial rulings have affirmed this principle.

The application of the least cost principle needs to be better framed in the current legislation, in order to ensure the conditions for an affective and consistent application of preventive and alternative measures. To this end, we need to reflect more on what could be the best model for Depositor Preference and what priority should be given to DGSs which subrogate the reimbursed depositors (Super Depositors Preference). Should they have priority over other unsecured creditors or be treated *pari passu* with them, participating in the losses of insolvency?

This second approach would favour interventions other than depositor payout.

The EDIS. To complete the EU Banking Union, a single Deposit Guarantee Scheme (EDIS) must be established in the Eurozone. This issue has been hotly debated. Much work is still required to reach an agreement on the main features of an EDIS: its financing, its relationship with national DGSs, its interventions and costs in national banking crises. EDIS would have to merge and consolidate national practices and experiences in solving banking crises, especially those in small and medium-sized banks.

Only with EDIS is it possible to break the vicious cycle between banking risk and sovereign risk.

Harmonisation of insolvency rules. Deposit guarantee and insolvency rules must go hand in hand. The primary mandate of DGSs is the repayment of depositors of banks in liquidation, to which national insolvency laws apply. We must look into proposals for the harmonisation of insolvency rules and the creation of a European liquidation procedure in line with the FDIC model, which is called for in the current debate.

The crisis of banking groups. Closely connected with the harmonisation of insolvency law is the need to establish a specific framework for banking group crises, at national and European levels, to eliminate uncertainties in dealing with cross-border insolvencies. Currently, there is no legal framework for handling insolvent groups. As a consequence, liquidation and resolution are applicable only at legal entity level, under national insolvency law (*territorial approach*). This can lead to different treatment between creditors located in the different countries in which the group operates.

Therefore, resolution authorities cannot resolve a banking group as a whole, with an integrated and universal approach.

What is the best way to deal with NPEs? The Italian experience has shown that a common element of restructuring banks in crisis is the transfer of deteriorated loans to other institutions (through outright sale or securitisation) to clean up the balance sheets of banks and reduce risks.

The Italian model in this field has been successful, based on the activation of many instruments, some with public support (AMCO, REV, GACS, fiscal benefit).

There are currently concerns about the possible evolution of the pandemic and other systemic crises and their negative effects on the quality of credit of European banks. New instruments have been envisaged, such as the creation of an Asset Management Company at European level or a network of national AMCs. This is a priority for managing possible banking crises.

Putting the best rules and practices together. The crisis management system should be redesigned to meet the needs of a complex financial system operating in ever-changing markets and regulatory frameworks. It must uphold the requirements of legitimacy, credibility, predictability, effectiveness, practicability, accountability, flexibility and timeliness.

In-depth analysis and experience are essential to understand the current weaknesses in the framework and draft an action plan to correct them.

The process under way to revise the legislation by the European Commission represents an important step to improve the regulation of bank insolvency. The scope of the proposed regulatory review must be verified, since the views of individual European countries are very different. But the initiative is significant.

A technical working table open to academics, regulators and practitioners would allow the best practices in national experiences in banking insolvency to be put together and new ideas, tools and solutions to be developed. It is up to the policymakers to translate technical suggestions into new rules and standards, within a common strategy for the present and the future.

Bibliography

ACHARY V., RICHARDSON M., Causes of the Financial Crisis, *Critical Review: A Journal of Politics and Society*, Vol. 21, No 2–3, July 2009.

AMCO, *Bilancio consolidato 2019*, March 2020.

BANCA D'ITALIA, *Questions and Answers on the Solution of the Crises at the Four Banks Under Resolution*, January 2016.

BANCA D'ITALIA, *Informazioni sulla soluzione della crisi di Veneto Banca S.p.A. e Banca Popolare di Vicenza S.p.A.*, Memoria per la VI Commissione Finanze della Camera dei Deputati, July 2017.

BANCA D'ITALIA, *The "precautionary recapitalization" of Banca Monte dei Paschi di Siena*, December 2016.

BANCA D'ITALIA, *La crisi di Veneto Banca S.p.A. e Banca Popolare di Vicenza S.p.A.: Domande e risposte*, July 2017.

BANCA D'ITALIA, *Financial Stability Report*, No 1, April 2020.

BANCA D'ITALIA, *Annual Report for 2018.*

BANCA D'ITALIA, *The Annual Report of the National Resolution Fund*, Roma, March 2017.

BANCA D'ITALIA, *The Annual Report of the National Resolution Fund*, Roma, March 2018.

BANCA DEL FUCINO, *Banca del Fucino S.p.A.: il Consiglio d'Amministrazione approva il nuovo Piano Industriale*, press release, November 2020.

BANCA DEL FUCINO, *Relazione e Bilancio al 31 dicembre 2018.*

BANCA POPOLARE DELLE PROVINCE CALABRE, *Bilancio 2013.*

G. Boccuzzi, *Banking Crises in Italy*, Palgrave Studies in Financial Instability and Banking Crisis Regulation,
https://doi.org/10.1007/978-3-031-01344-7

BANCA POPOLARE DI BARI, *Relazione illustrativa dei Commissari straordinari della Banca Popolare di Bari S.C.p.A. in Amministrazione Straordinaria, sulla Situazione Patrimoniale al 31 marzo 2020*, June 2020.

BARAVELLI M., *Dalla crisi al rilancio economico: evoluzione dei modelli di business delle banche italiane. Il ruolo del cambiamento organizzativo*, Banche e Banchieri, April 2015.

BARBAGALLO C., *Banca Monte dei Paschi di Siena*, Senato della Repubblica—Camera dei Deputati, Commissione Parlamentare di inchiesta sul sistema bancario e finanziario, Legge 12 luglio 2017, No 107, November 2017.

BARBAGALLO C., *Cassa di Risparmio di Ferrara, Banca delle Marche, Cassa di Risparmio della Provincia di Chieti, Banca Popolare dell'Etruria e del Lazio, Senato della Repubblica*—Camera dei Deputati, Commissione Parlamentare di inchiesta sul sistema bancario e finanziario, Legge 12 luglio 2017, No 107, Roma, December 2017.

BARBAGALLO C., *Veneto Banca e Banca Popolare di Vicenza*, Senato della Repubblica—Camera dei Deputati Commissione Parlamentare di inchiesta sul sistema bancario e finanziario Legge 12 luglio 2017, No 107, November 2017.

BAUDINO P., GAGLIANO A., RULLI E., WALTERS R., *How to Manage Failures of Non-systemic Banks? A Review of Country Practices*, Financial Stability Institute Insights on Policy Implementation, No 10, October 2018.

BAZOLI G., *La banca, un'impresa 'speciale'*, Lectio Magistralis, Cerimonia di chiusura del Master in Giuristi, Consulenti e Professionisti d'Impresa A.A. 2015/2016, Specialisation School for Public Administration Studies (SP.I.S.A.), Bologna, June 2017.

BOCCUZZI G., DE LISA R., Does Bail-In Definitely Rule Out Bailout?, *The Journal of Financial Management*, Markets and Institutions (JFMI), January 2017.

BOCCUZZI G., DE LISA R., *The Changing Face of Deposit Insurance in Europe: From the DGSD to the EDIS Proposal*, XXI Rapporto sul Sistema Finanziario, *The Changing Face of Banking*, Ass. Rosselli, July 2016.

BOCCUZZI G., *Il Regime Speciale della Risoluzione Bancaria. Obiettivi e Strumenti*, Cacucci Editore, 2018.

BOCCUZZI G., *Il valore di una disciplina ben ponderata*, in Sole24Ore, June 2017.

BOCCUZZI G., *L'Unione Bancaria Europea*, Bancaria Editrice, 2015.

BOCCUZZI G., *La crisi dell'impresa bancaria. Profili economici e giuridici*, Giuffrè, 1998.

BOCCUZZI G., *La risposta europea alla gestione delle crisi bancarie: alcune riflessioni critiche*, Bancaria, No 4, 2016.

BOCCUZZI G., *Quali regole nella gestione delle crisi bancarie: la complessità in una fase di transizione*, in Tempo Finanziario, No 2 year VI, April–June 2016.

BOCCUZZI G., *The European Banking Union: Supervision and Resolution*, Palgrave Macmillan, 2016.

BOCCUZZI G., *Towards a New Framework for Banking Crisis Management. The International Debate and the Italian Model*, Quaderni di ricerca giuridica della Consulenza Legale, Banca d'Italia, No 71, October 2011.

BONETTI P., *Brevi note sui profili costituzionali dell'interpretazione conforme del decreto-legge No 99/2017 sulla liquidazione coatta amministrativa di due banche venete*, in *Rivista di Diritto Bancario*, No 10, 2018.

BONFATTI S., *Crisi Bancarie in Italia 2015–2017*, in *Rivista di Diritto Bancario*, No 4, April 2018.

BOVENZI J.F., *Inside the FDIC. Thirty Years of Bank Failures, Bailouts, and Regulatory Battles*, Wiley, February 2015.

BROZZETTI A., *Il Decreto Legge No 99/2017: un'altra pietra miliare per la questione bancaria italiana*, in *Rivista Trimestrale di Diritto dell'Economia*, No 1, 2018.

CACCIATORE E., *Riflessioni sull'efficacia verso i terzi del contratto di cessione previsto dal decreto salva banche venete*, in *Rivista di Diritto Bancario*, No 4, 2018.

CALANDRA BUONAURA V., *La disciplina del risanamento e della risoluzione delle banche. Aspetti critici*, in Orizzonti del Diritto Commerciale, year V, No 2, February 2017.

CAPRIGLIONE F., SEMERARO G., *Crisi finanziaria e dei debiti sovrani: l'Unione Europea tra rischi ed opportunità*, Utet giuridica, July 2012.

CASSA DI RISPARMIO DI CESENA, *Bilancio al 31 dicembre 2015.*

CASSA DI RISPARMIO DI RIMINI, *Bilancio al 31 dicembre 2016.*

CASSA DI RISPARMIO DI SAN MINIATO, *Bilancio al 31 dicembre 2016.*

CEPS, *Options and National Discretions Under the Deposit Guarantee Scheme Directive*, November 2019.

COMANA M., *SREP 2019: i business model delle banche al centro delle valutazioni della Vigilanza*, Diritto Bancario, February 2020.

CONGRESSIONAL BUDGET OFFICE, *Report on the Troubled Asset Relief Program*, March 2020.

CONSOB, *La crisi finanziaria del 2007–2009.*

COSMA S. (et al.), *I modelli di business delle banche: letteratura, nuove regole e implicazioni strategiche*, Bancaria, December 2016.

COSTANCIO V., *Challenges for the European Banking Industry*, Lecture at the Conference on *European Banking Industry: What's Next?*, University of Navarra, Madrid, July 2016.

DAVIES G., DOBLER M., *Bank Resolution and Safeguarding the Creditors Left Behind*, Bank of England, London, Quarterly Bulletin, September 2011.

DE GIOIA CARABELLESE P., Bail-In: Do Italians Do It Better (or Worse, or Not at All)?: Case Studies and a Reflection on the Italian Approach to the BRRD: The Bail-With, *European Business Law Review*, Vol. 32, No 1, 2021.

DE GIOIA CARABELLESE P., *Crisi Bancarie e Aiuti di Stato. La Sentenza Tercas: Brussels versus Italy?*, Ordine Internazionale e Diritti Umani 686–718, October 2019.

DE GIOIA CARABELLESE P., *Crisi della banca e diritti dei creditori*, Cacucci editore, July 2020.

DE GIOIA CARABELLESE P., *La ricapitalizzazione bancaria interna*, Studium edizioni, 2020.

DE GROPEN W.P., *Precautionary Recapitalisation: Time for a Review*, Centre for European Policy Studies (CEPS), June 2017.

DE SURY P., ROVERA C., *Il bail-over italiano*, Banche e Banchieri, No 3, 2016.

DELL'ATTI A., MIGLIETTA F., *Il sistema bancario e la crisi finanziaria*, Cacucci, 2014.

DESLANDES J., DIAS C., MAGNUS M., *Liquidation of Banks: Towards an FDIC for the Banking Union*, Directorate-General for Internal Policies, February 2019.

DI ANTONIO M., *I modelli di business nel settore bancario: un'analisi da ripensare*, Bancaria, 2018.

DIAMOND D.W., DYBVIG P.H., Bank Runs, Deposit Insurance, and Liquidity, *Journal of Political Economy*, June 1983.

DOBLER M.C., EMRE E., GULLO A., KALE D., *The Case for Depositor Preference*, International Monetary Fund, Technical Notes and Manuals, No 2, December 2020.

DOBLER M.C., MORETTI M., CHAVARRI A.P., *Managing Systemic Banking Crises: New Lessons and Lessons Relearned*, International Monetary Fund, Departmental Paper No 5, February 2020, page 13.

DOLMETTA A.A., MALVAGNA U., *Debiti (non) ceduti e insinuazione al passivo. A proposito delle "banche venete"*, in Rivista di Diritto Bancario, No 3, March 2018.

DONATI I., *La ricapitalizzazione "interna" delle banche mediante bail-in*, in R. LENER, U. MORERA, F. VELLA (eds.), *Banche in crisi. Chi salverà i depositanti?*, in *Analisi Giuridica dell'Economia*, No 2, 2016.

ENRIA A., *Audizione al Senato della Repubblica Italiana*, Commissione Finanze e Tesoro su Il 'pacchetto bancario' CRD 5/ CRR 2/ BRRD 2, July 2017.

ENRIA A., *Public Hearing at the Committee on Economic and Monetary Affairs*, Brussels, October 2020.

ERZEGOVESI L., *Il decreto 237/2016 e la ricapitalizzazione precauzionale di MPS del luglio 2017*, Università di Trento, September 2017.

EUROGROUP, *Letter of the President of the Eurogroup to the President of the Euro Summit*, December 2019.

EUROPEAN BANKING AUTHORITY, EUROPEAN SECURITIES AND MARKETS AUTHORITY, *Statement of the EBA and ESMA on the Treatment of Retail Holdings of Debt Financial Instruments Subject to the Bank Recovery and Resolution Directive*, EBA/Op/2018/03, May 2018.

EUROPEAN BANKING AUTHORITY, *Final Draft on Valuation for the Purposes of Resolution and on Valuation to Determine Difference in Treatment Following Resolution Under Directive 2014/59/EU on Recovery and Resolution of Credit Institutions and Investment Firms*, EBA/RTS/2017/05—Final draft RTS on valuation before resolution, May 2017.

EUROPEAN BANKING AUTHORITY, *Final Draft Regulatory Technical Standards on Independent Valuers Under Article 36(14) of Directive 2014/59/EU*, EBA/RTS/2015/07, July 2015.

EUROPEAN BANKING AUTHORITY, *Opinion of the European Banking Authority on the Eligibility of Deposits, Coverage Level and Cooperation Between Deposit Guarantee Schemes*, August 2019.

EUROPEAN BANKING AUTHORITY, *Opinion of the European Banking Authority on Deposit Guarantee Scheme Payouts*, October 2019.

EUROPEAN BANKING AUTHORITY, *Opinion of the European Banking Authority on Deposit Guarantee Scheme Funding and Uses of Deposit Guarantee Scheme Funds*, January 2020.

EUROPEAN BANKING AUTHORITY, *Guidelines on the Types of Tests, Reviews or Exercises That May Lead to Support Measures Under Article 32(4)(d)(iii) of the Bank Recovery and Resolution Directive*, EBA/GL/2014/09, September 2014.

EUROPEAN BANKING AUTHORITY, *Risk Dashboard Q4 2019*, April 2020.

EUROPEAN CENTRAL BANK, *Completing the Banking Union with a European Deposit Insurance Scheme: Who Is Afraid of Cross-Subsidisation?*, Occasional Paper Series, No 208, April 2018.

EUROPEAN CENTRAL BANK, *Convergence Report*, June 2020.

EUROPEAN CENTRAL BANK, *ECB Deemed Veneto Banca and Banca Popolare di Vicenza Failing or Likely to Fail*, press release, June 2017.

EUROPEAN CENTRAL BANK, *Guidance to Banks on Non-performing Loans*, March 2017.

EUROPEAN CENTRAL BANK, *Opinion on the Liquidity Support Measures, a Precautionary Recapitalisation and Other Urgent Provisions for the Banking Sector*, February 2017 (CON/2017/01).

EUROPEAN CENTRAL BANK, *Opinion of the European Banking Authority on a Proposal for a Regulation of the European Parliament and of the Council Amending Regulation (EU) 806/2014 in Order to Establish a European Deposit Insurance Scheme* (CON/2016/26), April 2016.

EUROPEAN COMMISSION, *Banking Union: Restoring Financial Stability in the Eurozone*, April 2014.

EUROPEAN COMMISSION, *Communication from the Commission on the Application, from 1 August 2013, of State Aid Rules to Support Measures in Favour of Banks in the Context of the Financial Crisis ('Banking Communication')*, paragraphs 79–82, July 2013.

EUROPEAN COMMISSION, *Communication from the Commission Temporary Framework for State Aid Measures to Support the Economy in the Current COVID-19 Outbreak*, 2020/C 91 I/01, March 2020.

EUROPEAN COMMISSION, *Communication to the European Parliament, the Council, the European Central Bank, the European Economic and Social Committee and the Committee of the Regions on Completing the Banking Union*, COM (2017) 592, October 2017.

EUROPEAN COMMISSION, *Commission Authorises Precautionary Recapitalisation of Italian bank Monte dei Paschi di Siena*, presse release, July 2017.

EUROPEAN COMMISSION, *Commission Decision C(2015) 9526 Final of 23.12.2015 on the State Aid SA.39451 (2015/C) (ex 2015/NN) Implemented by Italy for Banca Tercas*, December 2015.

EUROPEAN COMMISSION, *Commission Notice on the Notion of State aid as Referred to in Article 107(1) of the Treaty on the Functioning of the European Union*, C/2016/2946, July 2016.

EUROPEAN COMMISSION, *Financing Bank Resolution: An Alternative Solution for Arranging the Liquidity Required*, November 2018.

EUROPEAN COMMISSION, *How to Provide Liquidity to Banks After Resolution in Europe's Banking Union*, ECON, November 2018.

EUROPEAN COMMISSION, *Review of the Bank Crisis Management and Deposit Insurance (DGSD Review), Public Consultation, European Union Website.*

EUROPEAN COMMISSION, *State Aid: Commission Approves Aid for Market Exit of Banca Popolare di Vicenza and Veneto Banca Under Italian Insolvency Law, Involving Sale of Some Parts to Intesa Sanpaolo*, press release, June 2017.

EUROPEAN COMMISSION, *State Aid: Commission Authorises Restructuring Aid for Italian bank Monti dei Paschi di Siena*, press release, Bruxelles, November 2013.

EUROPEAN COMMISSION, State Aid SA.45664(2017/N)—Italy—*Orderly Liquidation of Banca Popolare di Vicenza and Veneto Banca—Liquidation Aid*, C (2017) 4501 final, Brussels, June 2017.

EUROPEAN COMMISSION, State Aid SA.47677(2017/N)—Italy—*New aid and Amended Restructuring Plan of Banca Monte dei Paschi di Siena*, C (2017) 4690 final, Brussels, July 2017.

EUROPEAN COMMISSION, State Aid SA.50640 (2018/N)—Italy, published in Official Journal, November 2018.

EUROPEAN COMMISSION, *State Aid Scoreboard 2019*, March 2020.

EUROPEAN COMMISSION, *Targeted Consultation on the Review of the Crisis Management and Deposit Insurance Framework*, 26 January 2021.

EUROPEAN COUNCIL, *European Judicial Systems—Efficiency and Quality of Justice*, Cepej Studies, No 26, May 2018.

EUROPEAN COUNCIL, *Remarks by Mário Centeno Following the Eurogroup meeting of 4 December 2019.*

EUROPEAN COUNCIL, *Terms of Reference of the Common Backstop to the Single Resolution Fund*, December 2018.

EUROPEAN COURT OF JUSTICE, *Judgment of the General Court (Third Chamber, Extended Composition) Joined Cases T-98/16, T-196/16 and T-198/16*, March 2019.

EUROPEAN PARLIAMENT, *How to Provide Liquidity to Banks After Resolution in Europe's Banking Union*, eds. M. DEMERTZIS, I. GONSALVES RAPOSO, P. HUTTI, G. WOLFF, November 2018.

EUROPEAN PARLIAMENT, *Liquidation of Banks: Towards an FDIC for the Banking Union?*, Economic Governance Support Unit (EGSU), February 2019.

EUROPEAN PARLIAMENT, *Precautionary Recapitalisations Under the Bank Recovery and Resolution Directive: Conditionality and Case Practice*, Directorate General for Internal Policies, July 2017.

EUROPEAN PARLIAMENT, *Precautionary Recapitalisations: Time for a Review, In-Depth Analysis*, Directorate General for Internal Policies, July 2017.

EUROPEAN PARLIAMENT, *The Financing of Bank Resolution—Who Should Provide the Required Liquidity?*, Economic Governances Support Unit (EGOV) Directorate-General for Internal Policies PE 624.420, June 2018.

EUROPEAN STABILITY MECHANISM, *Draft Board of Governors Resolution on the Granting of the Backstop Facility*; December 2019.

EUROPEAN STABILITY MECHANISM, *Draft Guidelines on the Backstop Facility to the SRB for the SRF*, December 2019.

EUROPEAN STABILITY MECHANISM, *Draft Pricing Guideline*, December 2019.

EUROPEAN STABILITY MECHANISM, *The Reform of the European Stability Mechanism*, Discussion Paper No 14, September 2020.

FEDERAL DEPOSIT INSURANCE CORPORATION, *Crisis and Response. An FDIC History, 2008–2013*, November 2017.

FERNANDEZ DE LIS S., GARCIA J., *Funding Before and In Resolution A Proposal for a Funding in Resolution Mechanism*, May 2018.

FINANCIAL STABILITY BOARD, *Key Attributes of effective Resolution Regimes for Financial Institutions*, October 2014.

FINANCIAL STABILITY INSTITUTE, *Bank Failure Management. The Role of Deposit Insurance*, FSI Insights on policy implementation, No 17, August 2019.

FINANCIAL STABILITY INSTITUTE, *How to Manage Failures of Non-systemic Banks? A Review of Country Practices*, October 2018.

FIORDIPONTI F., *Le aspettative restitutorie di azionisti e creditori ai tempi del bail-in*, in Analisi Giuridica dell'Economia, il Mulino, pages 527–550, 2016.

FORESTIERI G., *I modelli di business delle banche italiane. Alla ricerca della sostenibilità*, Banche e Banchieri, No 4, December 2014.

GALBRAITH J.K., *The End of Normal. The Great Crisis and the Future of Growth*, Simon & Schuster, November 2015.

GEITHNER T.F., *Stress Test. Reflections on Financial Crises*, Crown Publishers, May 2015.

GOODHART C., AVGOULEAS E., *A Critical Evaluation on Bail-Ins as Bank Recapitalisation Mechanism*, Centre for Economic Policy Research, Discussion Paper 10065, August 2014.

GOODHART C., HARTMANN P., LLEWELLYN D., ROJAS-SUAREZ L., WEISBROD S., *Financial Regulation: Why, How and Where Now?*, Routledge, May 1998.

GRAZIANO A., FRANCESCA V., FONTANA S., DELLA PERUTA M.R., *Look Who's Talking: Banking Crisis, Bail-In and Mass Media*, 9th Annual Conference of the EuroMed Academy of Business, Warsaw, Poland, September 2016.

HADJEMMANUIL C., *Limits on State-Funded Bailouts in the EU Bank Resolution Regime*, European Economy, No 2, December 2016.

HIGH LEVEL WORKING GROUP on a European Deposit Insurance Scheme (EDIS), *Chair to the President of the Eurogroup—Further strengthening the Banking Union, Including EDIS: A Roadmap for Political Negotiations*, December 2019.

HUPKES E.H., Insolvency. Why a Special Regime for Banks? *Current Developments in Monetary and Financial Law*, vol. 3, IMF, 2005.

HUSER A.C., HALAJ G., KOK C., PERALES C., VAN DE KRAAIJ A., *The Systemic Implications of Bail-In: A Multi Layered Network Approach*, Working Paper Series, European Central bank, No 2010, February 2017.

INTERNATIONAL ASSOCIATION OF DEPOSIT INSURERS, *Chart Pack Research Unit*, June 2020.

INTERNATIONAL ASSOCIATION OF DEPOSIT INSURERS, *Core Principles for Effective Deposit Insurance System* (CPs), October 2014.

INTERNATIONAL MONETARY FUND, *Euro Area Policies—Financial System Stability Assessment*, July 2018.

INTERNATIONAL MONETARY FUND, *Financial Stability Assessment Program*, June 2019.

INTERNATIONAL MONETARY FUND, *Resolution Funding: Who Pays When Financial Institutions Fail?*, August 2018.

INTERNATIONAL MONETARY FUND, *Staff Report for the 2013 Article IV Consultation*, September 2013.

INTERNATIONAL MONETARY FUND, *United States: Financial Sector Assessment Program-Review of the Key Attributes of Effective Resolution Regimes for the Banking and Insurance Sectors-Technical Note*, July 2015, page 58.

INTESA SANPAOLO, *Annual Report 2017*, press releases, June 2017.

INTESA SANPAOLO, *Annual Report 2019.*

INZITARI B., *BRRD, bail-in, risoluzione della banca in dissesto, condivisione concorsuale delle perdite* (d.lgs. 180/2015), Ildirittodegliaffari.it, May 2016.

KERN A., *Principles of Banking Regulation*, University Press, Cambridge, May 2019.

KIM D., SANTOMERO A.M., Risk in Banking and Capital Regulation, *The Journal of Finance*, Vol. 43, No 5, December 1988.

KING M., *The End of Alchemy, Money, Banking, and the End of the Global Economy*, March 2016.

KÖNIG E., *Developments in the SRB: Setting MREL and Safeguarding Operational Continuity*, Speech to the BPFI in Dublin, January 2019.

KPMG, *I Non Performing Loan in Italia, Trend in atto e prospettive future*, 2018; PWC, *The Italian NPE Market, Ready to Face the Crisis*, June 2020.

KRUGMAN P., *End This Depression Now!*, Norton & Company, April 2012.

LEONE P., NATALE S., NICASTRO R. (a cura di), *Risoluzione di una crisi. Le Good banks tra regole, mercato, territori e risparmiatori*, Bancaria Editrice, July 2019.

LEWIS M., *The Big Short: Inside the Doomsday Machine*, Norton & Company, January 2011.

LLEWELLYN D., *The Economic Rationale for Financial Regulation*, FSA, 1999.

LUBERTI M., *Le recenti crisi bancarie in Italia*, in Rivista Bancaria, No 4–5, Minerva Bancaria, July–October 2017.

MAJNONI D'INTIGNANO G., DAL SANTO A., MALTESE M., *The FDIC Bank Crisis Management Experience: Lessons for the EU Banking Union*, Notes on Financial Stability and Supervision, No 22, August 2020.

MALINCONICO A., *Npl: scenari e prospettive post Covid-19*, Bancaria Editrice, No 5, May 2020.

MCDONALD, ROBINSON, *A Colossal Failure of Common Sense: The Inside Story of the Collapse of Lehman Brothers,* Crown Business, New York, October 2010.

MCLEAN B., NOCERA J., *All the Devils Are Here: The Hidden History of the Financial Crisis*, Penguin Books, August 2011.

MECATTI I., *The Governance of Deposit Guarantee Schemes and Its Impact on the Use of Alternative Interventions in Banking Crises*, Il Mulino—Rivisteweb, Banca Impresa Società, August 2020.

MERSCH Y., *The Limits of Central Bank Financing in Resolution*, IMFS Distinguished Lecture Series Goethe University Frankfurt, January 2018.

MINISTERO DELL'ECONOMIA E DELLE FINANZE, *A inizio 2020 presentazione piano dismissione partecipazione Mef in Mps*, press release No 234, December 2019.

MINISTERO DELL'ECONOMIA E DELLE FINANZE, *Relazione generale sulla situazione economica del Paese*, 2008.

MONTE DEI PASCHI DI SIENA, *Progetto di scissione parziale non proporzionale con opzione asimmetrica di un compendio di crediti deteriorate da parte di MPS in favore di AMCO*, press release, June 2020.

MONTE DEI PASCHI DI SIENA, *Relazione finanziaria e Bilancio Consolidato 2017*.

MONTE DEI PASCHI DI SIENA, *Relazione finanziaria e Bilancio Consolidato 2016*.

NUOVA BANCA DELLE MARCHE SPA, *Situazione al 31 dicembre 2015*, June 2016.

NUOVA BANCA DELL'ETRURIA E DEL LAZIO SPA, *Relazione e Bilancio 2015*, May 2016.

NUOVA CASSA DI RISPARMIO DI CHIETI SPA, *Bilancio di esercizio al 31 dicembre 2015*, June 2016.

NUOVA CASSA DI RISPARMIO DI FERRARA SPA, *Bilancio separato al 31 dicembre 2015*, June 2016.

ONADO M., *La Banca come impresa, Manuale di gestione Bancaria*, il Mulino, October 1996.

OSTERWALDER A., PIGN€Y., *Creare modelli di business*, Milano, FAG, June 2012.

PANETTA F., *Finanza, rischi e crescita economica*, Equita SIM Benchmarking the UK market: A way to create an efficient and effective capital market in Italy, Milano, January 2016.

PELGANTA E., PIERIGE' M., PROSPERI L., *Le variabili determinanti della redditività e i loro fattori di cambiamento: profilazione delle banche nel contesto (new normal) post crisi;* intervento al convegno AIFIRM di Roma, August 2018.

PERRAZZELLI A., *Esame del disegno di legge C. 2302, di conversione in legge del decreto-legge No 142 del 2019, recante misure urgenti per il sostegno al sistema creditizio del Mezzogiorno e per la realizzazione di una banca di investimento*, Camera dei Deputati VI Commissione (Finanze), Audizione della Vice Direttrice Generale della Banca d'Italia, January 2020.

PERSAUD A.D., *Why Bail-In Securities Are Fool's Gold*, Peterson Institute for International Economics, No PB14-23, November 2014.

PHILIPPON T., SALORD A., *Bail-Ins and Bank Resolution in Europe: A Progress Report*, Geneva Reports on the World Economy Special Report 4, CEPR, ICMB International Center for Monetary and Banking Studies, March 2017.

PIERIGE' M., *Banche, il business model che verrà*, Risk Management Magazine, Anno 13, numero 3, September–December 2018.

RESTOY F., *How to Improve Crisis Management in the Banking Union: A European FDIC*, Lisbon, July 2019.

RISPOLI FARINA M., *La soluzione della crisi delle banche venete nell'ambito della procedura di risanamento e risoluzione delle banche italiane. Uno sguardo di insieme*, in Innovazione & Diritto, No 2, 2018.

ROUBINI N., MIHM S., *La crisi non è finita*, Feltrinelli, Milano, 2012.

SANTONI G., *La disciplina del bail-in, lo stato di dissesto e la dichiarazione dello stato di insolvenza*, in LENER R., MORERA U., VELLA F. (a cura di), *Banche in crisi. Chi salverà i depositanti*, Analisi Giuridica dell'Economia, Il Mulino, 2/2016.

SINGLE RESOLUTION BOARD, *Operational Guidance on Bail-In Implementation*, August 2020.

SINGLE RESOLUTION BOARD, *Summary of the SRB's Decision in Relation to Banca Popolare di Vicenza*, June 2017.

SINGLE RESOLUTION BOARD, *The SRB will Not Take Resolution Action in Relation to Banca Popolare di Vicenza and Veneto Banca*, press release, June 2017.

SIRONI A., *The Evolution of Banking Regulation Since the Financial Crisis: A Critical Assessment*, Baffi Carefin Centre Research, Paper No 2018-103, November 2018.

SMITH D., *The Age of Instability. The Global Financial Crisis and What Comes Next*, Profile Books Ltd., January 2010.

SORKIN A.R., *Too Big to Fail. The Inside Story of How Wall Street and Washington Fought to Save the Financial System—And Themselves*, Penguin, October 2009.

SORKIN A.R., *Too Big to Fail: The Battle to Save Wall Street*, Penguin, September 2010.

STANDARD & POOR'S, *Continued Bank Bail-Outs Stretch the Credibility of Europe's Resolution Framework*, February 2020.

STIGLITZ J., *Freefall: America, Free Markets, and the Sinking of the World Economy*, Penguin, October 2010.

TALEB N., *The Black Swan: The Impact of the Highly Improbable*, Random House, May 2010.

TUCCARI F., *La crisi economica mondiale 2007–2013*, Zanichelli, September 2013.

VESTAGER M., HILL J., *Letter of the Commissioners on the Solution of the Crisis of the Four Banks*, November 2015.

VISCO I., *Fact-Finding Inquiry on the Italian Banking and Financial System and the Protection of Savings, pdf 246.2 KB also Regarding Supervision, Crisis Resolution and European DEPOSIT INSURANCE.* SIXTH Standing Committee of the Italian Senate (Finance and Treasury)—Testimony, April 2016.

VISCO I., *The Governor's Concluding Remarks for 2015*, Report 2015, page 15, May 2016.

VISCO I., *The Italian Economy and Banks: Implications of the Pandemic and Outlook*, September 2020.

VISCO I., *Workshop on Stability of the Banking System*, Keynote speech, Florence, May 2016.

Index

G. Boccuzzi, *Banking Crises in Italy*, Palgrave Studies in Financial Instability and Banking Crisis Regulation,
https://doi.org/10.1007/978-3-031-01344-7

The manufacturer's authorised representative in the EU is Springer Nature Customer Service Centre GmbH, Europaplatz 3, 69115 Heidelberg, Germany. If you have any concerns regarding our products, please contact ProductSafety@springernature.com

Printed and bound by CPI Group (UK) Ltd, Croydon, CR0 4YY
22/09/2026
02221054-0010